MARRIAGE AND FAMILY

Better Ready Than Not

James P. Trotzer, Ph.D.

Toni B. Trotzer, M.A.

ACCELERATED DEVELOPMENT INC.

Publishers

Muncie,   Indiana

MARRIAGE AND FAMILY

Better Ready Than Not

Library of Congress Catalogue Card Number: 84-70097

International Standard Book Number: 0-915202-50-6

Technical Development: Tanya Dalton
Judy McWilliams
Sheila Sheward

Cover Design: Janet Pasakarnis

Artist Statement: The theme of the cover design is people emerging. As individuals emerge from the crowd of family, friends, and acquaintances, their identity is formed. Then individuals meet and marry, coupleness emerges, preparing the way for the family. The family then develops through the life cycle, producing the context for individual emergence to be recycled. Janet Pasakarnis

For additional copies order from

ACCELERATED DEVELOPMENT INC., PUBLISHERS
3400 Kilgore Avenue, Muncie, IN 47304
(317) 284-7511

DEDICATED

TO THOSE WHO CAME BEFORE

OUR PARENTS

ROGER AND BETTY   PETER AND ANNA

TROTZER   NARDINI

AND THOSE WHO CAME AFTER

OUR CHILDREN

TRACI

DANIEL

BENJAMIN

FOR WHOM OUR MARRIAGE

IS

THE BRIDGE

PREFACE

This book brings the reader into face-to-face contact with the realities of marriage and family life as a means of facilitating the preparation, enrichment, and remediation processes that enhance the success of marriage and family living. The need for and content of this book has emerged as a result of our professional practice as marriage and family therapists and our personal experience as marital partners and parents of three children.

Most people will eventually marry and a vast majority also will become parents. The expectation to marry and have children may be communicated quite early in life but the actual prospect of marriage usually emerges in some realistic form during late adolescence and early adulthood. At this juncture in life and later, people begin to respond to the need for intimate relationships which in the course of development tend to culminate in marriage.

Given the fact that most people will marry and engage in parenting, we are amazed at how little societal institutions (schools, families, churches, and so forth) do to help people prepare for such eventualities. Although everyone recognizes that the two major choice areas in every person's life are career and marriage, much stress is placed on preparation for the former and little attention is paid to the latter. The accelerating divorce rate, the increase in single parent families, the growing number of remarried families, the rising demand for marriage and family therapy, and the requests for other family services indicate that simply getting married does not insure happiness. The question then is, can anything be done to better prepare people for marriage and family life thereby reducing the potential for eventual marital and family breakdowns?

To assist people in living more fulfilling marital and family lives, we believe that materials should be made available through reading, classes, and programs which will

1. equip people to make effective decisions regarding intimate relationships and the subsequent choice of a marriage partner;

2. develop awareness of the realities of life after marriage, its developmental crises, joys, and difficulties;

3. provide knowledge and skills for enhancing family life and working on its problems in a constructive way; and

4. accentuate one's past and current life experience as both a resource and a limitation in the preparation for and experience of marriage and family life.

Whether married, anticipating a marriage or a remarriage, or even if marriage is not an imminent goal, this book will present readers with information and considerations that will develop their assets, expand their options, and provide a solid foundation for making better decisions both before and after marriage.

The content of this book bridges the trade-text reader populations on one hand and the consumer-professional populations, on the other. The trade population consisting of self-help readers will find the content to have personal appeal and to contain material that can be integrated into their ongoing lives. Young adult to adult readers will find the book meeting a need by addressing problems with which they currently are dealing.

The book also is designed to serve as a text for courses, programs, and classes which emphasize marriage preparation and enrichment to assist persons through more formal means of dealing with marriage and family issues. The professional reading population including counselors, psychologists, social workers, clergy, and other helping professionals will find the book is a resource for providing marriage and family counseling and that it may be adopted as a text in classes or programs they conduct. The content and format lend merit to the book as a resource in bibliotherapy.

The age range of readers extends from high school through adults. The content provides readers with resources in terms of knowledge, awareness, understanding, guidelines, and skills needed to engage effectively in marriage and family life. Content drawn from theory, research, clinical practice, and personal experience is integrated into a psychological framework for viewing healthy marital and family functioning.

Marriage and family life can be a fulfilling, satisfying lifetime experience. People do marry with intentions of making it together and raising healthy, responsible children. However, all too frequently things go wrong. Couples and families find themselves in a quagmire of problems and feelings from which they cannot extricate themselves in an intact manner. Even though family, friends, therapists, and concerned others extend help, it is often too late.

Increased awareness, better understanding, and more adequate preparation are effective antidotes to the current stress in marriages and families. At a time when society is beginning to take a long hard look at the whys, wherefores, and why nots of marriage and family life, *Marriage and Family: Better Ready than Not* can be a helpful and useful instrument for enhancing the growth and development of fully functioning individuals who are effective in meeting the challenges of marriage and family life.

CONTENTS

4 ENVIRONMENT AND CULTURE: DIFFERENT STROKES MAKE DIFFERENT FOLKS 65

5 FAMILY OF ORIGIN: YOU CAN'T LEAVE HOME WITHOUT IT 95

6 FAMILY OF ORIGIN TO ORIGIN OF FAMILY: THE DATING AND COURTSHIP PHASE OF MARRIAGE 121

7 THERE'S LIFE AFTER MARRIAGE: YOUR WEDDING AND BEYOND 151

ACTIVITIES

FIGURES

EXAMPLES

ACKNOWLEDGEMENTS

Just as marriages and families need outside support systems to succeed, we have many to thank for their part in making this book a reality. A cadre of typists including Priscilla Mundfrom, Evelyn Dadmun, Dorothy Crosby, and Judy Bassett deserve special thanks. Dr. Jo Ellen Thomas, whose Nubblewood retreat in Maine served as our headquarters for writing the last five chapters and adding the finishing touches, is owed a debt of gratitude. To Toni Gleeson who did the background research for Chapter 10, we express our thanks. To our friends and colleagues who kept asking, "Is it done yet?" We say emphatically "yes!" and "thanks for keeping up the pressure." Our clients who had the courage to share their problems and pain with us deserve special acknowledgement. In large measure any help that this book supplies to the readers must be credited to them.

Over the years we have collected, and students, clients, and friends have supplied, quotations, brief commentaries and poems, some by famous people, others by not so famous people and some anonymous. Many of these pearls of wisdom and wit have been integrated into the content of our book. Where possible we have located specific sources, but in some cases, the name of the original author only is provided and in some cases the entry is simply anonymous. We wish to acknowledge those who have provided us with these literary maxims and believe they contribute significantly to the relevance and readability of the book. However, we also wish to acknowledge any oversight that may have occurred by using names as sufficient source or when sources were anonymous or unknown to us.

A special note of appreciation is deserved by Andy and Janet Pasakarnis for their insightful input in designing the cover, and especially to Janet who did the art work and graphics.

We are grateful to Joe and Pat Hollis for their confidence in us and encouragement along the way. Although Pat's death has left us saddened and feeling a sense of loss, her influence is certainly reflected in the finished product. We also thank the editing and technical staff at Accelerated Development for their conscientious support and professional assistance.

We wish to acknowledge the presence of a loving and caring God in our lives who is the foundation of our relationship and who gives the resources to be who we are and do what we do.

And we want to recognize our parents and our children to whom we have dedicated this book. Their influence is immeasurable in terms of who we are, what our marriage is, and how we parent.

Authors' Personal Note

The genesis of this book occurred a few years ago when Jim had taken a sabbatical for the purpose of immersing himself in training, research, and clinical practice in marriage and family therapy. We had moved our family to Philadelphia where Jim had an appointment as a post doctoral fellow in the Family Psychiatry Department at Eastern Pennsylvania Psychiatric Institute. Toni planned to enhance her training by taking advantage of the numerous opportunities available and the children were excited about living in a big city for the first time in their lives.

Ten days after our arrival Toni developed appendicitis which went undiagnosed until emergency surgery was required and peritonitis had set in. This close brush with death drew us together and gave us a deeper sense of appreciation for life, each other, and our family. Throughout the long months of slow recovery many hours were spent in conversation and reading because little else could be done. During those times together the idea of writing this book emerged.

Now as the book reaches publication, we realize that writing this book was a metaphor for a marriage. The initial excitement and enthusiasm propelled us into the project. However realities soon set in and we had to face the fact that writing takes time and is hard work. As other aspects of our lives were constantly interrupting, we would have to set time aside to give writing first priority. The process of writing became embroiled in our relationship as we grappled with issues such as who should do the "important work" and who should do the "menial tasks." We learned we had to communicate and negotiate or we would get stuck.

As each chapter was completed, we would experience a lift and then become discouraged as we realized we had more chapters to go. Even when the final chapter was written, we could not celebrate fully because the editing, revising, and support work had to be done to reach final completion. So just like a marriage, always another stage brings with it joys and problems and requires continued effort.

Our purposes in writing this book were quite ambitious and often had to be compromised, but we believe we were able to retain their essence. We wanted to translate our training, our professional evolution (from individual, to group, to marriage and family therapy), our clinical experience as marriage and family therapists, and our personal experience as marital partners and parents into a practical resource that would have both preventive and problem-solving merit. Finally we wanted to convey a sense of hope and positivity relative to marriage and family life. Writing this book has helped us along our pathway of marriage. We now present it to you with our best wishes that you too will find it meaningful.

James P. Trotzer

Toni B. Trotzer

THE CASE FOR BEING PREPARED

The need for and purpose of the book is presented. The case for preparation relative to marriage and family life is made and personalized to the reader. Concepts relative to individual growth and development and the movement toward intimacy are presented with emphasis on the teenage, young adult, and adult phases of the life cycle. An overview of the book's content and how to utilize it are given.

THE FACTS OF LIFE

If you are reading this book and live in the United States, the following is very likely to be true of you. Chances are excellent that you will marry—95% of all Americans do (U.S. Bureau of the Census, 1984).

Once married, the likelihood of your becoming divorced is substantial. Statistically 53% of all marriages end in divorce rather than death (Saxton, 1983). If you do divorce, the potential for remarriage is 80% (Saxton, 1983) and, if you do remarry, 48% of those marriages will end in divorce (Cherlin, 1981). In addition to marriage, the potential for becoming a parent also is high since the average family in the United States is now 3.26 persons (U.S. Bureau of the Census, 1985a).

These U.S. Bureau of Census figures may appear startling at first glance. However, a quick perusal of your own experience in relation to marriage and family life will reveal a good deal of evidence confirming that the statistics are plausible. When you look around, particularly at people who are over twenty-five, you notice that the most salient characteristic of these people is that they are married. In addition, as you think about people you know, you will not have look very far to find evidence that marriages have failed to fulfill expectations of the mates. You may not have to look farther than your own family or relatives. Few families in the U.S. today escape the turmoil of marital breakdown. According to U.S. Census Bureau figures, the single parent family rate doubled between 1970 and 1984 jumping from 13% to 26% (U.S. Bureau of the Census, 1985b). Consequently, one family in four is headed by one parent. In other words, the experience of being in a family or marital relationship that breaks down is rapidly becoming as common an experience as being in a marriage and a family.

However awesome these figures may seem, they still tend to mask the even more crucial realization that people's lives are deeply affected. Holmes and Rahe (1967), in examining stressful experiences, indicated that the second most stressful experience in life, next to the death of a spouse, is divorce. Given the fact that marriage and family life in and of themselves produce most of life's difficulties, adding the dimension of breakdown to those experiences makes the impact even more intense. Yet in spite of the foregoing gloomy statistics, researchers, after performing study after study, have indicated that marriage and family are still considered to be the best alternative we have, as Americans continue to marry in record numbers.

Let's look at more of the realities. If you are a male, you will likely marry by the time you are 24 or 25 (U.S. Bureau of the Census, 1984). That means you will spend most of your adult life—male life expectancy is 71 years (National Center for Health Statistics, 1985)—as a husband in one of the various forms (husband, ex-husband, or widower). In the course of that 45 plus years, the probability is that you also will become a parent in one of the various forms (natural or adoptive father and grandfather). Therefore, the majority of your life will be carried out functioning as a husband/father. If ways exist to improve your effectiveness and satisfaction in performing those various roles, you will benefit from making use of opportunities to learn and perfect them. That is the reason we are writing a book such as this— to provide you with resources that will enhance your effectiveness as a male functioning in the various roles you will enter into as a husband and father.

What if you are a woman? The same holds true for you but the picture of your future is somewhat more predictable though more complicated (Sheehy, 1976). You probably will marry at age 22 or 23 which is younger than your male counterparts (U.S. Bureau of the Census, 1984). If you are working, you will leave the work force shortly after marriage to become a mother (something most males do not have to expect). Then, if you are a typical American female, you will face re-entering the work force at about thirty-five when your children are in school. The implications of your becoming a wife/mother are even greater since a larger percentage of your life will be spent in various forms of these roles (wife, ex-wife, widow; natural or adoptive mother and grandmother). Because women marry earlier and live longer than men—life expectancy for women is 78.3 years (U.S. Bureau of the Census, 1985a)—your involvement in the marriage and family enterprise is more extensive than men. Thus, efforts to prevent or circumvent problems via preparation can only increase the potential for greater effectiveness and satisfaction in living your life as a wife/mother.

Before going any further, we wish to point out that exceptions do exist to all rules. Some of you may in fact neither marry nor become parents. Others of you may at this time in your life "think" you will never marry or become parents. That opinion is not uncommon at certain periods in all of our lives and constitutes a phase of many people's experience who end up in the 95% category—married at some time in life. However all of you are a part of a family—a reality which is difficult to deny given the biological explanation of each of our existences. That being the case, reading this book may give you some understanding of your own family experiences facilitating more adaptive and satisfying relationships even "if" you never venture on the path of marriage and parenthood.

WHY THIS BOOK?

Given the fact that most of you will marry and engage in parenting, we are concerned about how little societal institutions (schools, family, churches, government, and so forth) do to help people prepare for such eventualities. More than any other aspect of our lives, marriage and family are left to chance as far as preparation is concerned. People engage in marriage and family life entrusting their experience to fate. Another typical attitude is that we should learn about marriage and family life by a process similar to osmosis. Just being around marriage and families is sufficient to absorb what is essential to get started. Another attitude is that you have to take your bumps and learn from experiences. This "school of hard knocks" syndrome sends us out into the world of marriage and family experience with the idea that if you are strong you will survive. Most likely we will survive but at what price?

Anyone to whom you talk will confirm that the two major choice areas in anyone's life are career and marriage. However, the discrepancy in preparation for the two is astounding. Formal education is a legal requirement for all U.S. citizens. Schools and parents are held responsible for preparing young people for entry into the job market. Pressure is placed on all of us to choose a life's work, but this pressure is accompanied by a host of supportive programs and opportunities. Training programs for career preparation abound; tests, inventories, and other evaluative tools have been developed to assist in the career choice process. Vocational counseling programs and career development curricula are common in schools and community agencies. But what about the marriage and family preparation area? Basically we learn about marriage and family by growing up in our own families of origin. We learn by a process called modeling. This is probably the most effective way to learn since it is a long term experiential process. Yet it sometimes is insufficient and may be a negative experience. It also may not account for adapting to a rapidly changing society. Little is done formally or informally to supplement the family in helping people prepare for marriage.

Common sense tells us that advance preparation is mandatory for effective and maximally satisfactory performance in all areas of life. Education, training, and practice are essential requirements for successful performance in jobs, athletics, the arts, and every other aspect of our lives—why not marriage and family life? We believe that more attention must be given to getting ready for this vital and basically inevitable aspect of life.

The growing divorce rate, the increase in single (one) parent families, and the growing demand for marriage and family therapy are evidence that simply getting married does not ensure living happily ever after. However, most people still marry with the intent of staying together "till death do us part." The question is, can anything be done to better prepare for marriage and family life thereby filling a vital gap in preparation for life and reducing the potential for eventual marital and family breakdowns? Our response and effort to answer that question has resulted in this book.

OUR PURPOSES

We believe that you have the right and the responsibility to do what you can to be prepared in the best way possible for marriage and family life. The right is yours because you are the one who must live out that experience "for better or for worse." Also you have a responsibility because how you live out the experience affects not only you but your husband/wife, your children and (believe it or not) your parents. Our goals (purposes) then are to engage you in a process that will stimulate your thinking, develop your awareness and understanding, and enhance your abilities and skills in areas that pertain to marriage and family. We believe that such an experience will be helpful to you in the following ways:

1. You will become aware of the impact of your current ongoing life experiences on your progress toward and experience in marriage and family living.

2. You will become better equipped to make more effective and satisfying decisions regarding intimate relationships and the subsequent choice of a marriage partner.

3. Your increased awareness of realities of life after marriage including developmental crises, joys and common problems will give you a sense of predictability about your future which will better prepare you for responding to them and handling them as they arise (and they will arise).

4. Your acquired knowledge and understanding of family life including how families change and grow, typical problems, implications of parenting and lifestyles, and essential skills will increase your potential for constructive action in family living.

Even if marriage is not an imminent goal, the focus, topics, and activities of this book will help you develop your assets, expand your options, and provide a solid foundation for making better decisions both before and after marriage.

FOR WHOM THE BELLS TOLL

One of the surest ways to get a rise out of people who are known to be involved to some degree in a relationship with a member of the opposite sex is to put a sly smirk on your face and mention something about "wedding bells." Such a comment is sure to obtain a reaction such as a vociferous denial, an irritable brush off, a revealing blush, a subtle acknowledgement, or any number of responses that indicate you have touched a live wire in the person's life.

The reason for such a volatile response is due to the fact that you have raised an issue that has rather far reaching implications for each of us, and which in most cases is always associated with some ambivalence and ambiguity. The issue is one of readiness for intimacy and the dilemma is one of commitment. Obviously this problem is more likely to occur at certain times during our lives than others and is more associated with circumstances under which we are single rather than when we are married.

What sets the stage for this movement toward becoming intimately involved with another person and what ignites the process that moves us toward and along the path of marriage? Part of the answer lies in the fact that as human beings we grow and change. Within the context of our development lies the potential for and realization of intimate relations with people outside our family, the nature of which ultimately raises the question of marriage. Let's look at what goes into this process of development and how that relates to marriage and family life.

ON BECOMING A PERSON

The fact that we all change is undeniable. We are different now than we were five years ago. Five years from now we will be different than we are today. These changes occur in many dimensions: physical, emotional, intellectual, moral, and vocational. The process is inevitable. Our appearance varies as we age; our thinking and feelings change as we acquire new knowledge and experience; our skills, lifestyles, and values change. But the one saving feature that predominates through all this variation, that enables us to maintain our sanity, is that predictable patterns do characterize our change process. Through all these changes, a person surfaces who is a unique blend of characteristics—some of which are like every other human being, some of which resemble certain groups of people, and some of which are special traits that only that person possesses.

Willa Cather once wrote that "there are only two or three human stories and they go on repeating themselves as fiercely as if they had never happened before" (Sheehy, 1976, p. 19). Each of us is unique and experiences life in the first person apart from anyone else. However, realizing and understanding that our development occurs in a sequence similar to another person gives us a sense of order and stability and provides a context that allows for predictability and control. Knowing these patterns, therefore, is helpful in understanding and preparing for life's eventualities.

THE PROCESS OF DEVELOPMENT

The analogy of a lobster depicts the process of human growth and development. Each year the lobster discards the old hard shell which enables it to expand in size. During the period of time it is without its hard shell, it is extremely vulnerable. However without taking that risk it would be trapped in a shell that allowed no growth. As human beings we engage in the same process. Just like the lobster, we feel an urge to grow but to do so involves risk, insecurity, confusion, and sometimes anxiety. However, once we begin to grow (at birth or even before) we become more and more capable of dealing with life's experiences through participating in the developmental process. Any interference which prevents us from risking (risking any or all of ourselves, our status, our self concept, and so forth) or causes stagnation at any level only bodes ill for our future adjustment, effectiveness, and satisfaction.

Psychologist Erik Erikson (1963) has described the basic stages of human development. He pointed out that every human being goes through the same stages in the same sequence although the pace may vary. These stages are infancy, childhood, adolescence, and adulthood. The adult stage is further delineated into early adulthood, middle adulthood, and the aging years. He explained that each stage is organized around a dominant theme and that behaviors at one stage are qualitatively different from those at earlier or later stages. A basic ground rule is that a person cannot achieve a later stage before going through an earlier one. As such, the process is prescribed relative to order although it can vary relative to the rate at which any one person moves through the stage.

An additional feature of these stages is that each one is characterized by certain developmental tasks that involve crucial behaviors and experiences with which persons must deal effectively before moving to the next stage. Confrontation of these tasks is often referred to as a developmental crisis. *Developmental crises* represent turning points in a person's life which introduce a combination of increased vulnerability and heightened potential. The Chinese character for crisis combines both danger and opportunity creating a definition that is highly appropriate because these crises are not only predictable but desirable since resolving them results in growth.

Since late adolescence and early adulthood are the typical times for the initial consideration of marriage, we will focus on the nature of development as it relates to these stages. Remember, however, that events which occur in infancy and childhood have a far-reaching impact and provide the foundation for what occurs in adolescence and adulthood. Some of the implications of the early years will be specifically discussed in later chapters in the book when we talk about the family of origin and parenting.

TEENAGE YEARS
(THE NEW MODEL ME)

Adolescence is frequently described as the period of life when the most predictable characteristic is unpredictability. Adolescence is a confusing, frustrating, exciting, and varied collage of experiences which in the course of development produces an adult. Adolescence as we know it today is really a contemporary phenomenon. Technological advancement in our society has caused the time period between childhood and adulthood to be expanded by making increased demands on young people in terms of education, training, and overall preparation for handling responsibilities of the adult world. In primitive societies the transition from being a child to being an adult may be as brief as a ceremony at a certain age after which the young person is viewed as an adult and accorded the full complement of privileges and responsibilities that come with that status. Not so in our society.

Termination of adolescence is no longer associated primarily with age. Rather the evidence of being adult is related to financial independence, completion of education, and establishing some form of autonomy from parents. Thus the stage of adolescence may extend well into the twenties if a person chooses to complete a college education and advanced professional training. Although adult privileges such as voting, drinking, and marrying are established by law, the actuality of being an adult is much more ambiguous.

Since no clear guidelines for the beginning of adulthood exist in terms of a specific age, the exact nature of the stage is difficult to determine. On the one hand, the extended nature of adolescence gives a person more time to prepare for the future and gives opportunity for exploration that can lead to better and more satisfying choices in one's life. On the other hand, it also produces a longer period of conflicts and vascillation between dependence and independence. This in turn produces tensions, frustrations, and anxieties that affect both the adolescent and significant adults in his/her life. If you are experiencing typical adolescent feelings of being "in-between," very likely your parents are also experiencing them which is why the adolescent phase of development is often the most stressful for parent-child relationships. Since neither parent nor child knows for sure what the status of the young person is, knowing how to act becomes difficult. One father of three teenage boys, upon observing the antics of a group of young people including his sons, was heard to murmur in a rather resigned tone of voice, "Youth is so precious, it's a shame to waste it on young people." This sentiment of envying and appreciating the energy and vitality of adolescents but being skeptical of their actions is common.

Erikson (1963) described adolescence as a period of time in which the young person strives to attain an identity. If successful, an integrated image of oneself as a unique person emerges which gives a sense of security and self-confidence. If one's identity does not get clarified, the result is a sense of confusion which effectively undermines one's confidence, self esteem, and general ability to function effectively in dealing with life's tasks. A person who does not succeed in developing a strong sense of identity has much difficulty making commitments and developing loyalties both of which manifest themselves as negative factors in the context of marriage and family experience.

The means of developing identity during adolescence are closely allied to interactions with peers and others outside the family. Since the family has been the primary influence in the child's life up to adolescence, the child's image of self is primarily in terms of a family frame of reference. As adolescence emerges, the young person tests that image against the view of others. Of particular importance are the views of one's peers. As a result the young person begins to throw off allegiances and loyalties to the family in exchange for the more preferred approval and relationships of friends. This process then sets the stage for contacts with persons outside the family which in turn produce relationships that raise the potential for intimacy and closeness.

Parallel to the development of identity, other changes also are occurring which feed into the adolescent experience both perpetuating it and causing problems. Sexual development generates drives and physical changes in both sexes. Initiated with the onset of puberty (at about twelve for girls and fourteen for boys), males and females develop physical sexual characteristics and capabilities that interject new dimensions into their interpersonal relations with one another. Encounters with the opposite sex generate feelings and emotions that take on greater significance. Friendships and experiences with others are affected. As a result the groundwork is being established that will facilitate or interfere with satisfying sexual relations in the context of intimacy.

Vocationally the adolescent is confronted for the first time with the question of earning a living. This becomes a serious focus not only because of its impact on producing autonomy but because one's career choices affect personal satisfaction. Also, career choices have a significant influence on one's relationships because careers tend to create contexts in which relationships develop and exist. This point is brought out in a book entitled *If You Don't Know Where You're Going You'll Probably End Up Somewhere Else* by David Campbell (1974). Your career choices lead you into environments and experiences that influence who you are and with whom you will get along. Therefore efforts (or lack of efforts) to clarify your vocational goals and move toward them certainly will affect who you meet and how your relationships develop.

The formation, testing, and solidification of values are other dimensions of adolescent development. By the time we reach adolescence most people have the capacity to think for themselves and to engage in reasoning in both concrete and symbolic terms (Piaget, 1963). Part of the testing that takes place is associated with seeing how those values learned in the family fit with experiences of living outside the family. Adolescents take on many roles and try out many behaviors in their search for an identity. The end product of this experimentation is the result of successful or unsuccessful experiences which in turn translate in part into values that the person holds and acts upon. Lawrence Kohlberg (1969), who has extensively studied moral development, pointed out that adolescents generally function on a level which is characterized by seeking approval. In other words, they act in a manner which they feel conforms to expectations of important others. In this way good relations are maintained and experiences of approval are more likely.

As the person matures, the impact of legitimate authority (government, laws, and so forth) becomes more important as a guide to actions. Thus a person behaves in ways that avoid censure and guilt. Pinpointed here is the typical process that occurs where the young person moves from acting in accord with peer values to responding more in terms of values that will facilitate adjustment in the adult world. In some sense then holding to adolescent group identity (though important during transition) only postpones forming an adult identity. In any case one's values will be a significant factor in forming and maintaining relationships since the stability of intimate relationships is contingent on value systems between people that are compatible.

All these developmental factors serve to prepare the way for pulling up roots and moving away from tasks and experiences of childhood onto those of early adulthood. It is as if adolescence is the practice field on which the various skills and strategies are learned for the game of being adult. And just like an athletic contest, the conditions of a game often differ from what was anticipated in practice. However, the better the preparation, the more likely the possibility that the individual will be able to adjust and cope effectively with variations from those expected. In terms of marriage and family, the way you handle the experiences of adolescence in which the issues of interpersonal closeness are first raised will to a large extent affect your capability and experiences in making the specific choice of a partner and spouse.

Coming Into Your Own

While adolescence progresses in most cases under the protective custody of family and the watchful eye of teachers and other significant adults, the early adult years mark the beginning of life on your own. Generally between the ages of eighteen to twenty-two efforts are directed at breaking away from parents, physically and emotionally. While this process is occurring, the cushion of support provided by the peer group transforms into more substantial relationships associated with the pursuit of one's goals and the specific nature of one's environment. New relationships are formed in different contexts (college, work settings, military, travel, and so forth).

Erikson (1963) described the main task of early adulthood as developing the capacity for intimacy and making commitments. People who handle this problem effectively attain the ability to form close and lasting relationships and to make commitments to careers and persons that are dependable. If unsuccessful, the result is isolation and loneliness. During early adulthood most people commit themselves to an occupation and marry or form intimate relationships. Gail Sheehy (1976) in a book entitled *Passages* pointed out that young people in their twenties expend most of their energy in trying to do four things: (1) shape a dream for themselves, (2) prepare for life work, (3) find a mentor—that is someone to whom or something to which to attach as a means of gaining direction, and (4) form intimate relationships without losing oneself. These efforts produce changes and conflicts in one's life.

These changes include the fact that individual relationships (partner, close friends, spouse) become more important than group relations (hanging with one's crowd). The arena of one's actions tends to change. No longer does the action take place in the primary context of one's family. Rather the majority of time is spent in work settings, educational settings, and living quarters other than the family home. More time is spent in the pursuit of "special relationships" rather than with family or friends. These changes obviously allude to greater autonomy and signal the arrival of adulthood.

Along with adulthood come conflicts and problems. Most of these conflicts involve decisions that reflect polarities of choice along a continuum that tends to either lock one in or keep one floating. In fact, the biggest issue is one of commitment—when, to what, and/or to whom. Every choice made during this time seems to have a forever quality to it which at the same time makes it desirable from a security standpoint and undesirable from a flexibility point of view. If I get serious with this person, am I committing myself to a relationship for life? If I take a certain program or job, will I be doing that for the rest of my life? We are afraid that we are creating an irrevocable pattern that will be with us the rest of our lives. Now why is that so?

Within each of us apparently are two forces which motivate us. One force propels us to be separate, unique, different, and independent. We are particularly aware of that force as we strike out from home and vow to make it on our own. The other force is one which drives us to seek closeness, security, safety, and intimate relationships with others. Thus, one part of us seeks freedom to be an individual while another part is always searching for something to which to surrender our freedom. While we are breaking away from our family, we are becoming involved in intimate relationships and one or more commitments such as marriage and career.

If we commit ourselves, we gain security and risk getting locked in. If we do not commit ourselves, we are free to explore and retain flexibility but at the cost of living a transient life without any commitments Sheehy (1976) called the force toward others the "merger self" since it enables us to love and share intimately with another person. However, if we overindulge that part of us, we take no risks and experience no growth as a unique person. She called the other force the "seeker self" because it drives us towards individuation. If we cater too much to that force, however, it leads to self-centeredness which interferes with committedness to others. Thus, a balance between the two is necessary.

While adolescence gets us in up to our ankles, early adulthood gets us in up to our necks in regard to issues of intimacy, marriage, and family. As such, decisions made are critical because we will have to live with the consequences. Therefore "good" decisions are essential because later they will make the road easier to travel. Good decisions are based on conscientious efforts to know as much as we can before making them and then acting upon our best knowledge. Remember that *no decision is a decision,* and as long as you are aware of the consequences (it keeps you floating) you have "no decision" as one option. Additionally, decisions you do make are not necessarily irreversible. They are crucial but do not have the catastrophizing qualities we tend to attach to them which we then use to avoid commitments.

MOVING ON

Although many of you reading this book are likely to be in one of the two stages just described, a brief look ahead may not be a bad idea to give some sense of continuity. Everyone eventually gets to middle adulthood even though that appears to be a long way off to teenagers and people in their twenties. (We both can attest to the fact that time does move on—rather quickly in fact.)

The focus of the middle adult years is on providing for the next generation. People in this age group are the ones who run our society. Thus, they are concerned not only with day to day living but with the impact that quality of life has on future generations. Middle adulthood brings the family dimensions of one's life into full view. Energy and time is devoted to supporting and maintaining the family including both children and aging parents. The complexity of life increases because of the need to balance individual, marital, family, and non-family domains of living. Efforts to share responsibility and develop a lifestyle which is personally fulfilling and adequately prepares one's children for the future are paramount.

The course of human development we have briefly reviewed can be summarized simply as a process in which you move from being a child of your parents to being a parent of your child. This process repeats itself over and over with marriage serving as the primary mechanism that perpetuates one generation after another. We trust that you now have some sense of where you are in that process and will be able to use the information in this book to help you move from one stage to another in relation to the domain of your life that will carry you toward, into, and through marriage and family living.

OVERVIEW OF THE BOOK

Many forces, factors, and experiences affect your development as a person, as a spouse, and as a parent. In Chapter 2 the focus is on you as an individual. Answering the question "Who am I?" for yourself is essential based on the premise that self awareness and self knowledge are important in preparing for marriage and family life. In Chapter 3 the process and skills of relationship development will be explored in the context of evolving intimacy. In Chapter 4 cultural and environmental factors are presented that influence individuals and in turn play a significant role in marriage and family living. In Chapter 5 the family of origin as a primary influence in preparing you for marriage and parenting is investigated. In Chapters 6, 7, and 8 the content is concentrated on the usual progression of events which move a person from the ranks of the unmarried to marriage and parental responsibility. Courtship and Dating (Chapter 6) contains key issues relating to physical and emotional involvement and focuses on important questions that should be addressed during this phase of the relationship. In Chapter 7 the meaning and experience of marriage is addressed including the important elements that keep marriage alive and growing and typical problems of marriage. In Chapter 8 on family life, the normal development of a family is described and the focus is on roles and responsibilities associated with developing a family lifestyle. In Chapter 9 issues and concerns of remarriage and the blended family are presented. The concluding Chapter (10) contains resources available for help relating to issues raised in the various chapters. Each chapter contains suggested activities to help you understand and expand the information and apply it to your own experience and life. Additionally, if you are part of a class using this book, group activities conducted by the leader may complement each of the chapters.

USING THE BOOK

We suggest you treat each chapter as a unit, reading it and engaging in the associated activities before proceeding to the next chapter. Taking each chapter in order will allow you to move through a logical sequence that most typifies the experiences of living. Finally, do not hesitate to discuss and share the information and concepts in the book with partners (boyfriends, girlfriends, fiances, spouses, and so forth). Such efforts will make the material more relevant and personal.

The various chapters may appear to make the process of preparing for marriage and family an extremely complicated undertaking. After reading the book, you may feel it would be impossible to resolve all the issues raised before or even during marriage. We want to stress our primary goal is awareness and beginning the process of communication and conflict resolution which will continue for the rest of your lives together. The major determining factor in the success or failure of a marriage is not the mere existence of these issues but what each person does with them.

CONCLUDING COMMENTS

Although our individual growth and development paves the way for becoming motivated and involved in intimate relationships, the issue is much larger. A healthy society is predicated on the existence of a healthy family structure since the family unit is the core of any society. A healthy family depends on the existence of a healthy marriage. Therefore efforts directed at helping people make wise choices in regard to marital partners and acquiring the necessary knowledge, skills, and experience to function in marriage and family living will produce positive results. Our society will be stronger and more dynamic. It will be composed of families that generate productive, satisfied, and adjusted individuals who are capable of forming healthy marital relationships which in turn will produce healthy families and thus perpetuate a healthy individual—marriage—family—society growth cycle.

We believe that marriage and family life can be a fulfilling and satisfying lifetime experience. People generally do marry with intentions of making it together and raising healthy, responsible children. Evidence indicates that too often things go wrong. Couples and families find themselves in a quagmire of problems and feelings from which they cannot extricate themselves in an intact manner. Even though family, friends, therapists, and concerned others extend help, it is frequently too late. Consequently we feel that the preventive measure of preparation is a needed response to the increasing turmoil occurring in marriages and families.

When we were kids growing up in different parts of the country, we used to play the game "hide-n-seek" with our friends. As you know, this game requires one person to be "it" while the other people run and hide. Whoever was selected to be "it" would close their eyes and count to 10, 50, or 100. However, before he/she could begin the search, whoever was "it" was required by the rules to call out, "Here I come ready or not!" This was a warning that if you weren't settled into your special spot, you were now vulnerable and better get moving. In the game of life we also are given time to get prepared. We strongly believe that taking advantage of that time is an opportunity too often missed relative to one of the most crucial areas of our lives. For that reason we have chosen to title our book: *Marriage and Family: Better Ready Than Not.*

REFERENCES

Campbell, D. (1974). *If you don't know where you're going you'll probably end up somewhere else.* Niles, IL: Argus Communications.

Cherlin, A. (1981). *Marriage, divorce, remarriage.* Cambridge, MA: Harvard University Press.

Erikson, E. (1963). *Childhood and society.* New York: Norton.

Holmes, T.H., & Rahe, R.H. (1967). The social readjustment rating scale. *Journal of Psychosomatic Research, 11,* 213-218.

Kohlberg, L. (1969). *Stages in the development of moral thought and action.* New York: Holt, Rinehart, and Winston.

National Center for Health Statistics: Advance report of final marriage statistics, 1982 (1985). *Monthly Vital Statistics Report.* 34(3), Hyattsville, MD: Public Health Service.

Piaget, J. (1963). *The origins of intelligence in children.* New York: Norton.

Saxton, L. (1983). *The individual, marriage, and the family.* Belmont, CA: Wadsworth Publishing.

Sheehy, G. (1976). *Passages.* New York: E. P. Dutton.

U.S. Bureau of the Census (1985a). Department of Commerce. *USA statistics in brief 1985: A statistical abstract supplement.* Washington, D.C.: U.S. Government Printing Office.

U.S. Bureau of the Census (1985b). Current Population Reports, series p-20, No. 398. *Household and family characteristics: March 1984.* Washington, DC: U.S. Government Printing Office.

U.S. Bureau of the Census (1984). Current Population Reports, series p-20, No. 389. *Marital status and living arrangements: March 1983.* Washington, DC: U.S. Government Printing Office.

KNOWING AND BEING MYSELF

The case for knowing oneself as a basis for making effective choices in marriage and family life is presented. Topics addressed include personality traits, interests, abilities, values, vocational identity, personal habits, and sexual identity. The importance and process of knowing and expressing the "real me" is stressed and implications of one's individual identity in marriage are discussed.

*To thine own self be true
and it must follow as the
night the day, thou canst
not be false to any man.*

—William Shakespeare (*Hamlet*)

Long before psychology and the other social sciences had emerged stressing the significance of self knowledge, Shakespeare presented the above premise that being truly yourself is the best way to insure fulfilling relationships with others. Often in the social cauldron of relationships we find that the "I" or "me" gets lost or covered up, or we discover that we don't know ourselves well enough to make satisfying decisions; or we find that we have changed without really knowing how or why.

Many couples have come to us for counseling with the complaint that "My wife/husband isn't the same person I married." For all practical purposes that complaint is likely to be true. We already have confirmed that each of us is in a continual process of change throughout our life. Consequently, I am different now than I was five years ago, and without question I will be different five years from now. Many married persons who suffer from the malady of not knowing their spouse, married when one or both partners were in their teens or early twenties. At that point, their individual personalities and identities had not fully emerged before they began to work on living a life together. As they became involved in the busy world of obligations and responsibilities, they lost touch with the fact that each was changing until one day one or the other discovered it and began making demands that they go back to the way they were before. If one truth exists about human growth and change, it is that going back is impossible. As a result, they find themselves in a stuck place of either trying to get reacquainted or breaking it off and starting over.

How can such a situation be avoided? The answer lies in the importance of discovering, rediscovering, knowing, liking, and being yourself. This ongoing process is essential both as a preparation for intimacy and as a means of preserving that intimacy over a lifetime. William Glasser (1969), a well known psychiatrist, observed that the most important goal in a person's life is to attain an identity. If we do not do so, we lack self confidence and find ourselves in a downward spiral of failure, discontent, and discouragement. Knowing "who I am" places me at a distinct advantage because I can fulfill my needs and stand up to the pressures of others who are needing to fulfill their needs at my expense. People who lack self knowledge are often the ones most susceptible to being manipulated, used, and abused in their relationships with others.

Knowing yourself provides a solid basis for making decisions and for engaging in interactions which are mutually fulfilling to you and your partner. When you know yourself you know what you have to offer and can give of yourself with confidence and with the assurance that what you are giving is valuable and real.* In addition, increasing your self awareness enables your individuality to emerge. Self awareness helps you realize your similarities and differences with respect to others. Some one once stated that "Every man is in certain respects like all other men, like some other men, like no other man." Self knowledge provides the basis then for knowing what I have in common with all humanity and with certain groups of people as well as understanding my own uniqueness.

I JUST GOTTA BE ME

The rock song that belts out the words "I just gotta be me" captures the meaning of a basic characteristic within each of us, knowing and being oneself. It connects directly with our drive or need to become the very best person we can. This push from within, sometimes referred to as the need for self actualization or self enhancement, propels each of us to discover and use our personal resources to the greatest extent (Maslow, 1970). An inscription on a poster we came across recently expressed the essence of this drive:

All that a man can be he must be, if he is to be happy. The more he is fitted to do, the more he must do.

Sometimes this drive to be myself gets sidetracked by social pressures to conform or by placing my own self growth rather low on my list of priorities. Other times we sacrifice what we are to that which we wish to be. In either case we lose touch with ourselves and then become frustrated when we are not experiencing self-fulfillment. Remember that self-growth is a natural and essential element of being human and that self knowledge—its pursuit and expression—is a necessity to help us realize our fullest potential as persons.

---

*Quite often we ask our clients to give us a list of their positive and negative traits. They usually have no trouble with the minuses but have difficulty supplying the plusses.

THE RELEVANCE TO MARRIAGE

Possibly you have heard the clichés about self awareness many times. Self awareness is being pushed in education, by the media, and by a host of influential forces in your life. Such inundation does become tiring but that does not negate the importance of actively acquiring self knowledge as a basic task in your life. Self awareness is only a part of what this book is about, but an important part.

Who you are is the basic material with which you have to work in forming relationships with others. It is what attracts others to you and what turns them off. Consequently, a mandate is that you engage in introspection on a continuous basis, starting now even though you may not be currently involved in an intimate relationship. If you are already connected to someone, then doing so is even more important. Not knowing yourself, or worse, covering up what you know is only priming the pump for future personal frustration and relational hassles. If you do not know and cannot express who you are, your chances of getting any intimate relationship off the ground on a solid foundation are limited.

WHAT MAKES ME WHO I AM?

You may well ask the question, "If self knowledge is so important, what should I know about myself?" The following pages are designed to help you answer that question with particular emphasis on how each element relates to marriage and family living and how to acquire specific knowledge about yourself.

Personality

Each of us has a personality which has developed over time and is composed of certain traits and characteristics that tend to be consistent regardless of the circumstance or relationships in which we happen to be involved. The fact that we have personalities is attested to by comments like "he's always smiling" or "she never stops talking even for a minute." Statements such as these imply traits that serve as predictors of how we will likely act in our various interactions. This predictability gives a sense of security to ourselves (self confidence) and to others. We also know, however, that personality traits have the potential for generating reactions in others that run the gamut from negative to positive. In fact, a great deal of what we experience is a direct result of our personalities. Thomas Dreier (source & date unknown) once stated:

> The world is a great mirror. It reflects to you what you are. If you are loving, if you are friendly, if you are helpful, the world will prove loving and friendly and helpful to you. The world is what you are.

Your personality more than anything else is what tends to both generate and cement intimate relationships. Although we may be attracted to people because of physical appearance, position, proximity, or any other facilitative factors, what determines whether the relationship materializes is our personality. If our characteristics mesh, complement, or supplement each other in a compatible manner, we will grow together. If personalities clash, in spite of initial attraction, the ultimate experience in the relationship will be frustrating and unsatisfying.

Another fact about personality is that at certain periods of time it develops more rapidly than others. Some mothers contend that the nature of their children was evident to them even before birth. "When I carried John he was so active I couldn't even sleep and he never stopped being active." Whether that particular observation is true or not, a child's personality does become evident very early in life often containing basic elements by the time he/she reaches school age that prevail throughout a lifetime. However, in a personal sense, the period of greatest change occurs during adolescence and young adulthood. As we grapple with becoming independent and autonomous from our parents, we find ourselves having to rely more heavily on our own resources than on the resources of family and friends. In doing so we emerge with consistent patterns of behaviors, emotions, thoughts, and values which transcend the variability of events and relationships. Those patterns are our personality which continues to evolve throughout life but at an increasingly slower pace.

With this picture in mind let us consider some of the basic elements of our personality which both contribute to and have an impact upon the final product.

Interests

Interests are those stimuli that motivate us to act, to become involved in activities, to do things. They are translated into behaviors that provide excitement, enjoyment, and fulfillment and contribute to whom we are as persons. Robert L. Stevenson (source & date unknown) once said of our interests:

> To know what you prefer instead of humbly saying amen to what the world tells you you ought to prefer, is to have kept your soul alive.

Our interests can be determined in many different ways. One is to simply keep track of those things we like to do. Naturally we prefer doing things we like to those we don't like and consequently plan our lives accordingly. When we can't do so, we find ourselves becoming irritable and depressed.

We also can identify our interests by looking at what we do successfully. This does not give a definitive answer to interests because we often do well in areas we don't enjoy, e.g., we get good grades in English even though we hate writing essays. However, those things at which we are good tend to fan our interest in them because of the gratification we receive by being successful.

Another method of determining our interests is through the use of interest inventories which provide us with composite profiles based on our responses to questions designed to surface our likes and dislikes. Our responses then are compared either to categories of interests of persons working in certain vocations (e.g., dentist, engineer, secretary, and so forth) or to an interest profile showing comparative data relative to stronger and weaker interest areas. Several instruments are available from guidance and counseling services, employment agencies, and mental health agencies to help you obtain input on your interests. Two well-known interest inventories you can request are *The Strong-Campbell Vocational Interest Inventory* and *The Kuder Personal Preference Profile*. A point to remember, however, is that your interests do not necessarily reflect your abilities in the areas that emerge. Further assessment to determine your capabilities is necessary.

Why is knowing and developing my interests so important to intimacy in relationships? For one thing, common interests often provide the vehicle through which a relationship develops. You meet prospective partners while engaging in activities you enjoy. You develop your relationship through participating in activities about which both of you are enthusiastic, and you rely on mutual interests to enhance your togetherness. Additionally, your interests can be a contributive element to your partner's growth as you introduce him/her to new experiences. They also provide you with the means to step outside of the relationship to engage in activities that revitalize you, enabling you to interact with your partner in a more vigorous and enthusiastic manner. Seeking and maintaining the delicate balance between individual and mutual interests is a primary task in developing and maintaining an intimate relationship.

A common problem couples experience stems directly from differences in individual interests. Many couples during courtship and early marriage have a tendency to set aside personal preferences and interests for the sake of the relationship. Due to the excitement of being together and the emotional enthusiasm for each other, one or both willingly give in to doing things that in other circumstances they would not choose. As the excitement of the relational experience subsides one or the other begins to feel the urge to be doing things they prefer and becomes less accommodating to the other's interests. Subsequently, the partners start "doing their own thing" or begin to get resentful of the other's lack of cooperation. Barriers begin to grow, arguments ensue, and the amount of time spent together both lessens and becomes less enjoyable. If not confronted, this process can lead to extensive distance between the partners, severely jeopardize the relationship, and detract from its importance to the individuals.

Examples

Interest on Hold. In a counseling session, the wife complained that her husband had never bowled during their entire courtship of almost a year. Shortly after their honeymoon, he joined a bowling league and, at the point the couple came in for counseling, he was bowling 2 to 3 nights a week. The husband affirmed the fact that he had not bowled while they were dating but insisted it had always been a major interest of his. He had merely taken a sabbatical from bowling while he pursued his wife.

Interest Interrupted. Another couple, both skilled in tennis, started playing mixed-doubles as a way of being together recreationally and socially with other couples. However when an injury prevented the husband from playing and the wife was invited to play socially and in tournaments with other males, tensions arose. The couple had to reassess their original goals relative to tennis. They explored recreational alternatives that were possible considering their inability to pursue their interest in tennis together.

To avert conflict due to differences in interests, the important point is for each of us to know and communicate our repertoire of interests. Determining what interests will likely remain regardless of relational ties, knowing mutual areas of interest, and acquiring interests from each other are vital to the emergence of relational intimacy. In addition, the development of individual interests sustains us during times we must be alone and preserves our individuality which provides a crucial balance to togetherness in a marriage.

Abilities/Talents/Skills

Abilities, talents, and skills are the assets we develop and use to work toward a realization of our full potential. *Abilities* are those characteristics which provide us with the aptitude to do things well. When our aptitudes coincide with our interests and our motivation to develop them, we experience our greatest personal fulfillment. *Talents* are the inherent gifts which *each* of us receives from our heredity. John Ruskin (source & date unknown) said it best:" The weakest among us has a gift, however seemingly trivial which is peculiar to him and which worthily used, will be a gift to his race forever." This statement affirms that the true value of our abilities and talents emerges only when we develop and use them. This then implies the need for skills. *Skills* are learned and involve a personal choice. What skills you develop are the result of efforts you make to enhance and utilize your abilities and talents.

A realistic assessment of capacities is essential to developing and realizing your potential. Feedback in terms of grades, evaluations of performance in school, on the job or in training are important input. Standardized tests such as the *Differential Aptitude Test (DAT)* or the *General Aptitude Test Battery (GATB)* can be taken at your nearby counseling or employment service. This information combined with other specialized aptitude tests in areas of particular interest to you (e.g., music, art, engineering, and so forth) can give you a good basis upon which to make educational and vocational decisions. These decisions will in turn affect the course of your life not only leading you into circumstances that will help or hinder personal satisfaction but also lead to meeting people and relationships out of which intimacy may emerge.

Vocational Development/Career Choice

The natural outgrowth of matching our interests and abilities with educational and training experiences (skills acquisition) is career choice and vocational development. Choosing and developing your career may at first glance appear to be quite far removed from marriage and family decisions. But let us look a little deeper at the implications of your career choices and experiences.

Our work life has a direct bearing on our sense of self fulfillment. The more enthusiastic and involved you are in what you do in your career, the more likely you will have a positive attitude toward yourself and others. Work is the element that gives meaning and direction to our lives. Kahlil Gibran (1923) once wrote:

> When you work you fulfill a part of earth's furthest dream, assigned to you when that dream was born, and in keeping yourself with labour you are in truth loving life and to love life through labour is to be intimate with life's inmost secret. (*The Prophet*, pp. 25-26)

> Reprinted by permission of Alfred A. Knopf, Inc. Copyright 1923 by Kahlil Gibran and renewed 1951 by Administrators C.T.A. of Kahlil Gibran Estate and Mary G. Gibran.

On the other hand, to be engaged in a career or job that is not satisfying also can be one of the most negative personal experiences we have.

Not only is our career related to our individual well being, but it is intricately related to marriage and family relationships. Often through work we meet people with whom we become intimate. Natural factors in the work setting, such as time spent together pursuing common objectives, mutual experiences, and common relationships leading to marriage have their beginnings in a common career experience. Consequently, your career decisions may in fact set the stage for such eventualities.

Your career also will impact directly on your relationship once it develops. All couples must face the problems of integrating career and home. Arguments over how much or how little time is spent with the family because of career commitments are common. Many times the pursuit of success in a career is in direct opposition to development of a happy marriage and family life. Marriages are jeopardized because one or the other places career above family and the couple cannot work out an effective way to accommodate both. Partners become jealous of time spent and of relationships the other has in the work setting.

Example

> *Parting of the Ways. One common scenario involves couples who meet on the job and proceed to become intimate. As the relationship develops, marriage results, and subsequently, a family. Due to the wife dropping out to care for the children, the partners no longer "work" together and begin to lose touch with each other career-wise. As time goes on the husband develops close ties with his associates at work. These relationships become threatening to the wife who is now heavily invested in the domestic scene. Tension increases and arguments ensue around priorities and the importance of the career versus the marriage. If these issues cannot be resolved, the husband involves himself further in the job avoiding both the problem and the home. He finds supportive hearing at work and consequently transfers his emotional loyalty to colleagues which increases the conflict in his relationship with his wife. This type of spiraling cycle continues until a crisis point is reached where the couple has to face the problem, resign themselves to emotional distance in their marriage, or dissolve the marriage.*

Additional problems related to career choice have to do with dual career partners. Many couples currently are opting for a lifestyle that is based on both partners working in careers for which they have trained and are interested in pursuing. Time together and decisions relative to home responsibilities and family are crucial issues for these couples requiring extensive cooperation to resolve. In contrast, the more typical pattern of career-marriage integration is that which involves both partners working until children are born. The wife then drops out to become the primary care giver for the children until they reach school age. At that point the wife attempts re-entry into a career only to be faced with obstacles, such as the need for updated training, lack of mobility to attain desired positions, resistance from the family toward her leaving the home, and her own loss of self-confidence which has been eroded by her extensive involvement in the home.

We trust that you understand clearly that your career choices will continually intersect with and impact upon your marriage and family choices and experiences. Therefore, making effective career plans and being aware of the physical, emotional, and psychological benefits and demands of a career are crucial parts of preparing for intimate relationships and maintaining a healthy relational atmosphere as it develops. Engaging in career planning activities and classes as well as consulting with vocational counselors are valid and helpful ways of pursuing a career. A systematic study of your own interests and abilities along with collecting information about training opportunities and jobs are good first steps toward vocational fulfillment and dealing with the subsequent implications in marital and family relationships. As you do these things, however, we encourage you also to consider the ways in which your career goals and plans mesh with your marriage and family goals. Look at career preferences and opportunities in terms of your total life picture.

ACTIVITY: Specific Questions to Ask Yourself as You Think about and Plan Your Career.

1. **Time Commitments:** Since your work life will require a certain amount of time away from your spouse and family, the time requirements of the job relative to the time you want to spend at home must be considered.

    a. How many hours a week are you expected to work?

    b. Does the job require travel which takes you away from home overnight, for periods of time and over weekends?

    c. To be successful are you expected to put in extra hours on the job or take work home with you at night?

    d. Will the job require additional education which must be pursued on your own time outside of work hours?

2. **Policies and Benefits:** Work settings and careers have characteristics and standards which can either facilitate or inhibit marriage and family life.

a. Do fringe benefits encourage having families by covering medical, dental, and other costs as part of wages/salary or at reduced rates?

b. Are policies conducive to child-bearing and child rearing including such things as maternity and child care leaves for both mother and father, part-time work options, job sharing, flexible hours and on-the-job services for child care?

c. Do the financial benefits provide for the lifestyle you desire especially when expenses increase due to marriage and children?

d. Is vacation time sufficient to accommodate your relational and family needs?

3. **Mobility:** Where you work geographically has an extensive impact on your lifestyle both in terms of expenses and recreational activities.

a. Are opportunities for employment existing in the geographical area in which you wish to work?

b. Will the job require you to move either for purposes of advancement or because the nature of the job requires it?

c. Does the career you desire require acquisition of education or training that is not available in the area in which you live?

These are the kinds of questions that will enable you to incorporate marriage and family considerations into your career decision-making. Taking the time to find answers to them will pay extensive benefits in your vocation, your marriage and your personal satisfaction.

Values

Values are the foundation of our human experience. They not only affect what we do but also influence how we feel about what we do. Everyone has values. However, the nature of our values is not always clear either because we have not fully developed our value system or because we have not seriously explored what they are. Also our values can change based on experiences and choices we make in the course of living our lives. Raths, Harmin, and Simon (1966), noted values specialists, have described values as being the result of three processes: choosing, prizing, and acting. *Choosing* means thoughtfully considering the consequences of known alternatives and then freely making a personal choice. *Prizing* involves cherishing and being happy with the choice and being willing to affirm that choice publicly. *Acting* entails doing something with the choice repeatedly in the same pattern.

Often, however, our values get covered up, disregarded, or challenged when interacting in significant relationships. Parents express great concern about the influence of peers on their adolescent children. Married couples discover value differences exist that never surfaced in the course of their dating. Career and social demands introduce stress into our lives when we are faced with choices that seem to compromise what we believe. Consequently, the more aware and sure you are of your values, the more you will tend to express those values in your relationships. This in turn increases the likelihood of forming intimate relationships with persons compatible with you on a values level.

Values tend to emanate from our experiences in significant relationships. Values are derived from our family of origin, our education, and our religious or spiritual involvements. We will explore the impact of our family legacy in a later chapter but suffice to say that each of us tends to acquire values that are directly related to those of our parents. Education, as the second most influential social institution after our family, plays a significant role in forming our values. The impact of our religion, whether formal or informal, prominent or insignificant, also carries clout when it comes to values.

The most common tension producing incidents in marital relationships have to do with value clashes. No matter how much two people care about one another, the very fact that they were raised in two different families sets the stage for values conflict. The conflict may arise over an item as insignificant as having candy in the house or extend to major issues such as child rearing practices or choosing a church to attend. Sometimes individuals unknowingly disregard their values in the course of forming a relationship. Other times they choose to cover them in order to avoid making waves or in hopes of changing the other person once the relationship is secure.

Example

Ignoring values. A common example of avoidance of personal values occurs in marriages where each partner was raised in a different religion. Prior to marriage and during the early years of their relationship both concur that religion isn't important and they do not practice either of the partner's religions. This appears to resolve the problem until a child is born. Now the parents, out of a sense of responsibility, feel their child should have some religious training. When the question of where comes up, a deep conflict occurs which surprises the couple who thought they were above such feelings of loyalty to their original religious roots.

Our point is not to tell you what your values should be, but rather to stress the essential importance of knowing what your values are.

ACTIVITY: Stating Your Values and Beliefs

Engage in values clarification activities (see Simon, 1974, *Meeting Yourself Halfway)* and seriously explore what you believe and what you would not give up even under pressure. Explain your values to another person or persons with the ground rule that the other person(s) listen but not judge. Try to state clearly what you value and believe.

Physical Appearance

Social psychologists have confirmed the importance of physical appearance in human relationships. In a review of research studies, Rathus (1984) indicated that people react positively to physical attractiveness and that such reactions result in favorable first impressions that tend to carry over once the relationship has developed. In our counseling sessions, many couples state that physical attractiveness was the thing that initially brought them together.

Physical appearance also is directly related to personal feelings of self worth and self confidence. People who are embarrassed or uncomfortable with the way they look tend to be hesitant and more withdrawn in social situations. People who approve of and like their physical image tend to be more outgoing and assertive in relating to others. Such differences directly affect the potential for initiating relationships.

Physical appearance is a very ambiguous and at best a relative concept. Obviously natural beauty is not a common trait among all human beings. Expressions such as "beauty is only skin deep" and "beauty is in the eye of the beholder" attest to the fact that we recognize the importance of perception with regard to beauty. As for physical attractiveness, therefore, the question is not how much you have but rather how you use and develop what you have. Your physical attractiveness emerges as an asset only when you realistically assess yourself and take the time to make the best of what you've got.

Your attractiveness has more to it than just your physical features. It also consists of developing your own style. Your style includes your unique manner of expression, the way you dress, walk, and talk, all of which contribute to your physical self-image. Understanding and working with all these factors can enhance your physical presentation to the world.

Numerous resources on beauty, grooming, dress and poise in the form of books, articles, classes, and workshops are available to you if you wish to use them. For example, John T. Molloy (1976), author of the book *Dress for Success,* has made a fortune promoting the theory that your style of dress is a crucial factor in succeeding in your career. Carole Jackson (1980), who wrote *Color Me Beautiful,* contended that all people need to discover the colors which best enhance their appearance and discard all others. Whether you agree with these authors or not, developing a sense of appropriateness in dress relative to your physical features and the social expectations of certain situations will do much to inspire a feeling of ease and self-confidence. One of the most uncomfortable feelings is to arrive at a social gathering only to notice you are inappropriately dressed. Finding the balance between being comfortably similar and yet personally and creatively unique is a mark of a person who presents him/herself well.

One note of caution is that although important, physical appearance is not the embodiment of personal success. It is a creative expression of who you are but should not become an all-consuming preoccupation. Over-involvement in self-presentation leads to negative reactions in others who begin to view you as self-centered and "untouchable." Enhancing your physical attractiveness is important but emphasis must be balanced time-wise and value-wise in order to maintain a healthy perspective that makes it an asset rather than your total personality.

Physical attractiveness not only is a factor in initial relationship development but also is a significant issue over the course of a relationship's history. The motivation to present yourself attractively usually varies over time. Partners, who during courtship did their utmost to be attractive, lose that drive once the relationship is secure. The importance of physical appearance may be stimulated by other forces, such as career demands, but looking attractive for one's partner becomes less important. This change may have ramifications in terms of decreased excitement in the relationship and less satisfying sexual experience. A particular problem emerges when one of the two partners "lets him/herself go" physically which often occurs because of feelings of low self-esteem or a lack of confidence. If it does occur, then the other feels let down or hurt or may feel like he/she is being taken for granted. Tensions and conflicts result creating more distance between the partners subsequently eroding the strength of the relationship and commitment.

A husband in a recent interview angrily stated to his wife, "We made a promise never to let ourselves go physically and you didn't keep it," referring to his wife's having become overweight. Such issues can be avoided if you know how to present yourself attractively and are committed to doing so for your own sake without either manipulating others or allowing circumstances to undermine your commitment.

Health and Hygiene

Our health tends to be one of those things we seldom think about until something happens to threaten it. Yet, how we care for and treat our bodies has a profound impact on the nature and quality of our lives. A recent government news release indicated that Americans are taking better care of themselves which is a major factor contributing to longer life expectancy. This increase in health consciousness, however, tends to be associated with middle aged and older Americans. When we are young, to imagine being old or infirm is hard to do. We do not realize that what we do now will affect our lives ten, twenty, and forty years from now. Yet if our goals are to live a long life, to have a satisfying sex life, and to give birth to healthy children, we need to be aware of our health habits and their long term implications.

The negative ramifications of poor eating habits, smoking, alcohol, marijuana, and other drugs, whether acquired by prescription, over the counter, or illegally are well documented, both scientifically and experimentally. Through research, for example, has been demonstrated that "you are what you eat." Eating nutritious and balanced diets composed of natural foods minus additives and preservatives, avoiding excessive eating and junk food, and limiting intake of such items as sugar and salt are recommended practices. Much has been written about healthy eating habits, since it affects our psychological as well as our physical well being.

As Americans we are influenced by the media and the business world to be a consumer society. If you are reading this book, you most likely have been ingesting chemicals added to your food and drinks for at least 15 to 20 years without even thinking about it. A similar pattern also has emerged in areas such as smoking, alcohol consumption, and drug use. The fact that the pharmaceutical, alcohol, and tobacco industries are among the richest in our society attests to the reality that individuals are using their products at a consistently high rate. The explanation for this is not simple, but part of it certainly has to do with individual choices and the fact that habits are formed when young which carry over into adulthood where we become role models for others thus continuing the cycle. When we are young, we tend to think of tomorrow as a long way off and live life for the present. In reality, our experience often turns out to be the following:

> Drink and dance and laugh and lie
> Love the reeling midnight through
> For tomorrow we shall die
> (But alas we never do.)

> (Dorothy Parker, 1931, *The Flaw in Paganism*)

We generally pay the price for whatever excesses or negative habits we learn. So an important point is for us to concern ourselves with making choices relative to eating, drinking, and drug use that are healthy in terms of both short term and long term effects.

Physical exercise and rest also are vital components of good health practices. Recent medical researchers have pointed out that consistent physical activity has a positive effect in that it enables the body to cleanse itself of excessive and damaging substances which if left to accumulate will contribute to cardiovascular, gastrointestinal, and respiratory diseases among others. Consequently, developing recreational interests of an active nature and engaging in them on a consistent schedule will be personally beneficial.

Rest is another important element. Insuring your body has a suitable amount of rest not only will facilitate better health, but also will positively affect your attitudes and moods. Stress is the number one cause of anxiety and tension in our society. The inability to relax and rest is one of the most talked about problems. We often are unable to leave behind the pressures of work, school, or other situations in which we are intensely involved. As we continue to carry and accumulate responsibilities and obligations, we begin to squeeze extra time out of our rest, recreational, or even sleep time. Such a downward spiral eventually takes its toll on our physical bodies resulting in physical problems and health impairment. Maintaining a schedule of sufficient sleep, learning techniques of relaxation as well as planning specific rest times removed from the daily pressures of your life will be helpful. Researchers have proven that physical exercise, meditation, and even intensive prayer experiences worked into one's daily routine are healthy practices combined with actual sleep time.

How do our individual health habits intersect with marriage and family living? Since our own habits are usually difficult to change, the first thing we attempt to do is create a relationship which accommodates our habits. If that does not work (in many cases it doesn't), we then try to change our partner over to our way of doing things. Obviously, either of these efforts will generate conflict and tension. At a deeper level, however, couples tend to develop supportive relationships that affect the mental and physical health of each individual partner. If couples support each other's poor nutritional eating patterns, drug, drinking, or smoking habits, the relationship contributes to self-destruction. One of the major obstacles to marital therapy emerges when one partner wants to change a habit or behavior but the other does not. Friction and conflict develop which escalate to an unresolvable standoff which results in a breakup of the marriage. Other times one partner may solve their individual problem in an area such as chemical abuse or smoking only to find that the marriage is now in jeopardy. Such problems may be avoided if relationships begin on a positive footing regarding health and hygiene habits.

Example

When Habits Change. One couple in their mid-twenties came to therapy because they were embroiled in an impasse over the use of chemicals and natural foods. Prior to marriage they had mutually engaged in a counter-culture lifestyle that involved the use of marijuana and diets that primarily depended on natural foods. After marriage and her pregnancy, she became more committed to eating natural foods and would rage at him for purchasing foods such as ice cream which contained artificial colors or flavors. She began to abstain from smoking marijuana out of respect for her pregnancy and put pressure on him to stop his occasional use so as not to tempt her. Both felt mutually betrayed with these changes and were continually involved in arguments. When they came for counseling they were beginning to feel that these differences in their value systems were unresolvable.

SEXUAL IDENTITY:
I AM WOMAN—I AM MAN

As for individual identity, the one fact with which we each begin is that we are born either male or female. That difference has inspired excitement and controversy throughout human history and is an integral part of every man-woman relationship. Much has been written about these differences and similarities between the sexes with many of these writings attempting to resolve the issue once and for all. But of course, no definitive answer has been provided nor does one appear imminent. In a May 18, 1981, *Newsweek* report of research on sex differences was stated that differences between males and females go beyond the obvious ones of size, anatomy, and sexual function. Apparently "men and women experience the world differently, not merely because of the ways they were brought up in it, but because they feel it with a different sensitivity of touch, hear it with different aural responses, puzzle out its problems with different cells in their brains" (p. 72). In the article was added that "biology isn't destiny, but it matters... and that triggers a furor over the social roles of men and women" (p. 73).

Your own maleness or femaleness is certainly the result of both trait differences you inherit and cultural influences to which you are exposed. We will explore the what and how of cultural influences in Chapter 4, so for now we simply want to affirm their impact on you as a person. Too often we never think about or consider our sexual identity. It tends to evolve rather unconsciously through the acquisition of characteristics which line up quite effectively with "sex role stereotypes" of males and females. Consideration of sexual identity as a process involving "sex role choices" gets ruled out. Instead of thinking about what I want for myself as a man or a woman, I make automatic responses which further substantiate the differences between men and women. People thus relate to each other as roles (male role and female role) rather than as persons. This conflict becomes personalized and crystalized in the context of marital relationships.

The issue of sex roles in marriage and family life is a primary source of tension, irritation, and pain. The battle of the sexes is carried out to some degree in every intimate relationship. We certainly have experienced this in our own marriage. After a recent argument involving sharing household duties, Toni brought home a card which stated "the nicest thing about the battles of the sexes is that you can go to bed with the enemy." This message both affirms the inevitable existence of conflict, but also points out one of the means of resolving issues that stem from differing views of one's sex role in a relationship. The problem, however, is that sexual closeness is only a temporary solution and seldom resolves differences on a long term basis. Consequently, vitally important for you is knowing who you are as a man or woman because that knowledge will lead to knowing what you want in an intimate relationship with your opposite sex counterpart. Knowing and making sex role choices also will give you a better foundation for negotiating and developing sex role compatibility in your relationship. Acting to clarify and determine your own sexual identity thus will become a personal contribution to resolving the sex role controversy because you will settle it for yourself as well as introduce a better quality of relating in your marriage.

Although research and personal experience attest to the existence of differences between males and females, these differences are not absolute nor do they necessarily determine the course of our existence. The conclusion drawn in the May 18, 1981, *Newsweek* article was, "Perhaps the most arresting implication of the research is not that there are undeniable differences between males and females but that their differences are so small, relative to the possibilities open to them" *(Just How the Sexes Differ,* p. 83). Regardless of heredity or culture, you still have to live with your sexual identity. So rather than accentuating differences on a global level, by acquiescing to the norm, create your own identity by exploring, choosing, and acting upon sex role options that will enhance your own fulfillment as a person, a spouse, and a parent.

GETTING THE INSIDE OUT: EXPRESSING THE REAL ME

As you grow in self-knowledge and begin to understand who you are, the next step is to communicate that awareness to others. However, our ability to communicate our real self to others is often thwarted by fears of rejection, lack of self-confidence, and perceived pressures that seem to require us to be someone we are not. Sometimes expressing who I am is so confusing that it resembles the old TV program *What's My Line* where someone eventually asks, "Will the real (person's name) please stand up?" In our case, the real me is camouflaged in the interaction of three elements: what I know about me, what others want to know about me, and how much I am willing to let others know what I know about me. The process involved in getting the real me out is called self-disclosure. If I never engage in revealing the real me to others, particularly to those with whom I wish to be close, all my efforts to acquire self-knowledge are for naught. For a relationship to grow and develop, a mandatory requisite is that I *express* myself as well as *know* myself.

Benefits of self-disclosure are numerous. It enables you to overcome tendencies to be phony and eliminates facades which leave you frustrated and erodes confidence in your own identity. Being the real you, though not always comfortable and easy, will prove positive in the long run. Ultimately we have no choice but to let ourselves be known. Psychologist Everett Shostrom (date unknown) once said, "No matter how foolish, silly, or ridiculous I may be—that's me, and I've got to be patriotic to myself." This self-patriotism is a part of all of us.

Another benefit of self-expression is in terms of self-worth. When you let others know who you are, you affirm in your own mind your worthiness as a human being. You convey a positive attitude about yourself to others and confirm in their minds your value as a person. For years a quotation (date and source unknown) hung on the wall at Jim's office:

> I believe that if God thought highly enough of me to make me, there should be no reason for me to have any lower opinion of myself than He does.

One of the basic characteristics about healthy relationships is that they involve positive individuals, and positive individuals are persons who can express their self knowledge. Even when we deal with our faults and the negative aspects of our personality, positive feelings of self worth give a sense of confidence that change can occur.

Finally, just as self-knowledge provides inner security and self-confidence, self-expression involves a vehicle for control over the directionality of our lives. George Bernard Shaw once wrote:

> People are always blaming their circumstances for what they are. I don't believe in circumstances. The people who get on in this world are the people who get up and look for circumstances they want, and if they can't find them, make them. (George Bernard Shaw, *Mrs. Warren's Profession,* Act III)

The same is true with us. As we let others know who we are, we create an impact which generates circumstances compatible with our personhood. Non-revelation of self, particularly in the realm of intimate relationships, only results in others creating circumstances with which we then have to live or reject. Both of these alternatives can be frustrating and painful.

Genuine self-disclosure is an essential ingredient in intimate relationships and is a process that should begin before marriage and continue throughout the life of the relationship. It is the culminating activity of the self-exploration process and confirms our individuality in the context of our relationships. Self-exploration, self-disclosure, and the development of self assets are important activities in which to engage preparatory to and during marriage and family life. Current attitudes, interests, abilities, skills, and values may change in the future, but as long as you as an individual maintain an active practice of self-exploration and self-disclosure you will be prepared for accommodating to any circumstances you encounter and will be able to generate relationships that are truly person to person in their intimacy and fulfillment.

REFERENCES

Gibran, K. (1923, 1951). *The prophet.* New York: Alfred A. Knopf.

Glasser, W. (1969). *Schools without failure.* New York: Harper and Row.

Jackson, C. (1980). *Color me beautiful.* New York: Ballantine.

Just how the sexes differ. (May 18, 1981). *Newsweek,* pp.72-83.

Maslow, A. (1970). *Motivation and personality* (2nd ed.). New York: Harper and Row.

Molloy, J. (1976). *Dress for success.* New York: Warner Books.

Parker, D. (1931). *The flaw in paganism. Death and taxes.* In E. Partnow (Ed.), *The quotable woman.* Los Angeles, CA: Corwin Books.

Raths, L., Harmin, M., & Simon, S. (1966). *Values and teaching.* Columbus, OH: Charles E. Merrill.

Rathus, S. (1984). *Psychology* (2nd ed.). New York: Holt, Rinehart, and Winston.

Shakespeare, W. *Hamlet.* In T.J. Spencer (Ed.) (1981). New York: Penguin Books.

Shaw, G. B. *Mrs. Warren's profession.* In M. Peters (Ed.) (1981). New York: Garland Publishing.

Simon, S. (1974). *Meeting yourself halfway.* Niles, IL: Argus Communications.

INTERPERSONAL RELATIONSHIPS: TRAINING FOR INTIMACY

Interpersonal relating is explored as a foundation for the process of relationship development in the context of marriage and family life. Ingredients of healthy relationships, how relationships develop, and the implications of relational experiences on future relating are discussed. Communication skills, relating styles and patterns, and the importance of responsibility in relationships are presented.

No soul is desolate as long as there is a human being for whom it can feel trust and reverence.

—*G. Eliot (Date & source unknown)*

Without a connection with other people our very essence as human beings would be lost. Interpersonal relationships are the means by which we learn and confirm our humanity. They form the network in which we experience belongingness and come to know the meaning of community and intimacy. To the extent our relationships are able, they train us, teach us, mold us, and prepare us for life. Through the vehicle of interpersonal connectedness we acquire our expectations of others, learn relating skills, and meet our personal needs for trust, love, belonging, and respect. Consequently, relationships, their nature and development, constitute the training ground for obtaining skills and experiences that prepare us for forming and developing a relational bond that leads to marriage. These relationships give us the repertoire of resources necessary to make our marriage and family healthy and satisfying.

Our purpose in this chapter is to look at the general area of interpersonal relating as a foundation for the more specific process of relationship development in the context of marriage and family life. We will explore the general nature of interpersonal relationships identifying basic ingredients of healthy relationships. We will examine how relationships develop and present a model depicting the dynamics of that development. We will review essential interpersonal skills which are necessary to build and maintain relationships, and we will identify a variety of relational styles that characterize our interpersonal interactions. Finally, we will discuss the impact of relationship experiences and skills as both preparation for and the foundation of marriage and family relating.

OUR WORLD OF RELATIONSHIPS

Each one of us lives in a world of relationships which can be described as a three dimensional figure composed of concentric spheres emanating out from a central sphere representing our self (see Figure 3.1). Some of us have very large relational spheres while others of us have smaller ones. In either case, the circles closest to us represent those persons with whom we are most intimate. They are people who are our intimate confidants and who represent our closest interpersonal relationships. In most cases, only a very few people are in the inner circle. Often family members and eventually spouses or very intimate partners fill this space in the form of intimate dyadic connections. When that inner sphere is void of people, we feel lonely, detached, and isolated. Experiencing this void often propels us toward others in order to restore intimate connectedness with another person. To experience periodic lapses of intimacy is not unusual and only reaffirms the need and desire for that special closeness. However, if our inner circle remains empty for any reason, the ultimate result is isolation and the loss of access to a unique and special aspect of the human experience. In some sense, the inability to develop and maintain a close intimate relationship is analogous to a tree without a tap root to give it stability and strength in storms and high winds.

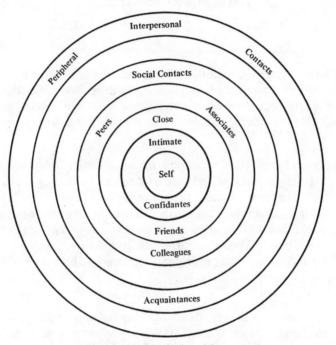

Figure 3.1. Relationship map.

As we move out from this center of our relational sphere, these relationships become less intimate but take on other important features. Close friends and peers help us meet our social needs and colleagues, co-workers, or fellow students form a relational milieu in which we pursue career/educational fulfillment. Other relationships form around interests and values while still others emerge from contacts with people who supply services and information relating to the necessities of living in a society. All these relationships are important to us and either help or hinder our coping on a day to day basis.

In the context of our relational network we know that certain relationships stand out as positive and constructive, and others tend to be negative and destructive. We need to be aware of the whys and wherefores in order to cultivate the positive and counteract or disassociate from the negative.

CHARACTERISTICS OF FUNCTIONAL RELATIONSHIPS

Generally speaking, relationships we construe as positive tend to be characterized by a number of common ingredients. These include trust, acceptance, respect, warmth, communication, and understanding (Trotzer, 1977). A brief discussion of each of these elements follows.

Trust forms the foundation of an effective relationship. It enables partners to feel safe and secure in sharing themselves with each other without fear of rejection or reprisal. It involves both trusting others and being trustworthy. As trust develops in a relationship it supplies the cement which strengthens the relational bond. Whenever trust is betrayed the relationship tends to be undermined and participants may learn to be more hesitant in their relating to others.

Acceptance is the experience of being fully and freely yourself in the context of a relationship. Who I am can emerge without the threat of judgment or the necessity to modify it simply to please another person. Victor Hugo captured the essence of this quality when he stated that "The supreme happiness of life is the conviction that we are loved, loved for ourselves or rather loved in spite of ourselves." Acceptance also has two dimensions—acceptance of self and acceptance of others. The Judeo-Christian commandment, "love your neighbor as yourself" implies a standard that we should accord others no less acceptance than we accord ourselves. On the other hand, it also indicates that the extent to which we can accept others is determined by our own level of self-acceptance. Cyrus once wrote, "All men

have frailties; and whoever looks for a friend without imperfections, will never find what he seeks. We love ourselves notwithstanding our faults, and we ought to love our friends in like
manner.'' While trust forms the foundation of the relationship,
acceptance provides the framework.

Respect is the quality in relationships that accentuates the worth
of the individual as a unique and special human being. When little respect exists in a relationship, then a poor prognosis exists
for growth or fulfillment. Carl Rogers (1951) coined the term
unconditional positive regard to describe this characteristic in
relationships. It means that we ascribe worth to persons because
they are human beings who are inherently worthwhile. Self-
respect also is an essential element in our attitude toward others.
If we do not value ourselves, then we have difficulty in ascribing
any greater sense of worth to others.

Warmth is a particularly human capability which cannot be
measured empirically but it is probably the life blood of any
important relationship. It encompasses caring, love, sensitivity,
closeness, prizing, liking, and a myriad of other elements that we
know exist by our inner experience as we relate to others. We
know it exists because when we feel it in a relationship we are
drawn to and attracted to the person. On the other hand, when
warmth is absent, we experience a sense of distance and coldness
which repels us or serves as a barrier to approaching the other
person(s).

Communication provides the means by which meaningful interaction among persons is facilitated. The most desirable type
of communication is two-way communication in which all persons involved have the desire and ability to initiate, respond, and
receive in the communication process. We will focus more
specifically on this ingredient later in the chapter.

Understanding is the ultimate dimension of an effective relationship. The ability of partners to see things from each other's
point of view is a trait common to relationships which have en-
dured the tests of time and circumstances. Carl Rogers (1951)
used the term *empathy* to describe this relational condition. He

defined it as the ability to understand another person as if you were that person without losing the "as if" quality.

Each of the qualities just described is really the positive end point of a continuum, the opposite of which is negative. While satisfying and fulfilling relationships tend toward the trust, acceptance, respect, warmth, communication and understanding side, unsatisfying and hurtful relationships tend to be distrustful, rejecting, disrespectful, noncommunicational, and nonunderstanding.

In our work with troubled couples, at least one and usually more of the preceding qualities are underdeveloped or missing in their relationship. Spouses distrust each other, do not accept each other, or demonstrate lack of respect for one another. Distance is evident in their relationship and little caring for each other is exhibited. Lack of communication is typically identified as their "problem" and each complains that the other does not understand. In such cases, the essential task is for the couple to get "back to the basics" which is to work at developing increased levels of each of these essential ingredients.

HOW RELATIONSHIPS DEVELOP

Relationships develop as a result of interaction between people in which information is exchanged. The extent to which a relationship develops depends on the intensity of the interaction involved and the nature and depth of the information shared.

Johari Window Relationship Development Model

Luft and Ingham (Luft, 1970) designed a relationship development model called the Johari Window to explain the process (See Figure 3.2). In any relationship, two person components—self and others—and two formation components—known and unknown—exist. Juxtaposed to one another a grid of four quadrants is created which can be used to graphically illustrate the nature of all relationships from initial contact or acquaintances to our most deeply intimate associations. Quadrant I is called the *Open* area and represents all information that is mutually accessible to all participants in the relationship. This information may range from the mere exchange of names with a first time acquaintance to a deep sharing of our innermost thoughts and feelings with an intimate partner. As relationships develop and grow, the open area expands. Referring back to the relational network we discussed at the beginning of this chapter, the inner circles of your relational sphere would be depicted as having large open areas while the outer circles of your network would be relationships with small open areas. Note that we have relationships of all degrees of openness, and that this model does not promote a value that "all" relationships should be "open". The model is only intended as a means of describing relationships. The open quadrant increases in size as a result of interactions where information drawn from the other quadrants of the grid is exchanged in the relationship.

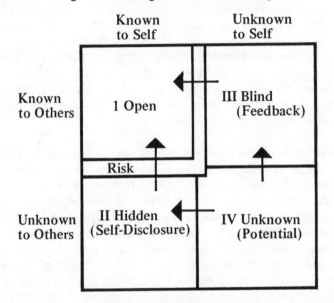

Figure 3.2. Johari Window.

From *Group Processes: An Introduction to Group Dynamics* by Joseph Luft. Reprinted by permission of Mayfield Publishing Company, copyright 1984, 1970, and 1963 by Joseph Luft.

Quadrant II is called the *Hidden* quadrant because it contains information that is privy to oneself but not to others. This area is the domain which houses the "real you". Only when you want others "to know" does information pass into the open quadrant through a process known as self-disclosure. The important characteristic of this area is that you control the nature and amount of information which is disclosed. You usually make the decision as to what and when based on the level of trust and acceptance sensed in the relationship. Any time you choose to self disclose you take a risk because now others have access to the information and as such you lose control of it. John Powell (1969) in his book *Why am I Afraid to Tell you Who I Am* discussed at length many of the barriers that hinder us in telling others about ourselves. However, the more we do disclose, the greater the likelihood that others will know us as we really are.

The other quadrant that provides information directly to the open area is called the *Blind* area (Quadrant III). This contains information that others know about you of which you are not aware. Each of us develops impressions of those to whom we relate. However, until we tell them what our perceptions are, that information remains part of the blind area in the relationship. The only way to remove this barrier in a relationship is through feedback. However, feedback involves risk just as self-disclosure does. Therefore, we usually hold back giving feedback until we are sure that the relationship will not be jeopardized or until we feel the relationship will improve because of it.

The obstacle of risk is an ever present phenomenon in our relationships no matter what the context. As human beings, we are endowed with self-protective defense mechanisms which intercede whenever we sense we are vulnerable to reprisal or rejection. Consequently, we do not unleash overly personal, positive, or negative information unless we are somewhat assured that we will not be punished or hurt or that the relationship will be able to stand it. However, a certain degree of risk-taking must occur for any relationship to grow. Benjamin Franklin's old adage, "nothing ventured, nothing gained," is applicable to the arena of relationships. Generally speaking, when we risk self-disclosure or feedback and experience positive results, we become more willing to do so again. Thus a positive growth cycle is initiated in the relationship. On the other hand, if we experience negative consequences, we are less likely to risk again which inevitably results in relational stagnation, deterioration, or termination.

The fourth (IV) quadrant labeled *Unknown* refers to potential information that only emerges as a result of a specific interpersonal interaction. For example, we all have the capacity to love. However, until we become involved in a relationship where we experience loving and being loved, that information is an unknown entity. Similarly, as we relate to others over time, aspects of ourselves emerge that neither we nor our partners knew existed. Married persons often attest to this fact when they say, "I was never like that until after I got married." The unknown is the resource domain in a relationship, and any information emanating from it is usually processed through the *Hidden or Blind* quadrants.

ACTIVITY: Utilizing Johari Window

A helpful way of understanding the Johari window model and applying it to your own life is to take a number of relationships from the various circles of your network and graphically compare them using the size of the various quadrants as indicators of closeness and intimacy. Form a continuum starting with a relationship that has a small open area (acquaintance) and a relationship with a large open area (intimate confidant). Place the other relationships between them according to your perception of openness.

Interpersonal Skills:
The Tools of Relationship Development

As human beings we are born with certain traits which effectively distinguish us from other living creatures and certain needs which must be met in order to ensure our survival. Our traits provide us with a blueprint for development and our needs motivate us to act. However, whether we realize our full potential as a human being and whether we meet our needs is a matter of learning. The domain in which that learning takes place is our relational network, and the primary means by which we learn is interpersonal communication. We can improve our chances for realizing our potential and meeting our needs by developing intrapersonal and interpersonal skills as the tools for enhancing our relationship development and improving our communication. We addressed the intrapersonal aspect extensively in Chapter 2 so we will concentrate on the interpersonal aspect here. Interpersonal skills can be differentiated into two main categories: (1) communication skills which pertain to the specific process by which information is exchanged in relationships, and (2) social skills which relate to how we act or behave in social situations. We will briefly address each of these areas.

COMMUNICATION SKILLS

Listening

Listening is probably the most important and the most underdeveloped communication skill we possess as human beings. The reason for this is that listening is something we all take for granted. With the exception of people who have hearing impairments, we automatically assume that we know how to listen. Although researchers have proven time and again that we are ineffective listeners, we continue to expend most of our time and energy on the development of our *expressive skills* rather than our *receptive skills*. The Simon and Garfunkel song "Sounds of Silence" made us cognizant of the societal impact of "people hearing without listening." More specifically, each of us is acutely aware when we are not being listened to and when we are not even being heard much less understood. The consequences in terms of loss of self-esteem and frustration as well as the confusion or conflict due to errors are evident.

Even though we give lip service to the importance of listening, it is usually the first thing to go when conflict arises, when pressure to perform increases, or when the need for personal expression becomes paramount. Yet when people are genuinely listened to a number of vital relational results automatically occur. When you really listen, you communicate interest, caring, acceptance, and respect all of which forge a stronger relational bond and a positive interpersonal atmosphere. When you listen, you increase the potential for understanding and subsequently pave the way for effective action if that is required. As such, effective listening acts as the catalyst for the development of positive relationships.

The impact of poor listening is seen in many marriages and families where, because of conflicts and hassles, the spouses or parents and children have stopped listening to each other. As this important channel of communication is severed, the potential for conflict resolution is reduced and family members begin to distance themselves from one another. When these couples and families come for counseling our first task is to help them start to listen to each other again.

The type of listening that is most effective in a relationship is the skill of "active listening." *Active listening* is a receptive process which requires the listener to verbally respond to the speaker in order to assure that the message being received is accurate and understood. It requires attending to the speaker until the full message is received rather than simply waiting your turn or preparing your response in your head while the other person is still talking. A common approach we all use is to listen passively until we hear something we want to hear, *selective perception,* or something that triggers a reaction. Then we close out the rest of the message while we get ourselves ready to express our viewpoint. Active listening requires the self-discipline to stay in tuned to our partner instead of getting distracted by our own thoughts and reactions.

Active listening involves four types of responses you can learn through practice:

Restatement is the skill of accurately repeating the basic content of your partner's message, usually in words similar to those used in the message. This confirms to the speaker that he/she is being heard and keeps the listener attending to the person speaking.

Reflection is the skill of expressing the meaning of your partner's message as you understand it. Reflection facilitates understanding because the speaker can confirm, correct, or modify the listener's reflections resulting in mutual understanding. It also assists the speaker in understanding his/her own meaning because of the process involved in getting to a point of mutuality.

Clarification is the skill of responding to confusing or unclear aspects of a message. Too often we hesitate to do this because we think it may seem redundant or reflect negatively on us. However, simply asking our partner to repeat a message or to say it in a different way will do wonders for communication.

Summarizing is the skill of pulling together important elements of a particular conversation and presenting them in capsule form. This skill is useful in both concluding a conversation and in facilitating transition to a new topic. A common communicational phenomenon in many marital and family disputes is that closure is never reached. People simply drop the subject instead of summarizing where things are. Even when something is not resolved, a good idea is to summarize the current status so that the communicators know where things stand and can move on to something else. Doing so also makes picking up on the issue at a later time easier thus facilitating the conflict resolution process.

Tindall and Gray (1985) in a book entitled *Peer Power: Becoming An Effective Peer Helper, Book 1,* provided activities for practicing these four skills. To learn these skills can and will be meaningful in all interpersonal relations including relating to your marriage partner.

Awareness

The Minnesota Couples Communication Program uses a model called the *Awareness Wheel* to assist in understanding the communication process and learning specific communication skills. It is based on the concept that information we wish to communicate comes from one or more of five areas in our life experiences. These five areas are as follows (Miller, Nunnally, & Wackman, 1975, pp. 29-52):

> **Thinking:** The cognitive part of us which manifests itself in interpretations of our experience and perceptions.

> **Sensing:** Information which emerges as the result of our sensory processes involving touch, taste, smell, sight, and hearing.

> **Feeling:** The affective part of us which surfaces in the form of feelings and emotions.

> **Wanting:** The intentions we manifest usually in the form of attitudes which move us toward or away from something.

> **Doing:** The realm of our actions or behaviors which are observable and concrete.

As we develop our awareness in each of these areas we are then prepared to communicate effectively with others using a series of specific skills (Miller et al., 1975, pp. 53-78):

> 1. **Speaking for Self:** Using "I" language to express the information drawn from one or more of the areas just described.

> 2. **Making Sense Statements:** The skill of describing what you see, hear, touch, taste, or smell.

3. **Making Interpretative Statements:** Presenting in a tentative or hypothetical manner what you construe your cognitive experiences to be.

4. **Making Feeling Statements:** Recognizing and owning feelings and then expressing them as directly and clearly as possible both verbally and nonverbally.

5. **Making Intention Statements:** Letting people know what you want on both a short-term and long-term basis.

6. **Making Action Statements:** Verbally describing your behavior in simple and concrete terms.

A more extensive discussion of this very helpful model is in the book *Alive and Aware: Improving Communication in Relationships* by Sherod Miller, Elam W. Nunnally, and Daniel B. Wackman (1975). Their ideas combined with the skill of "active listening" provide an excellent basis for effective communication. Other helpful resources on communication are *Interpersonal Communication* (1978) and *Human Communication: An Interpersonal Perspective* (1978) by Stewart L. Tubbs and Sylvia Moss. Another book entitled *Reaching Out* by David W. Johnson (1981) is recommended from both relationship development and communication perspectives.

Verbal, Nonverbal, and Meta-Messages

Since communication is the single most important factor affecting our relationships, knowing how we send and receive messages is important. The most obvious method is through the use of words or the verbal channel. As words convey meanings on which both the speaker and receiver agree, understanding results. However, words are sometimes inadequate or have different meanings resulting in miscommunication. Other times what is not said has more impact than the words. Gestures, body language, and inflection (tone of voice) often convey more than words. In fact, researchers have found that in two person communication more that 65% of social meaning is conveyed through nonverbal messages (McCroskey, Larson, & Knapp, 1971). When verbal and nonverbal signals match, the result is generally a very clear and precise meaning. For example, if a husband exclaims, "I'm so angry at my boss

I could quit right now," in a heated tone of voice, with a flushed scowling face, and clinched fists, his wife can be pretty sure he is angry and upset. However, if verbal and nonverbal signals clash, ambiguity and confusion result. A date who responds to your query as to whether he/she is having a good time by stating, "I'm really enjoying myself," in a dull voice while stifling a yawn will probably raise doubts in your mind about the authenticity of his/her words.

In order to communicate effectively special effort must be directed at sending verbal and nonverbal messages that are congruent. Because nonverbal cues have such impact and because they are inherently difficult to understand, learning the skill of "checking out" is a necessity. Whenever you get a message nonverbally or a mixed message, check out your perception rather than simply relying on your own assumptions or conclusions. Doing so will prevent miscommunication and keep communication channels open. Sometimes married couples fall into the trap of thinking they know each other so well that they stop checking as to whether or not their assumptions and perceptions are accurate. They begin to act on the basis of what they think they know only to find out later that they were inaccurate.

Example

Checking It Out. One elderly couple was struggling with what to talk about in a counseling session when the counselor suggested they tell each other something that they had thought about often but never said. After a pause the husband said, "I wish you would quit making me spinach omelets for lunch—I hate spinach omelets." The wife was stunned and replied that he always "seemed to like them." In this case she had assumed that his nonverbal demeanor meant he liked spinach omelets, and he did not want to hurt her feelings by either showing his distaste or saying anything. Even with someone you know well the process of checking out is essential.

Any comment in a conversation about how a person communicates is referred to as a *meta-message* (i.e., a message about the message). Many times in conversations instead of responding to the content of a message we respond to how the message is sent. A mother may direct her child to "get the dishes done" only to have her child reply, "I wish you wouldn't always order me around." The child in this case is reacting to the meta-message (ordering) rather than the verbal content (doing the dishes). Whenever we get into conversations about how we communicate, that is metacommunication (Watzlawick, Beavin, & Jackson, 1967). Couples often find themselves arguing about how they argue—one accuses the other of being too cynical or too disrespectful when they talk. Being aware of and discussing the meta-message aspect of our communication can be extremely rewarding because, once the meta-level is clarified, dealing with problem issues is easier.

SOCIAL SKILLS

Although the main emphasis of this book is directed toward the eventuality of intimacy in relationships, our relating in a social sense should not be overlooked or underemphasized. We need to develop social skills for relating to the vast majority of people with whom we come in contact. Social skills are door-openers to relationships which can develop into friendship and intimacy. Despite the fact that Emily Post is often lampooned certain social amenities communicate a basic respect and consideration for others based on a universal code of behavior which can alleviate the uneasiness of social encounters.

Social skills need to be developed within the context of one's cultural background and the milieu in which one is going to be functioning. Social skills encompassing standards of behavior relative to decency, propriety, etiquette, and decorum can be acquired through observation, classes, and reading. Expanding your sense of appropriate behavior along the entire continuum of informal to formal situations will prepare you to interact socially with ease and self-confidence. As such you will present yourself in a positive light as well as enhance your opportunities to develop new, exciting, and fulfilling relationships. Once integrated into your repertoire of behaviors, these skills will serve you well throughout your life fostering a sense of personal fulfillment and capability in your social relationships.

STYLE OF RELATING

Each time we encounter another human being we engage in a communicative event. Over time themes and tendencies emerge in our communication which can be construed as our style of relating.

Satir's Communication Styles

Virginia Satir (1972) author of the book *Peoplemaking,* maintained that the nature of our interactions with others particularly in the area of communication has a direct impact on our sense of self-esteem. She referred to this inner sense of self-worth as our "pot." When we have positive encounters over time the result is "high pot" and when we have negative experiences over time the result is "low pot." She described five typical communication patterns that are based on and affect our "pot." The first style is *Placating.* In this approach the placater's primary goal is to keep everyone happy no matter what the cost to one's self. To do this successfully one has to continually put one's own feelings aside and be willing to let others have their way. Any sense of positive self-worth is eroded because of the continual put down of self and the placater's belief that he/she is unlovable.

The second style is *Blaming.* In this approach the person takes an aggressive position of accusing others so as to be viewed as strong. This type of communication is based on the person's belief that nobody really cares about him/her and that the only way to have an impact as well as protect self is to yell. Not only is the blamer's "pot" low because of experiencing little receipt of love or caring from others, but his/her mannerism also destroys the self-esteem of the people to whom he/she relates.

The third style is *Super-Reasonable* otherwise known as "the computer." This style involves treating everything as if it is harmless. Nothing ruffles this person and everything is logical and rational. By keeping emotionally aloof and distant, any real sense of vulnerability is hidden and his/her "low pot" is not revealed. Connecting relationally with this type of person is difficult. They experience little closeness and seldom risk themselves as persons in their interactions with others.

The fourth style is the *Distracter* whose primary mode of interacting with others is to be irrelevant. Whatever this person says or does has little to do with what anyone else is doing or saying. Interacting with the distracter reduces both his/her self-esteem as well as yours because neither of you gain any positive results. Such behavior is based on the person's belief that he/she has no place and consequently fills his/her role in relationships by becoming detached and nonsensical.

The fifth style of communication is called *Leveling* which builds self-esteem as a result of interaction. In this approach, messages are direct and relevant expressing congruence between thoughts, feelings, and actions. Direct contact between two persons occurs and each partner knows where he/she is personally and in the relationship. Partners may experience differences or disagreements but they do not negate the sense of acceptance and respect communicated in the relationship.

In marriage relationships and families, individuals often adapt one of the first four styles of communication, e.g., one partner becomes the blamer while the other is irrelevant. Or, the full gamut of styles can be observed in a family. For example, mother may take on the placater role while father is the blamer. The oldest child may become the computer in order to moderate the encounters between mom and dad without getting hurt, and the youngest child may become the distracter in order to alleviate the tension in the family interaction. The final result is quite chaotic and unfulfilling, and the overall communication process is frustrating and unproductive. However, as individual partners learn and risk leveling in their encounters with each other, communication channels clear and the way is paved for mutually satisfying and growth producing experiences in the marriage and family relationship.

Berne's Win-Lose Continuum

Eric Berne (1964), father of transactional analysis (TA), described relational encounters another way. In his book, *Games People Play,* he described many different modes of interacting all of which impact on our perception of ourselves and our relations with others. He pointed out four possible results of our encounters with others. They are (1) No-Win, (2) I Win—You Lose, (3) You Win—I Lose, and (4) Win-Win. In the No-Win interaction both parties experience a loss personally and relationally. Partners cannot figure out how to connect in any but mutually self-destructive ways. Relationships become addictive and even though one or both know they are not growing or benefitting they cannot seem to extricate themselves from them.

In the I Win—You Lose and You Win—I Lose encounters, the competitive nature of the relationship requires that one or the other of the partners comes out a loser. You may set yourself up to lose so as to avoid responsibility or to prove that you are incapable, inferior, or unsuccessful. Or you may try to build your self-esteem at the expense of the person or persons to whom you are relating. Either way, relationships that continue in either of these two veins are unhealthy.

The Win-Win interaction is much like Satir's leveling. Both partners experience growth and personal fulfillment as a result of the interaction. On the esteem dimension, these four patterns can be designated:

I'm not O.K.—You're not O.K. (Both lose)
I'm O.K.—You're not O.K. (I win—you lose)
I'm not O.K.—You're O.K. (I lose—you win)
I'm O.K.—You're O.K. (Both win)

The goal in our relationships with others is to strive for the Win-Win situations. Thomas Gordon (1975) in his credo for relationships captured the essence of this goal well when he wrote:

> I respect your needs but I also must respect my own. Consequently, let us strive always to search for solutions to our inevitable conflicts that will be acceptable to both of us. In this way, your needs will be met, but so will mine—no one will lose, both will win. (p. 305)

Couples and parent-child relationships often demonstrate each of Berne's four patterns. As such an important task is to find ways of communicating which move relationships to a Win-Win position which are most growth producing for both the individuals involved and the relationship.

Shostrom's Manipulative Types

Our final example of relational styles was developed by Everett Shostrom (1967) and presented in his book *Man, The Manipulator*. He pointed out that one of the primary dynamics in relationships has to do with power and control. However, this does not imply that the person with the most strength is in the driver's seat. He contended that control can emanate from either a position of strength (top dog) or a position of weakness (underdog). Who controls depends on the extent to which a person masters the manipulative style(s) associated with each position. Figure 3.3 illustrates Shostrom's concepts. The inner concepts are the qualities of each of the styles while the outer circle represents the manipulative type involved when a person develops a relating style designed to control others as opposed to relating to others in an actualizing manner.

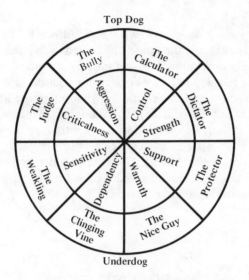

Figure 3.3.   The manipulative types.

Note. Adapted from *Interpersonal Diagnosis of Personality: A Functional Theory and Methodology for Personality Evaluation,* by Timothy Leary, copyright 1957, Timothy Leary, and from *Man the Manipulator,* by E.L. Shostrom, copyright 1967, Abingdon Press. Reprinted by permission.

Examples of each of these relating styles can be found in our own behavior and in the actions of others. Identify which of Shostrom's styles you use most and then assess your motives for doing so. Ask yourself such questions as the following: "Am I interested in controlling others for purposes of personal power or self-protection (the basis of manipulation) or am I sincerely interested in a mutually caring and respectful relationship that helps us both grow?" "Do I tend to function more effectively in a 'top dog' capacity or do I tend to interact with others from an 'underdog' position?" Answering these questions for yourself will help you learn a great deal about how you function in your relational spheres.

ACTIVITY: Personal Relationship Style

Although we have only touched briefly on a variety of relational styles, we suggest you use them to assess your interaction in relationships as follows. Construct a relationship map using circles to represent the various levels of relationships in your life (Refer to Figure 3.1).

Fill in the names of people who you believe fit in each of the categories. Then, using the models presented in this chapter, compare and contrast your relationships and identify characteristics about you and how you relate. Analyze whether your relationships are constructive or destructive and determine how you might be able to change those which are not satisfactory. Use the Johari Window, Satir's communication styles, Berne's Win-Lose continuum, and Shostrom's manipulative types as tools to develop your perspective on you and your relational world. Finally, tie these things together by deciding what aspects are most crucial and desirable for you with respect to an intimate relationship such as marriage.

RESPONSIBILITY:
THE BOTTOM LINE IN RELATIONSHIPS

Psychiatrist William Glasser (1965) has defined responsibility as the ability to meet your own needs without depriving others of meeting their needs. In other words, responsibility is an essential component of *all* our relationships because of the potential impact on our self and the self of others. How we act in even the most superficial contacts with others will have a direct bearing on how we will act in intimate relationships and vice versa. Be constantly aware of and working on your genuineness, candor, assertiveness, and honesty in brief interactions as well as in long-term encounters. The abuse or exploitation of any relationship is damaging to that connection as well as detrimental to the development of effective relating patterns. The ultimate results of acting irresponsibly in relating to others are personal loneliness, social distance, and interpersonal distrust. Often people tend to compartmentalize their relationships, acting responsibly toward certain persons and exploiting others. However, due to the nature of relationship dynamics such tactics increase the likelihood that when push comes to shove, the same exploitative patterns also will emerge in the intimate relationships. The same holds for one's actions in close interpersonal relationships. Sometimes people use each other for personal gratification, power, or need fulfillment without giving the other person a clear message as to their intention.

Common examples with often painful ramifications are male-female relationships where a man professes genuine interest and love for a woman for whom he is only experiencing sexual attraction, or where a woman uses sexual innuendoes and seductiveness to achieve relational closeness with a man. The potential of one or the other or both to realize negative results in such relationships is great.

A common discordant theme in many marriages is past motives and actions which have left scars because one or the other did not act responsibly in the course of dating, courtship, and marriage. On the other hand, developing the standard or principle of acting responsibly in all relationships including those with intimacy potential will produce relationships that will both grow and endure even under stress.

Marriage and family are essentially an outgrowth of our interpersonal relationships. From the time we are born, we are involved in the development of relationships in some way. Even if those relationships have been negative or created obstacles for us, the time is never too late to turn them around. Although statistics and clinical evidence tell us that people tend to repeat relational patterns from their background, our relational past need not be an excuse or explanation for continuing an unhealthy pattern. We all know of success stories where people have overcome their past by taking on the challenge of being responsible for their own lives.

In terms of relationships, our job is to perpetuate those qualities which are healthy, productive, and growth producing and modify, revise, or delete those qualities which are not. Developing the art of listening, communication, and social skills, and our relating style will lay a solid foundation for interpersonal relating and will serve as an effective springboard into the domain of marriage and family relationships. Add the relational bottom line of responsibility and you will not only enhance your present life situation, but will also be acting to prevent problems and insure effective relationships in the future.

REFERENCES

Berne, E. (1964). *Games people play.* New York: Grove Press.

Glasser, W. (1965). *Reality therapy.* New York: Harper and Row.

Gordon, T. (1975). *P.E.T.: Parent effectiveness training.* New York: Plume.

Johnson, D. (1981). *Reaching out: Interpersonal effectiveness and self actualization* (2nd ed.). Englewood Cliffs, NJ: Prentice-Hall.

Luft, J. (1970). *Group process: An introduction to group dynamics* (2nd ed.). Palo Alto, CA: National Press Books.

McCroskey, J., Larson, C., & Knapp, M. (1971). *Introduction to interpersonal communication.* Englewood Cliffs, NJ: Prentice-Hall.

Miller, S., Nunnally, E., & Wackman, D. (1975). *Alive and aware: Improving communication in relationships.* Minneapolis, MN: Interpersonal Communications Programs.

Powell, J. (1969). *Why am I afraid to tell you who I am?* Niles, IL: Argus Communications.

Rogers, C. (1951). *Client-centered therapy.* Boston: Houghton-Mifflin.

Satir, V. (1972). *Peoplemaking.* Palo Alto, CA: Science and Behavior Books.

Shostrom, E. (1967). *Man, the manipulator.* New York: Bantam Books.

Tindall, J., & Gray, H.D. (1985). *Peer power: Becoming an effective peer helper, Book 1.* Muncie, IN: Accelerated Development, Publishers.

Trotzer, J. (1977). *The counselor and the group: Integrating theory, training, and practice.* Monterey, CA: Brooks/Cole.

Tubbs, S., & Moss, S. (1978). *Human communication: An interpersonal perspective* (2nd ed.). New York: Random House.

Tubbs, S., & Moss, S. (1978). *Interpersonal communication.* New York: Random House.

Watzlawick, P., Beavin, J., & Jackson, D. (1967). *Pragmatics of human communication.* New York: Norton.

ENVIRONMENT AND CULTURE: DIFFERENT STROKES MAKE DIFFERENT FOLKS

The nature and impact of common factors which form the environment in which we live are investigated. Race, ethnicity, religion, socio-economic status, education, geography, mass media, the work world, and government are all addressed from the standpoint of implications for marriage and family life.

BEYOND MYSELF:
THE HUMAN ENVIRONMENT

Each person lives and grows in an environment which directly and indirectly affects the nature of the person's identity and influences the character of interpersonal relationships. The world outside of ourself sometimes referred to as our "outer reality" can be defined as narrowly as the neighborhood in which we live or as broadly as the universe. Regardless of how extensively we perceive our life space to be, it is composed of a multiplicity of factors which interact to form a social system and a culture which becomes the domain in which our individuality emerges and in which we form relationships. Each person in turn becomes a representative of and the creator of that culture in which he/she lives. Collectively, groups of persons share common traits, attitudes, behaviors, values, knowledge, and so forth which give the members a sense of belonging and a common heritage.

As cultural characteristics are passed from one generation to another, a legacy develops giving the culture both historical reality and contemporary meaning. Cultural traits emerge from both nature and nurture. Heredity accounts for certain aspects of racial, ethnic, and sex-linked cultural characteristics and is in turn altered or mutated by cultural and environmental changes. We learn our cultural identity through relationships with people around us. Family, education, and life experiences acquired in the course of growing up all serve to transmit and translate culture into personal characteristics that make us the way we are.

The purposes of this chapter are to investigate the nature and impact of the more common factors which interact to create the environment in which we live and to note their implications for marriage and family life. In doing so, we will look at factors such as race and ethnicity, religion, socio-economic status and education, geography, mass media, the world of work, and government.

Each of us reflects the impact of interacting environmental factors. As we learn to cope with these influences and understand how they affect our relationships with others, we lay a solid footing for making choices that lead to satisfying personal and interpersonal experiences. Intimate partners will exhibit greater or lesser degrees of similarities and differences emanating from environmental influences, and these similarities and differences in turn become the raw material out of which couples and families form. Consequently, we need to explore our lifestyle and understand our environment and culture in order to ease the pressures and tensions naturally associated with accommodating to cultural idiosyncracies in partners.

CULTURE AND THE FAMILY

Because the family is the single most influential institution in our lives, it plays a vital role in communicating our cultural heritage to us. Biologically we inherit racial, ethnic, and sex traits all of which are further developed and refined in a societal context. However, Salvatore Minuchin (1974), an eminent family therapist, pointed out that families actually serve two opposing purposes. They are both for the culture and against it. They are for the culture in that the family helps its members learn to accommodate to societal expectations and teaches them knowledge, behaviors, and attitudes which represent the culture. On the other hand, the family also protects its members from societal intrusion by preventing imposition of cultural dictates enabling individual members to have autonomy and the family to have an identity apart from society. In this way, the family protects individuals from infringement while at the same time passing the culture along to the next generation. Consequently, we are neither overwhelmed by pressures to conform to societal expectations nor are we ostracized as a member of society. We experience both separateness and belonging.

RACIAL AND ETHNIC HERITAGE

Marriages tend to occur between individuals with the same racial background. This happens most likely because of geographical proximity, day to day circumstances, personal preferences, and the catalyzing influence of common backgrounds and experiences. When people choose to cross racial lines in marriage, they are often met with strong objections and negative reactions from family, friends, and society. Some of these responses reflect a realistic concern that the couple will face insurmountable problems while forming their relationship and forging a family lifestyle. Other objections emerge from biases or prejudices and are expressed in comments like "think about your children—they won't know who they are," or "What's the matter, aren't our (Black, white, oriental, native American) men/women good enough for you?"

In spite of family and societal pressures cross-racial marriages can and do succeed. Couples considering such a marriage, however, need to be apprised of the realistic barriers they will have to confront. After the initial excitement, romance, and physical attraction wear off, the couple still needs to work out a lifestyle that is satisfying to both and accommodates their racial differences. Making an honest assessment of personal and environmental factors to determine if compatibility does exist regardless of race is a necessity. Consider the impact of racial background on perceptions of marriage and family life and look closely at each other's attitudes and biases toward racial differences and mixed racial marriages and families.

A common scenario of intimate relationships involving partners of different races goes something like this. The two persons are attracted to each other because of common interests, physical attraction, proximity, and mutually fulfilling experiences together. As the relationship materializes, caring and commitment develop leading to more time together and greater exposure of the relationship to family and friends. As significant others in each partner's life express doubts and objections and attempt to segregate either or both individuals, the partners put up defensive barriers and join together more closely in an attempt to preserve the relationship in the face of adversity. Consequently, the couple begins reacting to pressures against the relationship by forming a more intense connection which may lead to marriage. If the primary stimulus that cemented the relationship is the negative reaction of others to it, the couple will very likely experience severe setbacks and conflicts once into the marriage. On the other hand, if the relationship is founded on factors other than a defensive posture against the outside world, the couple will stand a better chance of working out their differences.

Examples

Interracial Marriage Dilemmas. The following are examples of conflicts we have observed in our contacts with mixed-racial couples. In oriental cultures the extended family still plays a significant role in family living. Consider the adjustment of a white female who was expected to live with the parents of her prospective oriental husband. Or conversely, imagine the shock of an oriental man whose white wife expected him to place his aging parents in a home for the elderly rather than care for them in their home.

Sometimes difficulties associated with racial differences do not emerge until children are born. For instance, consider the dilemma of a fifth grade son of a Black-white couple whose Black classmates were calling him "whitie" while his white classmates considered him Black.

Race is an important factor in your choice of a partner and such a decision should not ignore the realities that differences create. Although interracial marriages comprise less than 1% of the marriages in the U.S., the incidence is increasing (Saxton, 1983). This indicates that more mixed race couples are opting for marriage in spite of potential problems and also that social prejudices are changing enabling society to become more accepting of these marriages.

Ethnicity

Before considering ethnicity as a cultural factor we need to differentiate it from race. Racial differences emerge from categories based on skin pigmentation such as Black, white (Caucasian), yellow (Oriental), red (Indian), or brown (Hispanic). Ethnicity on the other hand encompasses groupings within races as well, usually tied directly to nationality and/or religious persuasion. As such, ethnic background and differences play a vital role in each of our lives, particularly if you live in countries like the United States or Canada.

America has been called the great "melting pot" of humanity. Due to our historical origins as a country of immigrants, a continual process has occurred of mixing, blending, preserving, and defending relative to ethnic heritage. Intermarriage between members of different ethnic groups has certainly contributed significantly to the blending process. Consequently, our American culture is a multi-colored tapestry composed of myriad racial and ethnic characteristics. Ethnicity is both preserved and modified to create a rich and diverse culture that represents mankind's greatest experiment in living together. No other nation in the world has attempted to create an identity out of differences on such a massive scale. Consequently, the diversity contained in our ethnic roots has a direct impact on each of our lives and must be considered in light of marriage and family living.

No matter where you live you are surrounded by ethnicity. Sometimes your exposure may be highly concentrated with one particular heritage. For example, if you live in Minnesota you cannot help but be affected by the Scandinavian influence. Minnesota telephone books are replete with "-son" and "-sen" surname endings. On the other hand, your community may reflect a diversity of ethnic groups. If you live in a city like Philadelphia, for example, sections of the city clearly are differentiated by the density of a particular ethnic group, e.g., south Philadelphia is known as the Italian section. Either way your life will be colored by the tint of customs, traditions, personality types, and folkways which form the composite of any ethnic group.

Traditions and customs in particular tend to be marker events which serve to perpetuate an ethnic legacy. As you learn these traditions, you carry on the legacy and as you begin to value them, you take responsibility for preserving them. Ethnicity gives a sense of belonging and pride to individuals, and most people value it highly.

However, at the time that intimate relationships are being formed in the late teens and early twenties, ethnicity is sometimes set aside or discounted in the quest for individuality and independence. If that occurs you can be sure it will reemerge after marriage. People who marry within the same ethnic group enjoy and value common experiences that reflect their heritage. Such commonality breeds closeness and togetherness. In contrast, manifestation of ethnic traits in individuals in a relationship also can generate conflict.

Examples

Impact of Ethnicity. One wife complained that her husband never showed his emotions. After describing in detail her frustration she capped it off with the comment "He's just a typical old Swede," which in her view explained his unemotional personality. The intriguing aspect of this situation however, was that she had been attracted to him because he was stable and quiet in contrast to her first husband who was volatile and often lost control of his emotions. This incident occurred while we were doing therapy in western Wisconsin near the Minnesota border. After moving to New Hampshire another wife described her husband in an identical manner but closed with the comment "He's just a typical Yankee." Apparently ethnic stereotypes are related as much to geography and density of the ethnic population as they are to the character of the ethnic group itself.

Sometimes ethnic influence also comes out in role expectations. A man of Syrian origin had adopted an American lifestyle in most ways except in his view of the role of women. In that area he held a perspective that was quite traditional and in keeping with the role of women in Syria. This proved quite troublesome in his relationship with an American woman of mixed ethnic background who was accustomed to functioning with much autonomy.

In many relationships ethnic differences provide complementarity and balance. For instance, one couple of German and Italian descent described their influence on one another: He helped her to learn to be more logical and rational—an outgrowth of his Germanic characteristics—and she helped him express his emotions—a contribution of her Italian heritage.

ACTIVITY: Exploring Ethnic Background

When it comes to ethnicity it is important for you to do two things in preparing yourself for marriage and family life. First, explore your own ethnic heritage emanating from both of your parents' ethnic backgrounds. Learn and understand the customs and traditions. Determine their importance to you and their meaning. Think about whether you want to carry the traditions, values, and customs over into your own marriage and family and decide whether or not you favor a common ethnic base in your important relationships. Second, explore ethnic groups other than your own. This can be a most exciting and enjoyable experience. Attend ethnic festivities and picnics, join in celebrations that occur in your community. Travel and visit places that have different ethnic populations. This type of exposure will not only increase your cultural awareness and broaden your perspective but will do much to enhance your respect for the cultural heritage of others. In this way you also will be determining for yourself what you can and cannot accommodate to in potential relationships with people who have an ethnic background different from yours.

RELIGION

Religion is a central influence in our lives. Its presence or absence, the meaning, values, beliefs, and traditions associated with a particular faith, the inevitable manner in which it is integrated into families, ethnic groups, and culture, all provide a backdrop for religious experience in our lives. Relative to marriage, one of the most commonly asked questions by young people is "Can interfaith marriages work?" No simple answer can be provided. Our religious beliefs and training whether acquired under the direction of our families, through an organized church, or on our own, find their most intimidating encounters in the context of intimate relationships. Dealing with religion is unavoidable because it represents a connectedness at a very deep level where differences and unresolved conflicts tend to permeate all other aspects of living together in one way or another. Religious beliefs have strong implicit and explicit values and expectations that direct behavior. In addition, basic tenets of a particular faith manifest themselves in traditions which have become interwoven into the lifestyle of ethnic groups and families. Thus, their influence is at times clear-cut but at other times very subtle in their effect on us as individuals.

Religious values may become submerged during adolescence when younger persons are struggling with gaining independence from their families in order to establish their own identity. Or, religion may become one of the major influences a young person rebels against in the course of growing up. Either way, most people at some point make their own conscious decisions relative to religion. Failing to do so restricts growth and autonomy and creates a situation where persons have not formed a foundation of their own beliefs. They become subject to being overwhelmed by pressures to conform which ultimately can lead to loss of individuality or spend their entire lives reacting rather than choosing.

In relationships, the religious issue is handled in many ways. Oftentimes a young person is surprised to find his/her religious beliefs reemerging after marriage to become a source of conflict and frustration in the relationship. Some of the common options couples use when encountering religious discrepancies in their relationships are as follows:

1. Partners agree to be different allowing each to practice their own faith without imposing it on the other.

2. One partner converts to the faith of the other.

3. Both partners agree that religion is a nonessential and/or an unimportant element in their relationship.

4. Partners consciously or unconsciously avoid the issue of religion so as not to create conflict or tension in the relationship.

5. One partner may go along with whatever the other wishes to do and at the same time have the hidden agenda of converting the other after marriage.

All of these options have built-in hazards that tend to surface under stress. Many couples who do not conscientiously work through the nature of their individual faith and beliefs in the context of their relationship find themselves embroiled in conflict later. A typical time for religious conflict to emerge is at the birth of the first child. Regardless of the option the couple selected or the agreement reached, religious loyalties tend to emerge. Even when partners have agreed that religion is not important, something about being a parent generates feelings of responsibility regarding religious training which in turn raises issues of if, what, when, and where. Subsequently, any unresolved issues relative to religion surface causing conflict and frustration.

Conflict over religious beliefs develops regardless of the nature of differences. Couples raised in different religions have the same problems as those who were raised in different denominations of the same faith or with different perspectives (liberal vs. conservative) in the same denomination.

Examples

Religious Differences. A Jewish couple came for counseling after a period of extended conflict over choosing a synagogue in which their child was to take his training leading to his barmitzvah. The husband had been raised in a liberal synagogue and the wife in a conservative one. Until they had a child it wasn't an issue because neither practiced their religion. However, the responsibilities of parenting and pressures from each spouse's family of origin had surfaced the conflict.

Another couple, both of fundamentalist Christian backgrounds, came for marriage counseling when the husband decided to live up to the letter of his beliefs after ten years of basically living a lifestyle which was quite counter to his stated beliefs. Since his wife was not ready to change to such a restrictive lifestyle for herself, a major rift was created in their relationship.

A third example is of a couple where the wife converted to her husband's faith only to find that her parents continued to put pressure on her for leaving their faith. The religion issue continued to affect their relationship as children were born and often spilled over into conflict between the husband and his in-laws.

ACTIVITY: Introspection Regarding Religious Beliefs

In preparing for marriage and family life we encourage you to look purposely and intensely at your religious beliefs. This confrontation with your faith may be the most significant element of your preparation because what you decide will become a part of your identity. Your choice may or may not reflect your parents' beliefs, but at some point it will be your own. In assessing your faith differentiate between that which is basic and that which has become a custom or tradition. Identify those actions, attitudes, and thoughts which are automatic based on exposure, practice, and habit in order to determine if they are meaningful to you or not. Personal work such as this will help you decide what is important for you and what you expect from a partner, and will help you gauge your flexibility and adaptability when it comes to developing a meaningful, personal and relational religious lifestyle in marriage.

SOCIO-ECONOMIC INFLUENCE AND EDUCATION

Sociologists have confirmed that a classless society does not exist and that two of the main determiners of class are socio-economic level and education. Extensive research has been conducted which affirms the existence of groups in society which have both intrinsic characteristics and a sequential place on a high to low continuum. The internal identifiers of class, however, tend to be more than just size of income, encompassing such elements as lifestyle, implicit and explicit expectations, rules, and the manner in which class members view the world. Because class lines are hard to determine specifically, most differences come to light primarily when these elements are compared relative to individuals who come from groups which are two or three steps apart from each other.

We all belong to a particular class and regardless of what we wish or aspire we are products of the group in which we were reared. Obviously, we can move into different class categories through channels such as education, career, business, marriage, circumstances, and so forth, but in most cases that mobility tends to be moderate. Movement is from one class to the next or possibly two steps. "Rags to riches" stories abound but for most of us someone else is usually involved. Movement also may occur over generations as parents pass on the goal or challenge to "be better off than we were" to their children.

Many marriages have a tendency to occur between individuals who have similar socio-economic and educational backgrounds. As such, the couple has a common foundation upon which to build their lifestyle. In other cases, however, partners may come from differing backgrounds which can present problems as the relationship evolves. In some cases, aspiration discrepancies account for conflict. One partner wants to be upwardly mobile and the other is satisfied where he/she is. Or one partner wants to de-escalate rather than escalate his/her mobility. More and more stories of couples and families "going back to nature" or "back to the basics" are being aired. In fact we may be seeing the demise of upward mobility because American society has evolved to a point where many children can no longer expect to be "better off than their parents." Consequently, expectations will have to be lowered to "doing as well as their parents." These dynamics will definitely affect you and your mate as well as have an impact on your children.

Let us look at some common examples of how socio-economic and educational factors surface. We can easily experience feeling "out of it" when for one reason or another we are projected into a group or situation where we are out of our element because the people around us are from another social or educational strata. An exception to this was dramatically illustrated in an Italian film entitled *A Brief Vacation* in which a woman of low socio-economic standing is thrust by circumstance into an upper class environment. In this situation, the woman finds she is very comfortable with the people with whom she is associating and they in turn resonate to her. A certain image and style begins to emerge and she finds she is actually more at home in the new situation than in the one she had lived all her life. Such stories help us remember that people cannot be pigeonholed and point out the importance of self-exploration and exposure to new experiences as a means of enabling our genuine selves to emerge.

Differing socio-economic background and educational experience also can be a source of strong attraction between individuals. Couples experience a magnetic compulsion to relate to one another and the challenge of heterogeneity becomes an exciting adventure in relationship development. Sometimes, however, the very differences that initially attract become the source of conflict. Other times, hidden agendas exist such as forging a relationship for purposes of upward mobility. In other cases, idealistic attitudes in the form of open-mindedness or egalitarian humanism which stress seeing people as people rather than as members of a social class provide the means for camouflaging real differences stemming from social class or education.

Too often in our counseling sessions we see couples where one pursued the other as a "conquest" or out of spite toward their parents and friends who made up their social circle only to find that once the marriage was consummated their perceptions, expectations, and actions were worlds apart. In conflict, the other person's background is often held against him/her. Statements like "I should have known better than to marry a girl/guy from the other side of the tracks" pinpoint a social diversity in a relationship.

Individuals in a state of rebellion against the values in their own families and social class may react by seeking out a partner who stands in direct contrast to those values. An almost certain method of doing so is to marry someone who is of a significantly different socio-economic or educational background.

Examples

Education Makes the Difference. A young couple appeared for counseling after three years of marriage. They had married after a stormy one year courtship. He had a high school education and was farming for a living and she was a junior in college. Although they had gone to the same high school, he described himself as a farm boy and she as a city girl. For him marrying a college girl had initially represented an achievement and for her marrying a farmer was demonstrative of her flexibility and non-prejudicial attitudes toward people who were not "educated." Living together, however, proved to be intolerable and under duress the many differences in their outlooks and expectations were accentuated.

Another case where educational differences eventually resulted in conflict is a couple who married in college. She dropped out to work and support him with the expectation that when he was finished she would complete her education. However, when he graduated and went to work, they decided to have children which cancelled her plans to return to school. Several years later he was offered a fellowship to do doctoral study which he accepted and completed. Consequently, the educational discrepancy between the two had burgeoned from a common level (both in college) to a Ph.D. versus a college dropout. In their conflicts she often noticed feelings of being put down because she was not as "smart" (educated) as he was.

Differences emanating from social class and education can be resolved through maintaining good communication and the practice of valuing and respecting one another in light of both similarities and differences.

ACTIVITY: Assessing Education and Social Strata

Education and social strata are so fundamentally tied to lifestyle that for anyone anticipating marriage the need exists to assess carefully (1) what his/her own background is, (2) what his/her aspirations are, and (3) what impact these two things have on the choice of a partner in marriage.

GEOGRAPHY AND MARRIAGE:
WHERE YOU LIVE IS HOW YOU LIVE

One of the inescapable facts of life is that where we live inevitably affects the kind of lifestyle we develop for ourselves. Obviously if ballet, opera, and symphony orchestra concerts are your first love, living in the heart of Iowa's farmland could be frustrating. Or if you love country life, rolling hills, and space, living in New York City may feel claustrophobic. All sorts of factors such as these affect the satisfaction you experience in your life. If you hate winter, it is ridiculous to live in Minnesota if you can avoid doing so and, if you value a full change of four seasons, you don't live in southern California. If mountain climbing is your main source of recreation, you locate near mountains not in the middle of the mid-western prairie. These kinds of choices are not only important to us as individuals but also vitally affect the lifestyles of couples and families.

Where you live becomes a first step in establishing roots for yourself and your family. Consequently, individuals, couples, and families often find themselves in a quandary which emerges out of the conflicting pressures that pull them back to where they came from, push them to leave where they are now, or both. Other factors such as job opportunities, family obligations, and loyalties also affect us directly and indirectly influencing our choice of geographical location.

Whenever we talk with families about where they live they seem to be in one of five categories:

1. **Wanting to Leave.** These families are not satisfied with where they live, have set goals to relocate, and are actively seeking an environment more appealing to them and more suitable to meeting family needs.

2. **Leaving or Arriving.** These families are in transition, either about to move or recently moved. They consequently have no strong ties to their geographical location as yet. Some families make a career out of being in this category. Examples are military families and corporate managers and executives both of which find relocating is part and parcel of their lifestyle.

3. **Settling In.** These families have located in an area where they intend to settle and establish roots. Although not an integral part of a community as yet, they are committed to the area for positive reasons. Families who relocate with school age children often fall into this category because parents are concerned about children having continuity and a secure relational base educationally and socially.

4. **Settled In.** These families have been living in a geographical area for two or more generations. Children and their children's children decide that the area is what they prefer and stay to marry and rear children there.

5. **Stuck.** These families are not satisfied or happy with their location, but they feel no alternatives are available so they neither set goals to leave nor actively pursue leaving. Rather they concentrate their efforts in either preparing their children to escape or merely learn to cope with their negative feelings.

Marriage often brings the geographical factor into focus because of ramifications associated with one or the other or both having to pull up roots and relocate. A typical situation occurs when two people from different parts of the country leave home to go to college. They meet, fall in love, marry, and move to the home base of one or the other. The displaced partner often has difficulty adjusting to the lifestyle, friends, family, legacy, and climate resulting in unhappiness and depression. The inequality in adjustment requirements between the two partners leads to tension and frustration and can become a major issue which the couple must resolve to create a mutually satisfying relationship.

The geographical location of your upbringing does influence your ideas of how and where you want to live. A person raised in a city constantly exposed to the hustle and bustle of people, mass transit, crowds, and commuting may consider the quietness of a small town to be quite lonely and unstimulating. This problem can be a major issue for a couple.

Example

Escape to Prison. A couple came for therapy because the wife had a history of depression which was jeopardizing the marriage. She had been raised in a large city and met her husband through her job when he was on a temporary transfer. After marriage they decided together to escape the city and set up a home in the country some 45 miles away from the husband's job. Because he commuted two hours each day and she was in charge of the children, she spent seven years "stuck" out in the country without access to any of the activities with which she had grown up. Consequently, she became withdrawn and depressed. In this case, the husband still had retained contact with both worlds—city and country—while the wife was totally cut off from her city roots and felt imprisoned in her rural home.

Some geographical locations are intrinsically attractive to people. California, for example, has been described as a state where everyone is from somewhere else. The lure of the west coast sunshine and lifestyle attracts many newcomers each year. Couples and families migrate in pursuit of better jobs, living conditions, recreational opportunities, and climate. When both partners acclimate to a place like California, loyalties and roots are forged quickly and social networks of friends develop to replace extended family ties. However, if one partner becomes committed to an area and the other does not, friction can arise in the marriage. On the other hand, married couples who make a mutual choice to relocate away from original family and friends may find the challenge and excitement of establishing themselves in a new place the very thing which forges a strong relationship between them.

Example

The Aftershock. We worked with one California couple who had relocated to Wisconsin after a severe earthquake. The wife developed such a fear of another occurrence that she pressured her husband to find another job. They moved to Minneapolis but the husband's heart was still in California. Following a series of setbacks economically, the husband despaired, formed a relationship with another woman who was interested in going to California, and left his wife and family. He moved back to the west coast.

Another common scenario involving geography and marriage is the "Returning to One's Roots" syndrome. Many young people grow up with their eyes on the horizon believing that "there is a better life out there somewhere.'' They actively pursue new places in their search for a better life. Marriage, family, and career all seem to fall into place, but for some reason disenchantment sets in making one or both partners feel something is missing. On closer examination, the missing elements are family and living conditions similar to those one or the other experienced while growing up. This realization can result in decisions to move ''back home'' particularly if job opportunities are available to provide for the economic well being of the family.

Many children whose parents own a business find themselves resisting being saddled with the family business during their young adult life, but at a later point, view involvement as an economic opportunity and desire to carry on the business to perpetuate the family name and reestablish themselves in the hometown community. Such circumstances can present problems in a marriage for the partner who does not happen to be from the hometown where the family business is located. Consequently, the couple must make efforts to insure ''moving back home'' is a mutually desirable and acceptable one.

The United States is a country where different regions reflect differences in the character and values of the people who live there. For example, something is unique about southerners when compared to midwesterners. Northeasterners differ from Westerners and so on. Additionally, people from areas within larger regions also have definable character traits conveyed in terms of accent, colloquialisms, attitudes, folkways, and appearance. For example, a Boston ''accent'' is certainly distinguishable from a Philadelphia ''accent'' and even a North Philadelphia accent can be contrasted with people who live in South Philadelphia. Most people take pride in their regional affiliation just as they do in their ethnic origin. Consequently, you need to know how you represent your own regionalistic group but also how you adapt to regional populations different from you.

ACTIVITY: Exploring Geographical Preferences

Preparing for marriage by knowing your geographical preference will help you make a better choice when the time comes to negotiate where ''we are going to live.'' Such preparation should take two different directions at the same time. The first is to explore and evaluate the area in which you live. Examine the importance of such things as climate, closeness of your roots, opportunities vocationally, and recreationally, and lifestyle. As you assess your connectedness to your geographical roots, place a value on its importance in a relationship. Communicate your feelings and values in this regard to the one with whom you have a relationship rather than either expecting your partner to assimilate your values or springing your expectations on your partner after you marry.

Second, explore other geographical areas whenever you can. The explorations can be achieved through such things as travel, summer jobs, education away from home, films, reading, and jobs which require relocation. Such activities will help you determine where you would like to live. More importantly, use such ventures to help you understand how flexible and adaptable you are. Try to verbalize and perhaps record what geographical areas have the most and others that have the least appeal to you. Use data obtained for comparing "home area" with other geographical areas to identify advantages and disadvantages of staying put or relocating.

MASS MEDIA:
WILL THE REAL AMERICAN FAMILY PLEASE
STAND UP?

Despite our own family experiences, mass media, in particular television (the adopted member of almost every American family), has a significant impact on our perceptions of what marriage and family living is all about. In fact, observing our own and other families proves boring indeed when compared to the tantalizing variety of marital and family relationships projected on the TV screen. Children, teenagers, parents, and grandparents sit for hours in front of the TV being bombarded with images of "real" family life. From reruns like *Father Knows Best* and *The Waltons* which present the traditional family to contemporary sitcoms like *Three's Company* depicting alternate lifestyles; from *All in the Family* with the dogmatic leadership of Archie Bunker to *The Jefferson's* who are an "average" American Black family; from the steamy intrigues of the Ewing family on *Dallas* to the single parent dilemmas of *One Day at a Time;* throw in *The Bill Cosby Show* and *Family Ties,* the mixed racial family groups of *Webster* and *Different Strokes,* the blended family dimension of *The Brady Bunch* and the father headed single parent family of *Silver Spoons* and you have just about every possible model to emulate as an ideal family. In fact, in a *Newsweek (*May 15, 1978) article was stated that the only thing that is missing is a "TV series depicting what the American family *really* does—and that of course, is watch TV" (p. 87). (The average American household spends 6 hours and 10 minutes a day doing it.)

TV images of marriage and family are much more appealing and exciting. This is not surprising if you consider how each episode proves that issues and problems can be clearly and cleverly resolved in 30 minutes to an hour including time for commercials and station breaks. Add to that, Madison Avenue commercials which promulgate the image of families in suburbia where mother, fashionably dressed at all times, works happily in an immaculate kitchen concerning herself with such important issues as the "whiteness" of her laundry and the "softness" of toilet tissue, and where dad and kids are excitedly pleased and amazed by mom's ability to solve their personal problems like "ring around the collar" and spaghetti stains on their baseball uniforms. This all adds up to a very positive and obviously "accurate" view of family life.

Though entertaining, the problem is that TV programs seldom communicate the reality of the ongoing struggle involved in living together in a marriage and family. "Yet a study prepared by the National Institute of Mental Health reported that a majority of adults and children use TV series to learn how to handle their own domestic roles" *(Newsweek,* May 15, 1978, p. 87). Children viewing the sitcoms and commercials grow up with the idea that what they see is how people really live and wonder why their family is not like that. They enter marriage with the idea of emulating what they have seen and when life doesn't turn out to be a well-edited screen play, they become discouraged and want to give up.

Often in our practice we have worked with discouraged couples who entered marriage with high ideals and romantic notions drawn from movies, TV, and reading. These notions had formed because in contrast to what their parents' marriages were like, they thought theirs would be different. One of the most painful discoveries these couples make is that their life mirrors their parents' life rather than fulfills the dreams they had molded for themselves from other sources.

The printed page is another source of influence in the marriage and family arena. As the education and literacy of Americans escalated, the publishing industry grew providing habitual and eager readers with ideas and information concerning marriage and family life. Daily and weekly news publications report tragedies and successes of families. Investigative reports on families and marriage present both the typical and atypical. Editorials and advice columns like *Dear Abby* and *Ann Landers* abound with suggestions and solutions to marital and family dilemmas. Self-help book sales have flourished as Americans have sought help and advice in coping with the turmoil currently affecting the institutions of marriage and family. Together these mass media missives compound and clarify the complexities of marital and family dynamics. They are resources to us when read critically and comparatively, and when information gleaned is integrated with our own situations and the requirements and demands of our day to day life experiences.

The real American family still remains an enigma to which the mass media can only allude and which only we as individuals can understand and experience as we marry, have children, and live through a lifetime of family interaction. Consequently, only that which is translated from the media into our own lives is real and the rest is merely a backdrop against which the nature of our family experiences are reflected.

THE WORLD OF WORK:
THE SIGNIFICANT OTHER IN A FAMILY'S LIFE

The relationship between the work world and the family can often be described as a marriage between incompatible partners who fail to acknowledge each other's existence and needs and where each believes the other is less important. As was noted in Chapter 2, choice of a career extensively affects the nature of your lifestyle and often determines the type of person with whom you may become intimately involved. Consequently, the two are inextricably involved with each other. However, since this chapter is on environment we will focus primarily on the work world rather than the family.

Business and industry have traditionally been insensitive to the family life concerns of its employees. They have operated on an impersonal basis requiring families to adapt to requirements and demands in the best interests of increased production and profits. More recently, the corporate structure has realized that stable, well adjusted workers are more productive and that the impact of the marriage and family domain on a worker's effectiveness is undeniable. In addition, the growing number of families with both parents working either because of economic need or personal career goals has molded the work place and the family into an even stronger partnership.

The work world has always valued and promoted marriage and family satisfaction and stability as an indicator of worker productivity. Hiring practices have been based on the logical "assumption" that married persons and persons with families are more dependable and responsible. Whether true or not, generally individuals with equal qualifications vying for the same position have often found that being married and having a family seemed to swing the balance toward the married person, all other things being equal.

Research into the validity of this assumption has been inconclusive but the practice continues. In recent years, however, court cases have required that hiring and promotion be based on individual ability, performance, and qualifications rather than personal characteristics such as race, sex, marital status, or value orientation. "Equal Opportunity Employment" practices have created at least a conscious level of fair treatment to all qualified individuals and "Affirmative Action" policies have been implemented to reverse the tendencies which years of discriminatory hiring and promotion practices have established. These policies may, in fact, have a direct bearing on whether or not you will be hired. In some areas, being a woman and/or a minority may be to your advantage while being a white male may be a drawback.

The impact of such policies will spill over into marriage and family life because they directly facilitate or impede the progress of an individual's career. Because of the direct relationship between work, money, and lifestyle, not only individuals but families are affected and in times of economic hardship, financial woes, and disappointments impinge upon marital relating causing serious problems.

Example

More Than a Job. One example is the M family where the father lost his job because the company closed. He had worked his way to a position of supervisor and had a prominent position in the union. When the company collapsed he went on unemployment. After several months he acquired a new job but at an entry level position which required extensive physical labor and had no seniority. As the primary breadwinner in the family, his loss of position resulted in depression and withdrawal from the family. His wife and two children found him continually irritable and described him as always being angry. When the youngest boy started getting into trouble in school, the family was referred for counseling and a number of these issues were surfaced and discussed. In this case, the work environment had directly affected the marriage and family relating patterns.

Many companies are now taking a serious look at the relationship of the family and the work world. General Mills published a report entitled *Families at Work: Stress and Strains* (1981) in which they surveyed a wide range of workers, family members, business and industry leaders, and social groups to determine the relationship between work and family in contemporary society. Of particular note was the study's interest in and affirmation of the increase of women working outside the home. More than five out of ten women living in families now work outside the home and the study indicated "a majority of women will continue to work outside the home, marriage, and family notwithstanding" (p. 9). This trend, although, often supported by employers, family, and society, directly affects the family. For instance, the majority of persons surveyed felt children would learn to be more autonomous and self-reliant but that they (the children) would also get into more trouble. Consequently, family members have to learn to adjust and deal with the new stresses and strains created by mothers working outside the home.

In addition to studies, companies are establishing programs contracting for services to deal with problems affecting employees and their families. One example is the rise of Employee Assistance Programs (EAP) offered to or sponsored by companies for their workers. Research has indicated that rehabilitation is far less costly than turnover and far more productive than retaining inefficient employees until they accumulate enough evidence to be fired. Many employees can obtain help with their alcohol or drug problems for themselves and their families directly from counselors in the company and company sponsored treatment programs. Programs such as these provide resources and assistance which not only improve productivity on the job but also aid marriages and families.

An entire book can be written on the relationship between work and family, but we would like to close this section with three typical examples of how the work setting and requirements directly affect marriages and family life. These examples are (1) dual career couples, (2) occupations, requiring travel, and (3) shift work. In our experience with families these three situations seem to cause unique problems that couples and families have difficulty resolving.

Dual Career Couples

Dual career marriages are defined as marriages between two persons both of whom are engaged in career pursuits primarily because of the personal challenge and satisfaction involved as opposed to both working primarily to enhance the economic well-being of the family. Since success and advancement in most careers require a primary commitment, persons engaged in a marriage where both place a first priority on career face a unique set of problems. Dual career couples often experience little difficulty arranging schedules and meeting each other's expectations as long as only the two of them are involved. Crises, however, sometimes arise when the decision to have children is approached. Couples may put off having children for the sake of their careers or may even decide not to have children. Either decision has implications for the marriage. Putting off children means that the parents will likely be older and more financially established. They also will have difficulty adjusting themselves to the less autonomous lifestyle required to raise children. Not having children means that the couple will cut off their biological legacy, a decision which either or both may have difficulty accepting and one which their parents and relatives may not look upon kindly. Either way, the issue of children is a primary one in a dual career marriage.

Example

Who Gets the Kid? One couple came in for counseling because although both wanted children, neither wanted to give up his/her successful career. They described their dilemma as a conflict between an "irresistible force and an immovable object." Neither felt they could give the time needed to attend to the child and both wanted the other to make the primary commitment to child-rearing. Both felt they could handle the role of breadwinner since financially either's job could provide for the family economically. So they decided to work on the impasse between them before simply jumping into a family—a very wise *decision and one which many couples in similar situations **do not** make.*

Another common problem associated with dual career couples is whose career takes precedence when promotion or access to job opportunities requires relocation. A not unusual situation is for partners to be faced with the choice of living in two separate locations in order to pursue their desired career goals. Such marriages may become weekend encounters with weekday communication restricted to phone calls and letters.

The key to effective dual career marriages and families is communication. Hidden agendas and expectations must be surfaced and faced in preparation for marriage and in regard to decisions within marriage. Not having the courage to face differences in each other's expectations only feeds fuel to the fire when circumstances require decisions and actions in the heat of conflict. Not facing the reality of work demands on dual career partners relating will only lead to dissatisfaction, anger, and bitterness in the marriage and will breed feelings upon which the relationship begins to dissolve.

Occupations Requiring Travel

Certain occupations require travel as a part of the job description. When a person is single, such a requirement is viewed as an advantage because the opportunities to spread one's wings and to experience new places and persons are exciting and stiumlating. In the context of a marriage and family, however, such a requirement may pose problems. In many families where one spouse travels as a part of the job, the family is forced to develop a minimum of three lifestyles: (1) weekdays with the traveling spouse gone, (2) weekdays with the traveling spouse home, and (3) weekends. More importantly these families must learn to work out the transition in an efficient manner so that spillover from one situation does not engulf the others. For example, if dad is gone all week and mom has had a rough time with the kids the scene is set for a potential blowout come Friday night. Dad comes home tired, looking forward to relaxing and enjoying his family; mom has negative feelings about the children, and dad's not being around to help out, and wants to get out of the house to socialize a bit. The kids having pushed mom to the limits have been warned to "wait 'til dad gets home" and consequently, they avoid contact with him when he arrives. Such is the scenario for many reunions in families where a spouse travels. Again, communication is a must, coupled with efforts to respect and understand each other's perspective. Another important ingredient is a strong sense of individual identity and self-worth in each of the spouses. The partner who is at home needs to be able to run the family and function independently deriving personal satisfaction and a strong sense of self, and the traveling partner needs to be able to change roles to function with sensitivity as a member of a family group.

Another area of difficulty in these families is when the traveler stays home. Especially if travel is the usual rather than the exception, the family develops a routine where "single parenting" is installed as the mode while the traveling spouse is gone. Rules, roles, customs, expectations, jobs, and so forth, are worked out which may not suit the absent partner. When he/she stays home during the week, friction and tension develop because the rest of the family continues to function under the "single parent" routine. In these families the transitions are of primary importance and couples must work on creating effective ways to say "hello" and "goodbye." Whenever possible, transitions should be celebrated to create a positive atmosphere. This requires a cooperative spirit even when emotionally, cooperation does not come easily.

Shift Work

Shift work has been called the "nemesis" of the blue collar family. As production efficiency and cost analysis determined that round-the-clock operations were most successful, workers were forced to accommodate to two, three, or even four shifts in their work schedule. Such changes also must be adjusted to by the families in which the worker lives. Given the potential interaction between shift requirements, school hours, and work obligations of the other spouse, often husband and wife, and father and children may go an entire week with little or no direct contact even though all reside in the same house.

In working with couples where one spouse, usually the male, is on shift work, a number of common elements have surfaced. First of all, the mood of the worker changes significantly dependent upon the shift often to the point where spouses almost agree not to interact until the next change in rotation occurs. One wife said, "When he's on the graveyard shift (11 p.m. to 7 a.m.), I simply ignore him until Sunday." Second, the business of the family gets shifted with the change in schedule. On certain shifts children are primarily the responsibility of mom because when dad's not working he is sleeping. Third, the routine and lifestyle of the home changes. Noise levels must be modified to facilitate daytime sleeping. A common experience of children in shiftwork families is to be confronted by a sleepy, angry, red-eyed father who appears on the scene to intrude in their lives because they are making too much noise. One of the wife's primary concerns becomes keeping the house quiet.

Members in these families learn to adjust effectively, but the special nature of the living situation generated by the shifts cannot be understated. Both the marriage relationship and the family structure is affected. Special efforts are needed to accommodate to shifting patterns and to keep lines of communication open between all members rather than relying on one (usually mom) to keep the others (usually dad and kids) in contact with each other. As more women enter the labor force, these roles may shift with mom being the one on shift work and dad being the one who is expected to "keep the others in contact."

A variation of shift work is *seasonal work*. This has often been described as too much or too little of a good thing. When the seasonal worker is gone or busy the spouse feels lonely and finds it difficult to function and run the family alone. Yet when the one on seasonal work is home all the time, the spouse feels that he/she cannot get anything done or do his/her own thing because the mate (seasonal worker) is always underfoot.

In this section we have pointed out how the work environment and marriage/family are intricately related. Be aware of the contingencies the work world introduces as you consider jobs and careers.

ACTIVITY: Recognizing Impact of Careers on Marriage

Think about the impact of careers on your marital and family relating and the implications for lifestyle. What about your working and your mate not working? How will this affect the relationship? What if the opposite is true with your mate working and you not? What if both of you work? What if hours of work don't agree (on different shifts, no common date off from work)? What if one or both travels? Identify and express your priorities so that your marital partner and your family will know from where you are coming and can adjust accordingly.

GOVERNMENT AND THE FAMILY:
BIG BROTHER DOESN'T MERELY WATCH!

In the literary classic *Nineteen Eighty-four,* George Orwell (1949) presented a convincing picture of government intrusion into individual and family life which repels the reader. Although we may not experience the "Big Brother" phenomenon in our society, the subtle and direct impact of government on our life is inevitable. Laws, policies, and regulations of federal, state, and local government create a framework in which we live. The political process which evolves from ideology to legislation to enforcement of the law has a direct bearing on family life. Everything from taxes to welfare has family implications. The income tax system though continually in flux at present appears to favor single working individuals as opposed to couples. A number of couples have protested this inequity by engaging in a continual process of divorcing and remarrying for tax purposes. Programs designed to "help" needy families often are directly responsible for their demise because of rules, policies, or qualifications necessary for participation. For example, welfare programs encourage absence of the father from the home by not paying benefits when a father is present. Another example is foster care programs which allocate funds for foster parents but do not provide comparable help for the child's real parents thus enabling the family to remain intact. Laws dictate what you have to do to become married and then regulate a large proportion of your life after marriage.

Every government, regardless of its nature, has a view of the family which is perpetuated by its laws and policies. This fact was finally recognized by President Carter who in 1979-80 convened the first White House Conference on Families (1980). His purpose was to "learn what American families believe is important to them," in order to provide a "catalyst for continuing and expanding action in the federal government." The conference focused on six major themes convening sessions throughout the country to obtain input. These themes were

1. family strengths and supports,

2. diversity of families,

3. the changing realities of families,

4. the impact of public and private institutional policies on families,

5. the impact of discrimination, and

6. families with special needs.

This conference served as a forum for input into government but more importantly it formally acknowledged the reality that government, whether democratic or autocratic, whether based on premises of republicanism, communism, or any other -ism, directly affects the substance and character of family life. Whether it is defining poverty, regulating inheritance, assessing taxes, or establishing social programs, the family is involved. In our private practice with couples and families, issues related to government surface in many ways. For instance, a survey conducted in Western Wisconsin revealed that contacts with divorce lawyers and marriage counselors significantly increased as the April 15 tax deadline approached.

Many families, particularly poor families, find themselves so encumbered and confused by government regulations, dictates, and requirements, that all semblance of a definable family unit is lost. Counselors find it almost impossible to work with some couples or families without involving a whole host of government sponsored agencies.

Example

A Host of Helpers? Recently, a family contracted for counseling which had the courts, corrections, social services, and welfare all dictating regulations to "help" the family. No less than one judge, three lawyers, three social workers, one parole officer, and one welfare officer were directly involved in the life of this family. Although the actions of the family and its members had certainly drawn the attention of these agencies in the first place, once involved, the extrication process was long and frustrating.

Not only does government impinge directly on your family life, but one's view of government can also cause problems. The old cliché, "never discuss religion or politics" has validity. Many family arguments between spouses and between parents and children can be sparked by political preferences and passions. Democrats versus Republicans, liberals versus conservatives, positions on political issues such as civil rights, women's rights, the private and the public sector all can be sources of intense emotional combat.

To explore and understand your own and your partner's political persuasion is essential because for some couples that may be the straw that breaks the camel's back in regard to their relationship. An excellent example of the impact of political differences was presented in the film *The Way We Were* in which two people (played by Barbara Streisand and Robert Redford) found that in spite of their many physical, intellectual, and emotional connections their values expressed through the political arena were incompatible.

CONCLUSION

The content of this chapter was presented to make you think about the myriad of contingencies in your environment that contribute to whom you are and to how they affect the nature of the relationships you form. Our hope is that you will explore and expand in these areas for yourself and discuss and confront them in your interaction with your significant other as a means of both improving your understanding of one another and increasing the basis upon which your relationship can grow.

Each of the environmental factors mentioned have an effect of some kind on each one of us, although its degree will differ qualitatively and quantitatively for each individual. Conversely, we also can have an effect on or change our environment in varying degrees. To think that two people coming together with all of these factors in their background can work out a mutually satisfying lifestyle is mind boggling. However, such factors are also the elements that create excitement and meaning in life, and prevent culture from becoming stagnant and inbred.

We can be thankful that human beings are remarkably flexible and marriages have been known to last. Consequently, we cannot be pessimistic about the viability of any possible combination jelling, nor can we plead ignorance or make light of these factors. First of all, we need to be aware of these factors. Second, we need to understand the nature of their influence: what makes us content, what we can and want to change, and how flexible we can be. Third, we need to address these factors with our prospective partner through the practice of mutual self-disclosure. These steps will increase the likelihood of forming and building a strong relationship.

REFERENCES

Families at work: Strengths and strains (1981). *The General Mills American Family Report.* Minneapolis, MN: General Mills, 9200 Wayzata Blvd.

Minuchin, S. (1974). *Families and family therapy.* Cambridge, MA: Harvard University Press.

Orwell, G. (1949). *Nineteen eighty-four.* San Diego, CA: Harcourt, Brace, Jovanovich.

Saxton, L. (1983). *The individual, marriage, and the family.* Belmont, CA: Wadsworth Publishing.

The TV fun house. (May 15, 1978). *Newsweek,* pp. 85-87.

White House Conference on Families. (1980). Report 1 (3) 330 Independence Avenue, S.W., Washington, DC 20201: U.S. Department of H.E.W.

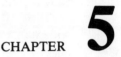

FAMILY OF ORIGIN:
YOU CAN'T LEAVE HOME WITHOUT IT

The impact of one's family of origin is explored. The development and impact of a family legacy are discussed in terms of implications, issues, and problems in marriage and family life. Suggestions for exploring one's roots and using one's family as a resource are given. Concepts such as ordinal position in the family constellation are presented. Nuclear vs. extended family dynamics and the process of breaking away are discussed.

The family . . . is inescapable. You may revile it, renounce it, reject it . . . but you cannot resign from it. You are born into it and it lives with you and through you to the end of your days. Not only that, but its memory will prompt you to fashion new families, of blood or water, either in its image or—just as tellingly—quite unlike it.

—Jane Howard, 1978, *Families*, p. 35

The very fact of our existence supplies irrefutable evidence that we are born into a family. That fact over which we have no control sets the stage for experiences which will influence our lives directly and indirectly regardless of the on-going nature of the relationship we have with our family of origin. Those unseen forces unleashed by our birth meld into a bond which we inherit and pass on to our children. That bond called "invisible loyalty" by Boszormenyi-Nagy and Spark (1973) produces a web from which we cannot extricate ourselves even if we try. Our family of origin not only influences who we are as persons but immensely affects our marriage and ultimately impacts on our family of creation. The purpose of this chapter is to take an intense look at the nature and dynamics of the family of origin as related to marriage and family life.

We will explore the meaning and nature of legacies, how they evolve and are passed from generation to generation. Concepts related to the loyalty connection and the family constellation will be discussed. How we deal with our family of origin experiences when intimacy emerges in our lives will be presented. The process of "breaking away" and the differentiation between nuclear and extended family will be addressed. Suggestions for extending your family of origin knowledge and understanding as a preparatory measure for marriage and family living will be integrated into the chapter along with examples of typical issues/problems that arise out of the legacy domain of each partner's experiences.

LEGACY: ITS MEANING AND IMPACT

An appropriate subtitle for this section might be "What you get is more than what you see." When two people fall in love a definite tendency is to either purposely or inadvertently disregard the fact that each comes from a different family background. Partners become so wrapped up in each other and the excitement of their growing relationship that all they can see and all that is worth seeing are encompassed in the personhood of their counterpart. However, when marriage occurs the reality of the matter is that not only are two individuals joined together but also two families are joined. The age-old rationalization often used by parents of marrying children, "I'm not losing a son, I'm gaining a daughter" is merely a camouflage for the fact that two different family domains are being merged through the individual channels of the marrying children.

Each spouse brings with him/her a *legacy* which has been taught, reinforced, refined, and integrated into the very character of each individual's personality. Consequently, many of the adjustments, tensions, and conflicts that arise in the marriage are not merely the result of personality differences but more likely than not are the result of legacy clashes. Some of the biggest problems that couples experience in marriage can be traced directly to how each partner was raised in his/her family of origin.

The dictionary defines *legacy* as "something received from an ancestor or predecessor or from the past." Our family legacy is passed to us both by our heredity and by our interactional experience in the family. In fact, by the time we have reached the age of majority we have already acquired the clinical equivalent of a Bachelor's degree in marriage and family living. Our family exposes us to values, traditions, customs, and traits which form our view of the world generally, but more specifically creates our expectations about marriage and family life. As to legacy, every family is unique. No matter how long you search or how carefully you pick, you will never be able to find a partner who has the same legacy as you. Consequently, anyone contemplating marriage needs to take an intensive look at his/her own family as well as the prospective partner's family as a preparatory step.

INVISIBLE LOYALTIES:
THE PRODUCT OF OUR PAST

Psychiatrist Boszormenyi-Nagy explained the inevitability of our legacies by differentiating between two types of relationships. The first type called *primary relationships* are those relationships where no choice is involved and where non-substitutability is the rule. These relationships are thus restricted to parent-child and sibling connections which are the result of a biological linkage. All other relationships including marriage, adoption by nonbiological parents, and friendships are termed *secondary relationships* because choice is involved. We choose who we will marry but we cannot choose who our biological parents or children will be. I cannot become an un-parent to my children nor can my children become un-children to me. This irreversible link provides the channel which inevitably supplies us with a legacy (Boszormenyi-Nagy & Spark, 1973).

From the moment a child is conceived he/she is the son/daughter of the conjugal parents and nothing can change that. The child inherits a biological blueprint for development and is placed in an interactional environment from which the content of his/her legacy is derived. Each child born represents the next generation of the parents and as such also must face the difficult task of combining the legacies of both parents. Marital partners merely have to learn how to be compatible but children have to internalize legacy differences into an integrated whole. Thus an *invisible loyalty* will always be operating.

Given this spark of inevitable loyalty, the link between us and our family is developed into a dynamic force that influences our actions toward our parents and family and toward others. We may grow up feeling we owe our parents a debt for their care of us, or we may feel we deserve more than we got from them. Depending on how we view that situation, either we have difficulty leaving our parents or we expect to get from others (usually our marital partner or children) what we didn't get from our parents. In either case problems can result if we do not deal effectively with our family of origin. All couples struggle with the problem of how to relate to the families from which they come. If one spouse is too tightly connected with his/her family, the other spouse feels slighted or jealous. If one spouse feels that his/her parents did not show enough affection, he/she may expect to get more love/caring than his/her spouse or children are willing or able to give.

At times spouses may need to place their parents temporarily on a high priority even above their spouse and children. For example, when a parent or parents experience health crises, become infirm due to aging, or experience loss, the married child may be called upon to give assistance and care. Under such circumstances the functioning of the marital pair is crucial. If the nonrelated spouse can support, encourage, and pick up the duties of the related spouse, a stronger bond will be generated in the marriage. If, on the other hand, the nonrelated spouse becomes resistant and chooses to place the related spouse in a position of choosing between parents and marital partner, damage to the marriage can occur. Caring for parents in need is one key way of paying back the debt we all feel to our parents. So, if that can be done without antagonism being created in the marriage, the related partner will in fact be freed up to relate more easily and fully in the marriage.

In some sense, marriage is an act of disloyalty to one's family of origin. It sends a message to parents that "I am choosing my husband/wife over you." While this is a very normal and natural process, repercussions often appear after the marriage when the parents sense that their child is doing things to please their spouse in opposition to pleasing them. This problem is part and parcel of that invisible loyalty we all have and an aspect of married life on which we will have to work extensively for it to be resolved.

On the other hand, family of origin connectedness can be inappropriate and can damage the marriage. A spouse who is overconnected emotionally to his/her parents may spend inordinate amounts of time with family of origin members and pressure the nonrelated partner to either "join" his/her family or take a second position in the relational hierarchy. "Running home to mother," a common malady in early married life can be a marriage threatening option if the other spouse interprets the act as a choice to put the family of origin above the marriage. Many couples enter therapy with one or the other issuing the complaint, "I thought I married a wife/husband but instead I feel like I'm married to the whole family." The joke that "at all times six persons are in the marital bed" is a clear expression of reality. Finding the appropriate relationship between being a son or daughter and being a husband or wife is a major achievement that must be accomplished for an effective marriage and family experience to occur.

CONTENTS OF OUR LEGACY

Our family environmental context builds content into our individual legacy. Values, traditions, customs, and traits are passed to us by a process called *attribution*. Our parents explain, model, and make rules which teach us what we are to be like, what is right and wrong, and what the world is like. Through the process of interacting with them we acquire knowledge and information about how to be and live. In addition, because our parents are our parents and because of their special influence derived from the loyalty connection, they also can *invalidate* other information we may receive about how to be, what is correct or proper behavior, and what the world is like. This further accentuates the process of internalizing our legacy. Finally, when faced with inevitable differences in viewpoints we are forced into making decisions about which values, beliefs, traditions, and perspectives of the world best explain life and best order its living. What we choose becomes our personal view of the world, and when we choose elements drawn from our family experience we become *inducted* into the family mold. Thus, what our parents passed to us are no longer their values, but now they are our own. This process of *attribution, invalidation,* and *induction* called *mystification* by psychiatrist R.D. Laing (1965) accounts for the specific ways in which we express our legacy in the context of relationships.

OUR FAMILIAL HERITAGE:
THE BLUEPRINT FOR MARRIAGE AND FAMILY
LIFE

Through the process just described our families provide us with a blueprint not only of our genetic make-up but also in terms of what is meant by being a man or woman, husband or wife, and father or mother. Although our decisions and experiences outside the family can alter, modify, or revise the blueprint, the original is still the primary referent. *The family of origin molds our expectations of marriage and family and provides us with the means and motivation to meet those expectations.* How this occurs will now be discussed.

Our familial blueprint tends to influence us in two basic ways which can be either positive or negative depending on how we decide to use it in our marriage. As we grow up in our family, we experience and observe firsthand the reality of marrige (our parents') and family (our own). From these two sources of information we deduce what marriage and family is all about and consciously and unconsciously decide what we want in our own marriage and family. These deductions and conclusions tend to fall into two categories: (1) those elements we wish to emulate and (2) aspects we wish to reverse or negate.

Things we wish to emulate stem from positive reactions and experiences which we have come to value and believe were good for us. Consequently, we generalize that these things also are good for others, especially our spouse and our children. We thus make a conscious effort to implement the same practices, customs, traditions, values, and so forth that we felt were positive into our own marriage and family. We do this by means of *adopting* or *adapting*. *Adopting* is the process of implementing something in your own marriage in exactly the same way that you experienced it in your family of origin. Doing so reveals the high value you place on what you experienced and also demonstrates your loyalty to your family or origin. However, it does not take into account the experience and feelings of your spouse nor make provision for the fact that you are now in different circumstances. As such you may find that your spouse is irritated and resistant to "doing things your way." Adopting is thus a process which discounts your partner's input into the way things are done in the marriage. Over time this can lead to tension and a consolidation against everything for which your family stands thus leading to continual conflict whenever family of origin issues arise.

Adapting is a constructive means of implementing our positive family of origin experiences into our family of creation. Adapting means that you take into account the input from your spouse and modify the things you want to do to account for your new circumstances. In this way your spouse does not feel discounted and the two of you begin to create your own version of a family which further identifies you as a couple while at the same time honoring the good aspects from your past.

Example

A Christmas Tree is a Christmas Tree!! An illustration of the process occurred shortly after we were married. Christmas rolled around and Jim took it upon himself to get the Christmas tree. He brought it home, put it in the garage, and proceeded to flock it completely white with artificial snow. Upon completion he called Toni to come out and waited expectantly for her to express her admiration. After commenting about never having seen one like it, she agreed that it was a beautiful tree. The next year Jim once again got the tree and was about to flock it when Toni appeared on the scene asking if he was going to do it again. After being offended at the question (because that's how Christmas trees were supposed to be), he asked if she didn't like last year's tree. Toni pointed out that she had grown up with a green tree at Christmas and would like to carry on that tradition. At that point we realized that while both families put up natural trees, Jim's family tradition was to flock the tree while Toni's was to leave it green. Consequently, we now alternate each year and have even come up with some versions of our own.

The family in which we grow up not only provides us with warm, satisfying, and fulfilling memories we wish to recreate, but also is the source of some of our most bitter and painful experiences which we want to avoid replicating. Part of the scariness and trauma of coming from a family which has traits that we have determined to be negative is the fear that we will turn out the same way even if we don't want to do so. Research has documented that certain traits like chemical dependency have a familial relationship (Barnard, 1981). Offspring of a chemically dependent family have a tendency to abuse chemicals themselves, marry someone who does and/or enable their own children to be users. Thus a generational phenomenon occurs where the thread or theme of chemical abuse is woven into the fabric of the family legacy.

However, our neative reactions to our family of origin experience are not limited to those traits socially undesirable. Every one of us has probably made a statement like, "When I'm married I'll never let my husband treat me like my father treated my mother," or "I'll never treat my children like my parents treated me." Such thoughts or statements reflect the second way we use our family of origin background in our own family. We attempt to respond to the negative stimulus by doing things differently. We can do this in two ways: opposing or rejecting/choosing.

If our family experience was particularly negative, creating emotional scars, we have a tendency to create a marriage/family structure which is dramatically *opposed* to what we experienced. A common example is choosing a parenting style. If you feel your parents were too authoritarian, totally disregarding your feelings and suppressing your individuality, you may rear your children in a totally permissive manner not because that is what your children need but because you wouldn't be caught dead being authoritarian.

The reverse of this also occurs where children of permissive parents revert to authoritarian methods when they become parents. Such actions in failies across generations result in each generation having opposing traits which serve to stimulate, fan, and perpetuate intergenerational conflict. Since the new parents disapproved of their parent's parenting, they do the opposite. This upsets the grandparents who do not approve of how their children are parenting their grandchildren. In addition, the grandchildren wo have a natural affinity for the grandparents who are "part-time lovers," tend to form a coalition with them agains the parents. Consequently, a great deal of tension is generated in the family all because of the strong negative feelings mom/dad had about his/her own upbringing.

Creating patterns in a marriage or family simply to spite your parents does not solve the problem, doing so only accentuates it. Thus an important question to ask yourself whenever you get caught-up in doing things that result in conflict between you and your family of origin is, "Am I doing this because it is best for me, my marriage, my family, or am I doing this because of my own hang-ups with my parents?" To answer that question honestly is to take a major step toward making the correct decision and engaging in actions that will be constructive regarding your negative past experiences.

The most healthy way of coping with our negative heritage is to evaluate the intent and content of those experiences, *rejecting* those elements we deem to be destructive and then *choosing* from other options what we want to do. This process expresses your desire to do things differently but does not necessarily set you up as an adversary to your parents. Neither does it continually remind them of their failures which creating opposing structures will do. By evaluating, rejecting, and choosing you differentiate your self, your marriage, and your family from your parents, but you do so in the best interests of growth and satisfaction and not at your parents' expense. In fact, if you can come to the realization that your parents did the best they could and can exonerate them from their failures, you will have a better basis for conducting your own family life as well as building positive relationships with your parents.

The Revolving Slate

Family legacy is like a revolving slate (Boszormenyi-Nagy & Spark, 1973) which passes from one generation to the next with certain consistent characteristics that personify the family but also with modifications and additions which each generation contributes to it. We receive the slate at birth with certain inscriptions already in place. Our family experience further reinforces elements of our legacy etching them indelibly into our conscious and unconscious minds. By the time we leave the family, we are fully schooled in the heritage of our family and prepared to pass it on. However, an additional process takes place before our job of passing it on is completed. That process is introduced typically through marriage. When we marry, our individual slates must be merged. In doing so we create our own version of the family legacy by producing a slate that reflects both partners' pasts and adding elements which emerge out of the marital experience. This new slate is then passed on to our children who learn and experience it and then modify it in turn as they marry and have children. Consequently, the more you know about your legacy, the better prepared you will be for forming a compatible marital relationship and passing a valued heritage to your children.

ACTIVITY: Explore Your Family of Origin

One of the best steps you can take to insure a happy marriage is to make a conscious and intense effort to explore your roots. Interviews with family members of both your maternal and paternal families of origin and representing as many generations as possible are a good start. Ask questions you always wanted to ask, and give those being interviewed a chance to describe their views of your family. Identify what your family traits, traditions, and customs are. Find out its cooking "secrets" and learn its special family recipes.

Each family has a personality of its own that is more than just the sum of its individual member's qualities and characteristics. Find out what that personality is and what makes it unique. Be particularly concerned about surfacing how your family views and deals with areas such as finances—who controls the money and how are financial decisions reached. Look carefully at your family's way of perceing men and women in their particular roles as husband/father and wife/mother. Ask yourself the questions "Of what am I proud?" and "Of what am I ashamed?" relative to your family.

Identify family expectations regarding how much or how little the "family" gets together. This will become a crucial issue when you marry, particularly if your partner's legacy is different from your own. If one person's family stresses getting together often and the other's seldom, a feeling of unbalance will soon emerge generating marital stress and conflict. If both sides emphasize getting together frequently, time alone as a couple or as a nuclear family unit may be severely curtailed.

Zero in on how your family celebrates. How do they observe holidays, birthdays, anniversaries, and other marker events in family life? Since every family has traditions and customs, family members grow up with the feeling that "of course it's always done that way." Imagine the chagrin of a wife whose husband expects ten different home-baked varieties of cookies at Christmas when her fmaily used to buy two or three basics at the local bakery. Or imagine a husband's irritation when his wife spends and "excessive" amount of money at

Christmas because filling the room with gifts was her family's standard fare.

In marriage a rude awakening can occur if your partner does not see things through your eyes. If you know from where your ideas came, the two of you can then discuss the matter and make decisions about how you want to celebrate, what traditions you want to continue, what role expectations you have of each other, how often you will visit your different parents, and how financial matters will be handled. Rather than treating each other's objections or differences as personal affronts, you can mediate your differences based on how the two of you want to carry on the family legacy in your own way. Instead of becoming adversaries you can become partners in the cooperative venture of legacy making.

YOUR FAMILY AS A RESOURCE

Not only is learning *about* your family of origin important but also essential is identifying how your family is a resource to you, your marriage, and your own family (Campbell, 1974). What assets do your family have which can be helpful to you as you assume responsibilities of adult living? The commonly experienced tendency of adolescents to reject family values and resources in the quest for independence often becomes an obstacle to treating the family of origin as a source of valuable information and assistance. In most cases, this rejection is transitional and temporary. As Mark Twain once said, "When I was a boy of 14, I thought my father was one of the stupidest mortals to walk the face of the earth; when I turned 21, I was amazed to see how much the old gentleman had learned in seven years."

In our day and age of rapid technological change, skills and information acquired by the parents often are obsolete by the time their children grow up. Although this may be true in the work world, it should not be generalized to the personal and interpersonal arenas. Adolescents and young adults who are able to overcome the taboo against asking their parents' advice more often than not come away with valuable help. Some of the best career assistance can be acquired right at home when you investigate the career aspirations and experiences of your parents (and grandparents). When the topic is dating and mating, asking parents for opinions and advice may seem awkward, inappropriate or embarrassing, but doing so alleviates uncomfortable tensions and pressures between you and them as well as opens channels of communication. At times your parents may appear "old worldish" if they attempt to introduce you to potential partners, yet "matchmaking" is one of the oldest of all family obligations and customs. Your family may know more about you than you realize and can actually expose you to a relationship that is potentially satisfying.

If your family has material assets they make available to you, make a point to use them responsibly to develop your talents and abilities in the best interests of yourself, your marriage, and your family. Maybe you will shun these resources to prove to yourself that you can make it, but they are still valid. Whether you use them or not, remember, your family for the most part wants you to succeed and be happy. They want to help if at all possible. Even though you may not want their help, remember that in the normal course of events you too will want to help your children. Therefore, although using your family's resources accumulates a debt (of loyalty or obligation as well as financial), you will have the opportunity to balance that debt when you respond in kind to the needs of your own children. Over the course of generations, then, your debt to your parents can be repaid by your giving to your children. So the ledger continues from generation to generation in the forming of your family heritage.

ORDINAL POSITION:
YOUR PLACE IN THE FAMILY

When we are born into a family, we not only acquire a legacy but we also are placed in a position within a family structure which influences who we are and how we view the world. This birth place referred to as our *ordinal position in the family constellation* provides us with our first experience in relating to other people (Toman, 1976). The things we learn as a result determine to a great extent how we relate as our relationship network expands. Several factors affect the formation of our "private logic." One is the specific position we hold in the sibling sub-system (oldest, youngest, middle, and so forth). Second is the number of siblings and, third is the sex of the siblings in combination with whether they are older or younger (e.g., younger brother of older sisters or older sister of younger brothers).

Walter Toman's (1976) classic work *Family Constellation: Its Effects on Personality and Social Behavior* provides extensive detail about ordinal position and its impact on individual development and relationship patterns. We will review some of the basic concepts here, but recommend reading Toman's book and studying Adlerian psychology if more indepth information is desired.

Each child born into a family forces the family to adjust and reorganize itself. How the family reacts to the new entry creates the context in which that new individual must pound out his/her own identity. In the struggle to find one's place in the family certain characteristics emerge as patterns which eventually become integrated into the personality and identity of the child. Part of the process in forging our identity involves how we deal with the position we hold and how we work out relationships with our siblings. Each position holds certain innate traits which a child may claim or disregard depending on how his/her identity is worked out.

Being an oldest child means that you are your parents first experience (and experiment) with being parents. Consequently, parents often have higher standards, ideals and expectations for their first child than for children born later. On the other hand, the first child often becomes the center of attention not only for parents but for grandparents as well. The combination between expectations and attention tends to produce responsible, achievement-oriented traits that may be presented to later siblings as a model to emulate. Parents also tend to place more responsibility on the shoulders of the eldest as the family expands and becomes more complicated. A common complaint of eldest children is that they wish they could have had more freedom and fun like their younger brothers and sisters. They also feel parents were unfair because they had more stringent rules than did younger siblings. On the other hand, eldest children do a great deal to pave the way for their siblings by testing the rules and providing parents with information upon which they can adjust their parenting of later children. A common complaint *about* eldest children is that they set an example by which younger children are judged and as such make the life of their siblings miserable because parents, teachers, and others are always expecting them to be like the eldest.

One of the facts about being the eldest, however, is that it is a position that cannot be altered. All other sibling positions have the potential of being changed by the birth of another child. Not so for the oldest. The oldest is always the oldest and consequently, the only options available are to accept and cope with those privileges and obligations of the position or to reject and rebel against them.

The biggest task of second children is to differentiate from the first and make a mark in the family that is uniquely their own. Often a great deal of competition exists between the first and second child. This may be tempered somewhat if the siblings are of different sex or a large age gap exists between them. Some of the options available to a second child include doing better at what the first child does, developing interests, skills, or abilities different from those of the first child or becoming the antithesis of the oldest (e.g., if the oldest got attention by being good in school, the second gets attention by being bad or vice versa). Second children also face a threat from younger siblings because as soon as another child is born they become middle children, losing some of the attention of being the youngest and still having to cope with the competition with the eldest. How a second handles these pressures and shifts affects his/her strength and adaptability as well as forges the type of personality he/she will have.

Middle children are in a position in the family that has the least clear-cut privileges or responsibilities. Middle children often feel like they were the invisible members of the family. Because they do not inherit privileges and responsibilities of the oldest or the attention and license of the youngest, middle children have to fend for themselves in the identity struggle. Consequently, they often become the most adaptable of family members and can enter into the role of peacemaker, moderator, or facilitator in family hassles. Middle children emerge from family life with the best ability to adjust to ups and downs and the variability of the real world outside the family. They have a sense of their own strength which is a resource that carries them through stress and disappointments. They also are able to see, understand, and respond to needs of others to a greater extent than siblings raised in other positions. On the other hand, they also may harbor resentments about not having gotten the attention or special treatment accorded the oldest or youngest sibling. In working with families we often ask children which position in the family other than their own they would like to have. Those positions most chosen are oldest or youngest and the position least chosen is middle. However, middle children tend to defend their position indicating it is the least pressured.

The youngest child inherits the most nurtured position in the family. Many youngest children grow up feeling like they had more than their share of parents because older siblings tended to parent them in addition to their adult parents. The special attention accorded youngest children produces expectations that others will bow to their desires and attend to their needs and wants. They tend to be pampered to some extent and have fewer restrictions and rules with which to contend. The youngest often becomes the "darling" of the family and finds that his/her parents can be made to feel good by giving them love and affection. The youngest position is often the most envied position among siblings, however the label attached to it is difficult to escape. Parents commonly will introduce their youngest child (even when they are in their teens, twenties, or thirties) as "my baby." Imagine the embarrassment of an adolescent who is introduced to adults and potential peer friends as the "baby of the family." Consequently, youngest children may get the picture that other people are eager and available to serve them, but they also experience difficulty getting out of the family and being treated as an adult in their own right.

The number of children in the family also affects the child's growth and development. An only child experiences life in a much different manner than does a child raised with siblings. Only children acquire the benefits of exclusive parental attention and tend to mature faster. Their input is given greater consideration in family decisions and they are often accorded equal status in the family quite early in life. However, only children may have difficulty relating to peers and may lament the fact that they did not have brothers or sisters. Only children, once married, often have several children simply because they do not want their children to be reared as an only child. One result of this is that parents of only children sometimes view their multiple grandchildren as unspoken criticism or disapproval of them as parents. Only children acquire privileges and obligations of both the youngest and oldest which can be a heavy burden to bear as they work out their identity. Later in life a residual obligation of an only child is caring for aging parents which must be shouldered alone since there are no siblings with whom to share the responsibility. This factor may place extensive pressure on a marriage.

Example

When Only Means Alone. The marriage of an only child was severely tested when her parents both contracted terminal illnesses leading to their deaths within several weeks of each other. During the two years it took the illnesses to run their course, the daughter who was married and had three school-age children, spent most of her time running back and forth between her parents and her children. While she was putting her parents affairs in order, dealing with their medical problems, and arranging for their funerals, her husband, feeling abandoned, became involved in another relationship which came to light a few weeks prior to her parents' deaths. The combination of losses accentuated the aloneness of the only child position but also revealed how being an only child cultivated an inner strength which enabled her to deal with the trauma of the losses and work on putting her marriage back together.

Whether the number of siblings is large or small influences each child's development. Children reared in small families of two to four siblings have different experiences than those reared in large families. Historically, children often were viewed as a family resource particularly when society was largely dependent on agriculture and family business. However, as industry, technology, and economic factors made family man-power less necessary, family size dwindled. Consequently, typical family units in contemporary society are between two and five members. Values you acquire relative to number will be important however. If you feel growing up in a large family was too complicated and you did not get the attention you feel you needed, you will likely decide on a smaller, less complicated unit. If you valued a large family and want to emulate it, you may find obstacles such as financial resources, your own physical capacities (if you are a woman), or your spouse's resistance stand in your way. Such expectations when not met may result in disappointment and even a sense of failure. Many couples in therapy express deep pain and bitterness over their inability to have as many children as they wanted or because a major difference exists between them over that issue.

In conjunction with number, the sex and position of each child in the sibling hierarchy is important to consider. An older brother of younger sisters learns to relate to women in a much different manner than does a younger brother of older sisters. Relating patterns formed in the sibling subsystem carry over into same and opposite sex relationships outside the family. Both ordinal position characteristics and the relational patterns between opposite and same sex siblings should be considered when trying to understand yourself, your spouse, or your prospective spouse. We will cite a few examples of typical combinations and their implications for marriage. As you read these examples, however, remember that they are not intended to suggest a formula for selecting a mate or insuring marital happiness. They are meant to help you consider and investigate your own and your partner's view of the world as a resource in choosing a mate and working out a compatible and fulfilling relationship.

When two people come together in marriage their identities and expectations relative to marriage and family life come with them. For example, two oldest children who marry may find their drives for achievement to be compatible but may run into obstacles in working out who is in charge since both have experienced that position in their family of origin.

An older brother of younger sisters may find it easier to work out a relationship with a younger sister of older brothers than with an older sister of younger brothers.

Two youngest children who marry may have mutual expectations that the other will give in to them since it is likely that both have been "spoiled." Another difficulty for them may be creating their own identity as a couple separate from their families of origin because of their mutual position of "baby" in their respective families.

Sometimes seemingly compatible traits that initially make each attractive to the other turn out to be irritations later. During courtship an "oldest" may enjoy going out of his/her way doing special things and making decisions which please the "youngest" partner. Such activities create a climate to which both are accustomed and intimacy develops leading to marriage. After marriage, however, the "oldest" tires of taking care of "youngest" and wants the "youngest" to "grow up," "be more responsible," "stand on his/her own two feet," or "stop being a baby." Or, the "youngest" wants to "do his/her own thing," "have a voice in decisions," or "be treated like an adult." These changes build tension and conflict into the relationship. In one counseling session with a couple involving an oldest and a youngest it became very evident that their fighting was much like an older brother-younger sister spat rather than two adults confronting a mutual problem.

Middle children often make effective marital partners because they have acquired a high degree of adaptability and sensitivity to others. In addition, the marriage provides a new arena where they can develop their identity in the new roles of husband/wife and father/mother. Consequently, they get an equal start and a new beginning which was not accorded them in the family. Their resiliency is an asset to the marriage even though they may still have to adapt to traits their partner may bring into the marriage having been in one of the favored family positions.

Although we will address parenting extensively in a later chapter, we want to point out here that the position you hold in your family also will affect how you parent and how you relate to your children. As an oldest child you may set higher standards for your oldest whereas if you were a middle or youngest child your standards would still be higher for your oldest but not as high as an oldest would set. As an oldest you may impose higher across-the-board standards for all your children than a middle or youngest. Or, if you are a second, you may pass on the dynamic of striving and fighting for what you want that was acquired in your own struggle for identity.

Example

The Hallmark Connection.One illustration which combines elements of legacy and family constellation was related to us by a woman who was married for twenty years and had two children. She and her husband were both oldest children; she the oldest sister of brothers and he the oldest brother of sisters. Soon after their marriage she began having trouble with her mother-in-law over the issue of sending cards to acknowledge family events such as birthdays, anniversaries, or holidays. In her family, sending cards was never stressed and was not a major custom of any importance. In her spouse's family, however, not only was it of major importance but it was also a designated woman's responsibility. So when they married both her husband and her mother-in-law automatically expected her to pick up the pen and dutifully send the cards "like the other sisters" in the family. Although she was never told this directly, whenever she would forget, she would get negative vibrations (the cold shoulder routine) from her mother-in-law. Several years passed before she identified the connection between the card sending ritual and her mother-in-law's reaction.

Additional variations in the family constellation which affect a child's experience in the family are when the age range of siblings is quite large and when children are born into the family in groups (i.e., two or more children born in close proximity age-wise followed by another child or children with a number of childless years interspersed between the two). When a large age spread occurs between children, younger children have older parents who often lack the physical stamina of their younger years. Or the younger children may get more attention than the older children because the parents are no longer immersed so heavily in making their way in the world. Advantages to counter the lessened activity of parents are greater financial stability and access to monetary benefits that were not available to the older children. These discrepancies may create tension between older and younger siblings and may even lead to distancing. However, older siblings often are given parenting responsibilities for the younger ones which may create a stronger bond but can also be the source of resentment later in life when the younger siblings want to get out from under the yoke of older siblings. Typical comments of younger siblings are "I never really knew my older brothers or sisters" or "I was really brought up by my older sister/brother."

The "first and second family" of the same parents' phenomenon creates a situation where the family is always in at least two different phases at the same time. For example, when different subgroups occur in one family such as teenagers and preschool children, parents must be able to switch gears in their parenting. Doing so not only is a challenge but also can create stress because younger children may pressure parents to give them the same privileges that older children are getting. Sometimes parents get tired and worn out by the time the second group arrives at adolescence. They may feel that the later children owe them an easier time of it but they also may be more concerned about preventing problems based on their experience with the older children. Where you were on the older-younger continuum and whether you were in the "first" or "second" family will make a large difference in your experiences and view of the world.

In closing this section we stress looking at the impact of your experiences in your family of origin. Look at them from the perspective of your legacy as well as your position in the family. Do the same for your partner. Doing so will help you understand the dynamics of your interaction and will provide you with not only insight and understanding but alternatives for resolving conflicts. Use the information to help you assess areas of strength where you can combine forces and areas of potential conflict which you can circumvent or work through to solidify and improve your relationship.

EXTENDED FAMILY:
ITS PLACE IN MARRIAGE AND FAMILY LIFE

Marriage merges the two spouses' families of origin and turns them into an extended family network. With the birth of children, the potential exists for as many as four or five living generations to comprise the extended family. The nature of the relationship (or lack of a relationship) between the new unit created by the marriage and the extended family will be an important facet of the marital and family experience. In some cultures and in some families the extended family is still the essential unit which constitutes family experience. However, in our society, the trend has been toward making the nuclear family (parents and children) the primary unit of family life.

Many factors have contributed to the evolution of the nuclear family as the typical family unit. The fact that America was a land populated by immigrants initiated a family pattern that was emulated throughout history as the frontier was pushed westward. People left home to establish a new life in a new country or part of the country. In doing so, they often had to sever relational ties with their extended family and depend on the smaller support unit of the nuclear family.

For immigrant families, a typical cycle was for the first generation to leave their country of origin and either marry in the new country or bring their spouse and children with them. The separation usually meant never again seeing their parents or brothers and sisters, thus tightening the nuclear family.

The second generation would be caught between cultures and would often attempt to submerge itself in the new culture by dissociating as much as possible from the old. The second generation, as a result of feelings of embarrassment and/or the desire to be a part of the new culture, would disregard customs and traditions and would downplay its bilingual status.

The third generation would become acculturated and in doing so would lose a lot of its ethnic connectedness as well as the language. The fourth generation often found itself at a loss to explain its cultural heritage and would have to learn the language of its original culture in school. In the course of the four generations, a new family base would be established. Thus, the extended family which had been truncated by the immigration would be filled out again. However the pattern of mobility would be repeated as members of the fourth and fifth generations would seek out new places to live and establish their families. Consequently, much of the cultural heritage of a family would get lost in the process. One of the amazing features of a book such as Alex Haley's *Roots* (1976) is that Kunte Kinte was able to keep his family legacy alive and pass it on even under the most adverse conditions of slavery.

The same patterns are evident in the westward expansion in the United States. The frontier spirit pushed people west to seek out and populate new domains, but the flames of independence and freedom took their toll on the family. The aura of mobility created by immigrants and pioneers was picked up by the industrialization movement which fostered easier access to new environs. Then, after World War II the advance in technology spawned by education and science firmly entrenched mobility as a primary characteristic of the American family. The gap between generations was exacerbated in terms of knowledge and experience as well as in geographical displacement. Keeping in touch with one's extended family has now become a major issue for most American families and is the reason we address it here.

A FAMILY DISINTEGRATION FORMULA

One of the explanations offered for the expanding divorce rate and increased levels of family turmoil has been the gradual erosion of the extended family as the primary support system in family life. Before declaring the institution of marriage obsolete or attempting to displace the family as the primary unit of socialization, a look at these changes that have weakened the family unit undermining its ability to cope with the world's increasing complexity is in order. We submit the following formula in explanation.

The formula consists of three factors: *Turmoil Within (TW)* the nuclear family, *Pressure From Without (PFW)* on the nuclear family and the *Extended Family Network (EFN)*. *Turmoil Within* the nuclear family is a normal condition associated with marriage and family life. It comes with the package along the joys and satisfactions. *Pressure From Without* is also a normal aspect of family living. The fact that a family must exist in a society means that it has to work out a relationship to that society and in doing so will encounter many obstacles and difficulties that generate pressure and tension in the family. The nuclear family therefore is in a situation where it must learn to cope with the internal and external pressures but must do so with fewer resources because of the unavailability of the *Extended Family Network*. Grandparents and relatives are not readily accessible to supply help and assistance as they have their own nuclear families about which to be concerned. So the formula which explains *Family Disintegration (FD)* is

$$TW \quad + \quad PFW \quad - \quad EFN \quad = \quad FD$$

Turmoil Within (TW) which is normal

plus

Pressure From Without (PFW) which is also normal

minus

Extended Family Network (EFN)

equals

Family Disintegration (FD)

Advantages of the nuclear family arrangement include being simpler, more flexible, and more mobile. Nuclear families experience greater independence and privacy and generally diffuse tensions earlier when personality conflicts occur between members of different generations. However, total dissociation reduces the resources available to the family which both undermines the family (due to the continued influence of invisible loyalties) and reduces its ability to cope with complexity in the world around it. Let us look at some typical examples that illustrate dilemmas caused by the nuclear family emphasis and the need to work for effective connectedness between the nuclear family and the extended family.

One of the major losses when the nuclear family and extended family are geographically or emotionally distant from each other is easy access to help in coping with day-to-day pressures of marriage and family living. Couples who opt for distance deny themselves a source of ready help when faced with decisions that require availability of a support system. Leaving the kids with grandparents for short or long periods of time is greatly facilitated if they live near. Being helpful to aging parents is much easier on the family if cross-country flights are not involved. On the other hand, distance also reduces obligations which may become weighty and disruptive. Some couples feel that utilizing their parents as resources incurs too great a debt because then parents expect certain concessions in return. One couple explained that they chose to use a babysitter instead of their parents even though both spouse's parents lived within a short distance. That way they did not feel so "obligated."

When distance geographically is great, all decisions to visit become major commitments in terms of time and money for both parents and grandparents. Being able to stop in to see both sets of parents on a holiday is easy to do if you live in the same vicinity. However, if distance is great, the decision involves days and dollars and also involves keeping contact balanced and fair. On the other hand, distance can make reconnecting more exciting and fulfilling as each occasion becomes a celebration unleashing the therapeutic power of the family reunion.

The issue of how much time should be spent with one's parents is always a major one in marriage. However, it can become a real crisis if spouses do not mutually recognize the importance of working out extended family relationships. This can intrude on the marriage causing negative feelings between spouses and can lead to distance in their relationship as well. Visiting one's family of origin alone can be a positive experience in terms of feeling at ease in reconnecting or working out unfinished business. However, permanent practices such as "you visit your parents and I'll visit mine" which grant a temporary reprieve to tension will usually generate bitterness in the long run because the underlying message sent is "I can't stand your family."

ACTIVITY: Considering Extended Family Implications

One important thing you can do in dealing with the issue of extended family is to determine and express the importance of extended family in your own and your partner's life. What is the importance, pro and con of the extended family to you? To your partner? Second, work together to give extended family involvement a valued and balanced position in your marriage and family. How can this be done? In what areas? Under what circumstances? Third, when the issue of contact with extended family does come up, in what ways can you as the non-related spouse serve a supportive role to your partner, thus encouraging extended family connectedness instead of becoming an obstacle that cultivates distance? Studying these questions and openly discussing them with your partner will reduce tension in the family system as well as make movement between the nuclear and extended family domains more feasible and satisfying.

BREAKING AWAY

The challenge of growing up and becoming an adult is part of the continuing saga of the generational war in which each succeeding generation fights its own battle in its own style in order to achieve the same goals—autonomy and individuation. The generation gap is not so much a fact of absolute difference but rather a process of making a difference. As for our families, we often find we can't live with them and we can't live without them. Jane Howard (1978) in writing about *Families* pointed out that "Families breed us, name us, succor us, embarrass us, annoy us, drive us off toward adventures as foreign to them as we can imagine and then lure us back" (p. 33). We strive to break away but then hope that we are not totally successful.

The goal of breaking away from our family of origin is to get out with some semblance of an individual identity without destroying the relational bonds in the process. To be able to move from a position of obedience to our parents to one of respect for them is often a difficult task. To be able to differentiate yourself from your parents before engaging in another form of intimate relating is crucial, yet the process of moving from being a child to your parents to being an adult in your own right without losing the essential elements of family ties is frought with difficulties.

The task of breaking away is a problem not only for the child but for the parents as well. Every parent of a young adult knows how hard it is to let go of their children. Some parents manage better than others, but almost all have difficulty. Parents know that their children need to establish their own adult identity and to make a break from home, but knowing that and doing something to help the process are two different things. For some people the process of breaking away is relatively easy, for some a struggle, for some a crisis, for some a transition, and for some a break is never achieved.

Many parents hold the viewpoint that marriage is the real marker event which symbolizes their child has grown up. However, marriage may only be a camouflage which covers the fact that real individuation has not occurred. Many couples learn too late that they have not experienced a sense of individuality and therefore feel burdened down with the cares and responsibilities of marriage and family life. Such a fact can be a fatal flaw that leads to loss of self-esteem. Women who move from their parents' home into a husband's are oftentimes simply transferring their status of being their parents' child to being their husband's wife-child. Marriage becomes a half-step, a way to leave home without losing home.

Gail Sheehy (1976), author of *Passages,* maintained that for both men and women a separation crisis though unpleasant is desirable. A successful work experience is most useful in helping a young person resolve the conflicts of dependency and establishing an independent identity. Even though the book you are now reading is about marriage and family, we urge young adults to experience a career of some sort before marriage. This is especially true for women who often cannot see themselves as anything but wives and mothers. We are stressing the word "career" as opposed to some filler job until one finds a husband. A technical school or college education, training, or experience in a personally desirable vocational field are worth the investment of time and/or money before marriage. If you are most likely going to be working anyway, doing something you enjoy and which gives you a sense of satisfaction is not only sensible but mentally healthy. It will increase your options, your assets, and your confidence that you can make it on your own. Male or female, when you have made that break from your parents, you will find that the struggle was worthwhile as you begin to see your parents in a new light and can relate to them on an adult-to-adult basis.

The problem with breaking away is that it tends to be complicated by another equally influential force which emerges at about the same time in our lives. The need for intimacy propels us into seeking new and meaningful relationships with those outside our family. So as we struggle to "break away" we also are struggling to "break in" to the relational arena which paves the way to marriage. Our next chapter therefore will focus on the transitional period in intimate relating often referred to as courtship.

REFERENCES

Barnard, C.P. (1981). *Families, alcoholism, and therapy.* Springfield, IL: Charles C. Thomas.

Boszormenyi-Nagy, I., & Spark, G.M. (1973). *Invisible loyalties: Reciprocity in intergenerational family therapy.* Hagerstown, MD: Medical Department, Harper & Row.

Campbell, D.P. (1974). *If you don't know where you're going you'll probably end up somewhere else.* Niles, IL: Argus Communications.

Haley, A. (1976). *Roots.* New York: Dell Publishing.

Howard, J. (1978). *Families.* New York: Simon and Schuster.

Laing, R.D. (1965). Mystification, confusion, and conflict. In I. Boszormenyi-Nagy and J. Framo, (Eds.). *Intensive Family Therapy.* New York: Harper & Row.

Sheehy, G. (1976). *Passages.* New York: E. P. Dutton.

Toman, W. (1976). *Family constellation: Its effects on personality and social behavior.* New York: Springer.

FAMILY OF ORIGIN
TO ORIGIN OF FAMILY:
THE DATING AND COURTSHIP
PHASE OF MARRIAGE

The process and experience of dating and courtship are explored. The bases of attraction, myths of mate selection, and typical patterns of intimate relating are presented. Concepts such as responsibility, honesty, and openness are discussed and important questions to ask yourself and your partner during courtship are posed. Variations in the courtship process created by pregnancy, family crises, and special needs are also addressed.

> *There are three things beyond my comprehension,*
> *Four indeed that I do not understand:*
> *The way of an eagle through the skies,*
> *The way of a snake over a rock,*
> *The way of a ship in mid-ocean,*
> *The way of a man with a maid.*

> — *Proverbs 30: 18-19*

These words from the Old Testament underscore the complexity and confusion associated with the focus of our current chapter. Even King Solomon, reputed by history to be one of the wisest men to have ever lived and the husband of 700 wives, was baffled by the process of how a man and a woman became intimate partners in marriage. On the one hand, the number of different tales of how one finds a mate may be as large as the number of couples. However, maybe only two or three basic variations are repeated over and over with each repetition seeming like it never happened before. Whatever the case may be, we do not presume to have the right answers relative to dating and courtship. Our purpose is not to give you a formula but rather to present ideas, concepts, illustrations, and suggestions for you to consider reflectively as you experience the transition from your family of origin to your family of creation.

In this chapter we will look at the process involved in moving toward intimacy. We will consider the various dynamics and sequences that tend to occur in dating and courtship. We will look at the bases of attraction and myths associated with finding a partner and discuss that nebulous commodity called love. Also, we will review factors affecting marital choice and discuss the implications of these factors relative to the process of moving from being a child in your parents' family to being an adult in your marriage. Finally, the chapter will conclude with our view of the role courtship plays in preparing you for marriage and family life.

SO IT BEGINS:
FROM CHILDHOOD TO INTIMACY

During middle childhood boys play with boys and girls with girls, each sex professing disdain for the other. In approximately sixth grade these aforementioned adversaries begin to notice each other, not knowing quite how to handle it. They begin to tease, fight, and act silly in each other's presence. Notes and gifts are exchanged, contacts are made through intermediaries and the first boy-girl parties occur. Thus a process begins of creating experiences that have become the theme for thousands of love songs, plays, novels, and poems. The media publicizes and propels the process creating its own kind of hype and image. Parents also play a part. Some parents, trying to live through their children, push the process. Others try to ignore or prevent it as long as possible. Peers talk about nothing else and physical changes are awakening. The process is the thrust toward intimacy—a special male-female relationship often referred to as love which ideally culminates in a marriage ceremony leading to a life together.

Since we have discussed relationships generally in Chapter 3, we will concentrate here on the special relationship between opposite sex partners that leads to intimacy. However, we wish to applaud young people and adults who are able to approach opposite sex relationships as equals and friends without having to resort to games, roles, and ploys that occur when each sees the other as a sex object or stereotype.

DATING GAME

Someone once said "The course of true love never runs smooth." An appropriate corollary might be "The course of true love is never predictable." Very frequently couples preface their description of how they got together by stating "we never thought we would end up with each other." Some relationships move from acquaintance to deep involvement very rapidly. Others evolve over a long period of time, sometimes years. Recently we worked with a couple who had dated each other almost exclusively for eight years before finally deciding to marry. On the other hand, another couple met, dated, courted, and married in a matter of two weeks. These examples are likely end points on a vast continuum of possibilities which we wish to acknowledge as a preface to discussing the phases of the dating process.

As male-female relationships develop from initial contact to intimacy, several phases tend to occur. The initial phase tends to be open-ended where potential for dating is primarily the result of circumstances, personal interests and preferences, attraction, and the push within each of us for social interaction. Some people approach this phase with the attitude of exploration and a desire to gain new experiences by meeting and dating a number of people. Others, even at this point, put restrictions on potential dating partners. Common restraints drummed into young people are in the form of parental edicts such as "never date a person you wouldn't marry" or "never date a person who isn't a(an)_____." (You fill in the blank.) In either case, the second phase of dating usually follows where dating is "semi-restricted." You begin to identify the type of person you enjoy, are attracted to, and can get along with and move to date that person or persons more extensively. During this phase the pull or push toward exclusivity usually surfaces. This force may come from within yourself or from the demands of your partner. Either way a decision point arises where you have to say yes or no. A yes answer moves the relationship into phase three which is "exclusivity." You decide to limit your dating to one person which thus begins what we would formally identify as the courtship period—the purpose of which is to determine if a mutual commitment to each other can be made.

COURTSHIP:
GETTING TO CLOUD 9 AND BEYOND

Courtship can generally be broken down into three phases: *Excitement/attraction, Cloud 9,* and *Reality.* The initial phase, *excitement/attraction,* may actually begin during dating when the relationship is in its forming state. This phase is often characterized by cautiousness, tentativeness, discomfort, embarrassment, role playing, and the games of flirtation. These experiences are understandable given the vulnerabilities associated with entering a new relationship, in particular the fear of being rejected. Although "flirting" is generally perceived with some amount of disdain, it can be a legitimate and socially acceptable means of conveying a message of personal interest in another person. Since most of us lack the confidence to communicate our intentions relative to intimacy directly in initial encounters, the subtle camouflage of flirting gives both the sender and receiver a modicum of protection and the opportunity to choose whether or not to respond without losing face.

Despite the ambiguities of the initial phase, courtship is fueled by excitement and attraction that propels us into the unknown. Efforts are made to get to know each other, to impress each other, and to appear confident. Ways and means of getting together are broached and worked out, and time and energy are devoted to making the relationship expand. Once the groundwork is laid, the middle phase or "Cloud 9" phase emerges complete with its unbridled emotional enthusiasm and unencumbered excitement for each other.

In the *Cloud 9 phase* courtship shifts relating into high gear. This is the real "high" of the relationship. The world is seen from a new point of view even though that view is quite restricted. Everything, even the mundane, is new and exciting when shared with the other person. Other people begin to see you as a "couple" and it is fun just being together. You don't even have to do anything and it is satisfying. Your consciousness of each other is almost total even though it is limited to only the positive elements. Issues and irritations don't even emerge or if they do, they are quickly swept under the carpet in the interest of enjoying each other.

To be married during this phase would be heavenly, and it is often this emotional high which prompts the question and act of marriage. It is certainly a time to be savored and enjoyed and hopefully, it is a time that is governed by openness and responsibility. However, waiting until your relationship has moved on to the third stage before jumping into marriage is usually preferable.

The third phase, *Reality,* is the time when the rose-colored glasses are removed and the two of you are brought back to the earthly realm of day-to-day living and interacting as two human beings complete with personalities and backgrounds that have elements which create conflict and problems. As reality begins to poke its head into your perceptions, your awareness of the other person's imperfections increases. You have your first arguments that don't get resolved quickly. You become cognizant of differences in each other's goals, values, habits, needs, lifestyle, preferences, and interests and you realize that these things have to be taken into account relative to the relationship. The courtship thus becomes a time of working on the relationship in addition to just enjoying it as it unfolds.

ACTIVITY: Relationship Assessment in Courtship

Important questions with regard to the relationship need to be asked and answered. The *reality phase* is the time for assessing where the relationship can and should go. Are there certain conflicts or issues which continue to emerge repeatedly without resolution? If so, probably they will not become resolvable simply by becoming married. What things are you willing to change in order to continue the relationship in an affable manner, and what do you expect your partner to change? Has each person given enough thought and consideration to his/her own identity, self concept, and life desires? Are you basically intact without the other person or is dependency present, perhaps too extensively? How do you get along in dealing with day-to-day decisions? Do you think alike? Do you complement each other or are little conflicts occurring in too many situations?

How do you work out conflicts and resolve irritations? What about relationships with others? They are necessary, especially after marriage. Does a balance exist between people he knows, she knows, and both know mutually? What about sex role expectations? Have you explored your cultural, religious, political, socioeconomic, environmental, and education similarities and differences? What about family of origin roots, patterns, expectations, and values? Addressing these and other questions may appear both overwhelming and arduous, but they are crucial elements of an effective courtship. Certainly all the answers will not come out in a compatible fashion but raising them will help you solidify your commonalities and anticipate conflict areas that can then be handled constructively. As answers to these kinds of questions are worked through in the context of the excitement, attraction, and growing bond of love in the relationship, the pathway to marriage is cleared and the foundation of commitment becomes established. On the other hand, if such efforts begin to undermine the bases of attraction and caring leading to a dissolution of the relationship, both parties will have benefited as well as saved themselves the pain of having to address these same areas after marriage where incompatibility is destined to generate bitterness, unhappiness, and the potential for divorce.

FINDING THE RIGHT ONE

Having generally reviewed the process of dating and courtship, let us turn our attention now to the elements that serve as cues and clues in making the determination of a life's mate. We will address this difficult topic from several perspectives including the myths of mating, bases of attraction, and associated strengths and problems in marriage, the nature of love and the factors that affect marital choice.

Myths of Mating

When couples come to us for counseling, we ask two standard questions regardless of how long they have been in their relationship together. The first question is "How did the two of you get together?" and the second is "How did you know you had found the right one?" Most couples are not prepared for these questions and have become so embroiled in their problems that they have forgotten about those times when they were attracted to each other and excited about each other. What these questions often raise are the myths each partner had held about marriage and how they would know if they had found the "right one."

One woman in responding to the first question said, "I was attracted to him because he seemed so smart. I didn't realize how stupid he was until I married him." The husband, not to be outdone, immediately replied, "You should have known that the minute I asked you to marry me." Evidently what this couple thought they were getting in a partner and what they got was quite different. Their experience confirmed the old adage that marriage is like a cafeteria—you take what looks good now and pay for it later. What are some of these myths on which people rely in choosing a partner?

The Magic or Fairytale Approach. Most of us somewhere along the line have gotten the idea that when the right person comes into our lives, we will automatically know it. We have been indoctrinated by the "knight in shining armor" syndrome. As one woman explained "He wasn't wearing shining armor, but he sure had a spiffy car." Parents and friends console and encourage us with statements like "Don't worry, you'll just know when the right one comes along," or "Your prince or princess will come," or "There's someone out there who is your Mr. or Ms. Right." One man whose dad's advice was "Don't fret, something will just pop and you'll know," told us "something popped all right—that's why we had to get married."

The myth that people will magically know when their partner is the right one is usually reinforced during the "Cloud 9" phase of courtship, and is one of the main reasons for waiting for both to come back down to earth. In most cases, a real person complete with flaws and faults is hiding behind that shining armor, and if you marry, he/she is the person with whom you end up living.

Luck of the Draw. Another idea that surfaces in our discussions with couples is that fate was the primary factor in bringing them together. Bad relationships and bad marriages are explained as an unlucky break or simply the "luck of the draw." One man whispered confidentially as we were leaving the room after the first session of marital therapy, "I never had much luck with women, and I ended up with a loser." Although this myth is useful in rationalizing why other people have good marriages when you don't, the fact of the matter is that "choice" is always involved. Knowledge is something which counters chance, and responsibility is the flip side of fate. Like it or not, we all *choose* our partners—that's one of the facts of life.

Osmosis. Some couples explain that they really don't know how they got together—" We sort of just rubbed off on each other." Their lives kind of came together and before they knew it, they were "involved." Osmosis works fine until one or the other becomes disenchanted and wishes to extricate himself/herself or wants to change the way things are. This osmosis idea is perpetuated by people around the couple who describe them as "the perfect match," "like two peas in a pod," or "they were cut out for each other." No matter how well the two people fit together, in marriage no such thing as the perfect match exists. Fitting together is something that requires conscious work and effort.

On the Job Training. Another common myth that couples carry into marriage with them is that they will work out their differences after they are married. They purposely put off discussing issues that cause them to differ because they are not married yet. They figure that they will have plenty of time and energy to deal with problems once they are together so why waste time on them now. This concept of on-the-job training is often espoused by parents who figure the couple will learn when they have to face the realities of living together. (To be fair, we must point out that giving any advice to a couple who think they are in love is about as foolhardy as trying to keep an ice cube from melting in 90 degree heat.) One young woman recounted having told her father as she was walking down the aisle with him that she thought her marriage was all wrong. Her father's reply was "you made your bed, now lay in it." The marriage lasted one year.

Although all marriages require on-the-job training, this school of hard knocks approach is much too risky if advance preparation is not made. That is why we are writing this book. Having the tools and skills before marriage and working through issues during courtship will turn the myth of on-the-job training into a realistic means of insuring a healthy marriage.

Bases of Attraction

Social psychologists have espoused at least three bases of attraction upon which relationships are built (Rathus, 1984; Hendrick & Hendrick, 1983). These are (1) similarities attract, (2) opposites attract, and (3) the exchange theory. Each of these general perspectives has application to the process of choosing a partner and implications for the nature of the marriage relationship that emerges.

Similarities Attract Perspective. This perspective holds that persons are attracted to each other because of commonalities in their characteristics, values, life experiences, and view of the world. Couples develop attachments because they enjoy similar activities, and have common interests, similar backgrounds, values, and beliefs. This homogeneity makes it easy to make decisions and pursue the relationship because their two lives have so many places to intersect. The commonalities form a solid foundation for the relationship and facilitate each partner moving into the other's world with a minimum of hassle and discomfort. Couples who begin their relationship on a similarities basis find that their marriage relationship is strong because of the mutuality they experience. They can work together, play together, and relate to each other's family of origin with relative ease. Most important, they can harness their energies together and work toward common goals they both value. Partners of similar race, ethnicity, religion, education, values, and other lifestyle dimensions are compatible and find it easier to understand one another—a key dynamic of a happy marital relationship.

However the similarities basis of attraction does have some drawbacks. One problem is that of "look alikes." During courtship each partner perceives the other to be the same based on outward appearances and actions. Each assumes the other thinks, feels, and sees the world in a similar manner. The problem is usually accentuated by mutual noncommunication. The couple doesn't really discuss or check out what they assume to be common areas between them. When marriage occurs and the facades of similarity are rubbed off through day-to-day living together, differences emerge causing conflict and disgruntlement. One couple explained their surprise at how different they were when after two years of marital bliss, they could not reach agreement on when to have children and how to reorganize their lives to prepare for a family. Both had simply assumed they would see things the same way, but when the decisions were discussed all kinds of different expectations and values surfaced.

Another common problem that emerges out of relationships based on commonalities is BOREDOM. A typical complaint of many couples after several years of marriage is the lack of excitement and stimulation. Partners who are too much alike have a tendency to settle into a routine quite rapidly only to find themselves stuck in a rut. Without the input that differences provide, the relationship stagnates. This sometimes results in one or the other or both looking for excitement outside the marriage which further erodes the relationship and may even jeopardize the marriage.

A major reason couples get to this point of no return is their fear of saying anything to each other about it. On the surface the marriage looks happy, but their experience in the marriage is painfully unfulfilling. One young couple had the courage to talk to each other about their boredom and decided to get counseling to assist them. However, they were so afraid to let their parents know they were struggling that they drove 50 miles to our "out of town" counseling service and told their parents they were taking a class together—an explanation not entirely untrue since they were engaging in one of the most important learning experiences of their married lives.

Opposites Attract Perspective. The counterpart of the similarities hypothesis is the opposites attract perspective. Like the forces of attraction between opposite poles in magnets, two people find themselves drawn to each other in spite of or because of their differentness. This type of attraction generates an exciting and adventuresome kind of relational experience. An extroverted and socially outgoing person is drawn to the reserved and introspective person. An active and athletic individual is attracted to an individual who is more meditative and observational in approaching life. These couples come together and form a complementary relationship with regard to traits that have polar dimensions. They balance each other. The quiet and reserved person is pulled out into the social arena; the outgoing socializer is pulled back and settled down. The active person enjoys and values the quiet support of the observing person, and the observer is stimulated by the activity of their partner. Differences in race, ethnicity, religion, and values can be quite interesting and expanding in the context of a relationship and both can grow because of the exposure to each other's variability.

Couples who come together on the basis of difference form quite dynamic relationships. They have and need a great deal of energy and enthusiasm. Continual stimulation exists and when complementarity is attained their experience in life is broad and intense. They develop qualities such as openness and respect and learn to value not only each other's differences but differences between people in general. They tend to be more flexible and take risks which spiral their experience cycle in new directions.

However, all is not peaches and cream for these couples either. In marriage their relationship requires continual attention because their differences tend to draw them away from each other. When the initial excitement of the relationship dies down, usually less willingness is shown to accommodate to differences in one another. In fact, the very differences that attracted them may become the issues over which they conflict. These couples find that once they expand their relating beyond each other, they are uncomfortable in the world of their partner. They feel that they don't fit in with their partner's family, friends, and activities. Thus instead of continually placing themselves in arenas where they "don't fit," they begin to follow individual courses of action which begin to undermine their relationship.

Tolerance of the other's differentness wears thin. One wife explained that she was attracted to her race car driver husband because of the excitement involved in his profession. He was her hero. After a few years of marriage and the arrival of children, she wanted him to quit racing. She found his continued involvement in racing both uninteresting and jeopardizing of the security of the family. He began to leave her home because she was always nagging him about quitting, and his performance was affected. They drew apart, each creating their separate worlds until the bond between them was very thin—a bond which was broken when they could neither recapture their excitement about each other nor change to accommodate to each other's wishes.

Exchange Theory. The exchange theory (Hendrick & Hendrick, 1983) presents relationships as a context that develops as each partner gives and receives in a manner that is mutually fulfilling and growth producing. Each partner comes into the relationship with different assets, needs, and characteristics which serve as commodities in transactions that form the relational bond. As exchanges are negotiated, the partners both grow together and acquire larger areas of mutuality and interdependence.

Several principles serve as guidelines in the exchange version of relationship development. First, the exchange must be balanced and equitable. Both partners must contribute to the other's well being. If one partner does all the giving and the other all the taking, the relationship will eventually become unbalanced and counterproductive. Second, each partner's resources and contributions must be respected and valued. If one partner's stock is considered more valuable than the other's, the relationship will eventually be undermined. Third, each partner must acknowledge what the other has contributed to his/her life thereby crediting their partner's account and reaffirming the merit of their working relationship.

Couples whose attachment is based on what each brings to the relationship experience a strong sense of their own individuality. This is a very important dimension because of the common tendency in marriage for one partner's identity to become completely submerged in the other's. This often occurs in traditional marriages where the wife's role is defined as supportive to and dependent upon the husband's vocational identity. For example, wives of successful professionals or business executives often experience severe identity crises. If, however, both partners contribute to each other's well being, are cognizant of that contribution and are able to develop their individuality outside the relationship as well as in the relationship, a balanced and satisfying exchange can take place.

Exchanges tend to result in acquisition and growth in each partner's personality, skills, and knowledge. For example, in our relationship, Jim has acquired an appreciation and knowledge of classical music, an area in which Toni has extensive expertise. This feature was introduced early in our relationship and has become more significant over the years. Jim, who had never been to a symphony nor even listened to classical music recently realized the interest had become his own when he found himself habitually listening to a classical music station even when Toni wasn't around.

ACTIVITY: Questions to Ask

The bases of attraction can certainly be refined and expanded beyond these three broad areas, but we can not do so here. The important point to know is what attracts you to your partner and what forms the basis of the bond that develops. The three most important questions that should be asked and thoroughly investigated during courtship are outgrowths of the three bases of attraction we have just reviewed. Each contributes a basic question.

1. **How are we alike?** Identify common areas of interest and enjoyment. Look into the deeper elements of values, life goals, family background, religion, personal ambitions, lifestyle expectations and dreams. The larger the areas of commonality, the greater the probability of stability in the relationship. Discuss with each other how you can pool your energies and direct them in mutually satisfying directions. All relationships need a substantial basis of commonality or eventual problems are likely.

2. **How are we different?** Just as important as your sameness is your differentness. Differences will likely lead to interpersonal conflict that can undermine the relationship. On the other hand, differences also generate excitement and growth. As you find ways to become compatible and complementary to each other, you expand the resources upon which you can draw. Together identify your differences. Then you can begin to negotiate mutually acceptable ways of dealing with them. All relationships will have inevitable differences that must be addressed, and the sooner you establish the expectation that these differences can be discussed together and resolved by cooperation the better chance you have for differences to become positive stimuli for growth instead of elements endangering the relationship or making it unfulfilling.

3. **What does each partner contribute to the other in the relationship?** Take stock of what you and your partner bring to the relationship. How do your assets relate to your partner's needs and vice versa? Do you experience greater fulfillment as a person because of what your partner contributes to your life, or do you feel used or pressured by your partner? A significant indication of a healthy relationship is where partners feel they can retain their own identity and also feel good about how they have changed as a result of their partner's influence.

When each of these areas has been seriously investigated in court-ship and when the results are in, the basis for deciding whether to move the next step into marriage will be quite clear. Have the courage to acknowledge, accept, and respect what you find and the wisdom to act accordingly.

This Thing Called Love

Here we are, some six chapters into this book on the topic of marriage and family and we finally come to the point of addressing the one element which is central to the whole process—LOVE. You may wonder why it took so long to get here. After all the only "real" reason people marry and have families is because they are "in love." Right? Throughout history, songs like the Beatles' "All You Need is Love" have espoused the idea that love is the most important ingredient in life and relationships. Yet love is such a nebulous and unexplainable force and has so many faces that trying to deal with it in a few pages may seem presumptuous.

If you did a survey simply asking the question "What is love?" you would probably come up with as many answers as number of people you asked. Yet when you ask couples why they got married, they will in-evitably tell you they were "in love." That explanation is quite accep-table by societal standards even though the meaning of being in love may be quite different for each partner. Certainly life would be much easier if love had one clear, distinct, and measurable definition. That not being the case, love remains the most meaningful, least understood, most im-portant, least controllable, most confusing, least measurable aspect of our lives. Let us look at this force and experience and draw together some ideas that will be helpful in assessing the nature of the affectional bond between partners.

George Bernard Shaw once wrote:

> When two people are under the influence of the most violent, most insane, most delusive, and most transient of passions, they are required to swear that they will remain in that excited, abnormal, and exhausting condition continuously until death do them part (Sheehy, 1976, p. 106).

He was evidently depicting his view of love and its relationship to mar-riage. However, we can be more definitive than to simply portray the am-biguity and unpredictability of love as a passion.

The English language is somewhat restricted when considering a definition of love. For example, the Greek language has at least three terms which mean love, each of which presents a different perspective. *Philos* is love which is characterized by attraction based on a deep, enduring friendship. *Agape* is love that has a self-sacrificing, nondemanding, spiritual quality where satisfaction is experienced when providing for another. *Eros* is love that is passionate and emotional and associated with sexual attraction. Certainly a relationship could be built on any one of these three definitions, but an enduring marital relationship must have elements of all three to insure longevity and fulfillment.

We have talked with many couples whose relationship was initiated and consummated on the basis of "Eros." Once the emotion and passion died down, they found more was needed to make the relationship work. The "more" needed was in the kind of love expressed by the "philos" and "agape" forms of love. Other couples who described themselves as "best of friends" found themselves drifting apart because of lack of excitement and physical attraction (eros) between them. That certainly can become a problem particularly if that aspect of love is sought outside the relationship. Other couples struggle because one or the other feels like he/she does all the self-sacrificing (agape). Over time, if not balanced, the relationship becomes one-sided and bitterness begins to accumulate leading to a negative attitude and atmosphere which harms the relationship.

The presence of all three elements is important in a relationship. They will fluctuate and grow, and one type of love will be more prominent at certain stages of life than at others. However, none should be lost or nonexistent. If that happens to be the case during courtship, serious consideration should be given to steering the relationship away from marriage. After marriage, often one or the other of these types of love have to be revived or revved up to give the relationship life.

In English, adjectives can be used to describe types of love that emerge out of the three perspectives just presented. The adjectives used with the word love include romantic love, passionate love, companionate love, and altruistic love.

Romantic Love. The romantic love concept depicts idyllic beauty as a predominant theme. Atmosphere, having things just right, appreciating and admiring your partner in a nonpossessive, almost unreal way epitomizes romantic love. The giving of gifts, the planning of special occasions, expressions of love in the form of poetry, cards, or special messages, all fall in this category. Sometimes the most disconcerting factor in a relationship is that after a few years everything becomes routine and predictable. Partners lodge the basic complaint that "the romance is gone." Some couples find they have to go on second and third (and more) honeymoons to keep that romantic element alive.

Passionate Love. While romantic love has an exotic quality, passionate love captures the erotic component. The physical and sexual aspect of the relationship is extremely vital. It not only relates to our physical needs and the urge to procreate but more importantly, it prompts us to engage in a deeper level of intimacy. This aspect of love is usually the most difficult with which to deal during dating and courtship. Passions and excitement draw you toward one another propelling you far ahead of the pace your relationship is moving. Consequently, passionate love must be tempered by responsibility, honesty, and respect for one another. This is such an important area that we will divert our focus briefly to discuss sexual intimacy during courtship.

Because psychological ramifications of sexual involvement before marriage are so difficult to determine, and because perspectives of the participating partners likely will be different, and because of the high probability of normal consequences (e.g., pregnancy), we believe that sex without the commitment of marriage is a risky activity in both a personal and a relational sense.

For example, men and women tend to perceive sexual intimacy quite differently. For women, the physical relationship is usually coupled with feelings of romance and commitment. For men, sexual attraction can be kept separate from love and is often a present-oriented, physiological, need experience. Both men and women, aware of this difference, have exploited it to get what they want. Men have professed love and strong feelings to soothe the apprehensions of the reluctant female, and women have used sexual relations and pregnancy as a way to seal their security.

When two people become emotionally involved, it is the responsibility of each to ask the following questions, and when the answers are in, to choose to act in a manner which is for the ultimate good of yourself and your partner. (You may begin to get a sense of how the various aspects of love as we have discussed them also provide a checks and balances system in our intimate relationships.) Key questions include the following: How open is our relationship? How well do we know each other as persons? Where are each of us right now in terms of sexual knowledge, age, maturity, attitude, honesty about intentions, feelings for the other, and religious and ethical considerations? What will be the probable consequences for my partner and what will they be for me? Sex is an area where exploitation can easily occur both consciously and unconsciously. Therefore any decision before marriage should be subjugated to the preceding considerations so that no violation of either partner's personhood or integrity will occur.

Companionate Love. Romantic and passionate love, when experienced in combination, are a tough act to follow. When a couple is feeling these emotions, they often believe they can live on love. Sometimes the fact that you can't continue in that state or have lost it is a difficult realization with which to cope. Romance and passion have a built-in tendency to burn out. When that occurs the relationship is precarious unless other elements of love have quietly grown along with the impulsive and more fickle aspects of love. Companionate love characterized by shared interests and enjoyment of each other's company is one of these quiet faces of love. Often men and women confide in a person of the opposite sex who is considered a friend, even sharing joys, and pains about another relationship in which they are "in love." This same sharing is not risked with the loved one for fear of jeopardizing the relationship or becoming vulnerable. Yet that type of sharing—friend to friend—is a necessity for a relationship to endure.

We have talked to numerous couples who have been married for many years who attribute both their longevity and their fulfillment to the fact that they were "best friends." In fact, friendship was the top reason given by both men and women in a poll conducted by *Psychology Today* that asked the question "What keeps a marriage going?" (Lauer & Lauer, 1985). If you can't be friends with your partner and do not enjoy each other's companionship, marriage will not make that happen. To marry without friendship is literally jumping from the frying pan into the fire. Take the example of a couple whose courtship basically consisted of going to a movie or some other activity and then going out and parking. They necked, petted, and eventually had sexual intercourse, but they seldom talked. Shortly after marriage (a subject she brought up and to which he agreed) they found out that they not only didn't know how to talk to each other, but they didn't really like each other that much as persons. Instead of splitting they came for therapy which essentially involved helping them complete their courtship by learning to communicate with each other and learning how to be friends. Fortunately for them, their intense physical attraction lasted long enough to get the relationship balanced, and they continued their marriage. We hesitate sharing an example such as this because it might give you the idea that things will work out even if you opt for the passionate approach. In reality, the more likely ending is for the marriage to fail.

Altruistic Love. The other quiet face of love is "altruistic love." This aspect involves each partner's desire to "do for" the other. One elderly man who had been married over 50 years said, "The key to marriage is each partner trying to please the other 100% of the time." Although that sounds very idealistic, it does capture the meaning of self-sacrifice in marriage. If during courtship you find yourself getting irritated when you give in to your partner or begin to sense that one is more willing to give in than the other, warning flags should go up. If caring and respect for the other's well being does not have a role of central importance in the relationship, the marriage will have difficulty being consummated in a psychological sense. You will likely become adversaries rather than partners.

Limerance. Research has provided three other concepts that have relevance in our consideration of love (Saxton, 1983). These are limerance, infatuation, and attachment. Limerance has been described as a sudden, inexplicable, overwhelming attraction and bonding to another. It is the phenomenon of being so intensely engrossed in a person that to think about anything else is difficult. Limerance usually lasts for some time but is not a permanent condition. The stricken person is referred to as being "love sick" or someone who has been bitten by the love bug. The average length of time for the limerant person or persons is about two years, i.e., long enough for the couple to marry, become pregnant, have a child, and start a family. The exclusivity of limerance ("I can't get her out of my mind") lasts long enough for the relationship to jell. One view is that it creates the atmosphere or arena in which the bond of love can develop and mature.

Limerance is also the stuff of which broken hearts and rebounds are made. As a relationship fails to cement, usually because of a lack of mutual limerance, one party becomes "love lorn"—a very painful experience indeed. However, limerance is very resilient accounting for the fact that most of us survive relational break-ups and find ourselves once again engrossed in another person starting the process all over again. The nice thing about limerance as a concept is that it preserves and protects our most valuable human resource—love—from being expended unwisely or wastefully. It reserves love for the more intimate aspects of the relationship once it is developed.

Infatuation. This is a much more fleeting experience of attraction. Ray Short (1978) author of the book *Sex, Love, or Infatuation: How Can I Really Know?* makes the point that infatuation gives you three false clues that are mistaken for love. They are (1) funny feelings in your stomach, (2) a gnawing need for nearness, and (3) a powerful pull to passion. He also indicated a number of ways to distinguish between love and infatuation. Infatuation is when you are attracted to a person because of one or a few factors, whereas, love is when you are attracted to many or most features of the person. If your interest in each other fluctuates, i.e., comes and goes, it is infatuation. If your interest is consistent over time, it is love. If distance (being away from each other) kills the relationship, it is infatuation. If the relationship survives distance, it is love. If you think of your partner as "he" or "she" it is infatuation; if you think in terms of "we" it is love. If the major attraction is "physical equipment," it is infatuation; if it is your partner's total personality, it is love. Finally, he points out that sex is NOT a basis upon which to determine love or whether to marry.

Attachment. This is a term associated with a relationship that takes on a life of its own in spite of the nature of that relationship in each partner's experience. Attachment is the continued sense of needing the other person even when personally and emotionally positive elements are no longer present. Many couples continue their relationship out of habit or routine long after either is experiencing any meaningful fulfillment. Some even make the terrible mistake of pushing on to marriage even though they know the life is gone out of the relationship. One woman said she knew for six months before the wedding that the relationship did nothing for her. She said she laid in bed the night of her wedding wondering "How could I have been so dumb to go ahead with it?" She was a victim of attachment. To become comfortable and predictable is fine in your relationship, but make sure it has life, excitement, and challenge before you put the stamp of marriage on it.

Figuring It All Out

Coming to grips with "love" in your relationship can be mind boggling. Do you trust your feelings, your thoughts, or your actions? Should

I respond to and express these impulses or keep them to myself? Do I wait for my partner to make the first move or do I? It's no wonder that people prefer to simply use the catch-all reason of being in love to justify their actions. Yet the elements of love we have just reviewed are important and should be considered. Lederer and Jackson (1968) in a book entitled *The Mirages of Marriage* pointed out that people like to think of themselves as being in love but most of the time they are really interpreting some other emotion such as a strong sex drive, fear or a hunger for approval as love. For that reason and the potential difficulties we have already enumerated, an essential aspect during the courtship period is for couples to figure out what the basis of their affectional bond is. This is crucial because love is sometimes not the real reason people end up married as we will discover in the next section.

FACTORS AFFECTING MARITAL CHOICE

The main function of dating and courtship, at least in our American society, is to determine one's marital partner. However, factors that go into that choice are often more complex than the nature of those interactions and emotions that occur between the prospective partners. After-the-fact analysis reveals influences that are more significant than the experience of being in love. We can't count the number of times that couples when queried about how they got into the marital condition in the first place, have shrugged their shoulders and said "Well, we must have been in love." On closer examination, however, they discover "other" factors that consciously and unconsciously influenced their decision to marry. We will discuss the motivation to marry in five different ways: Marriage as a finishing process, marriage as conformity, marriage as a tool, marriage as a response to crisis and marriage as impulse and evolution.

Marriage as a Finishing Process

James Framo (1982) an eminent marriage and family therapist, said that marriage is an attempt to complete the business of the family of origin. From this perspective the choice of a partner is tied into our experiences in observing our parents' marriage. We select a partner who will present us with the same problems our parents were unable to solve.

Consequently, we repeat their pattern even though our best intentions were to avoid it. A child reared in an alcoholic marriage will choose a partner with a drinking problem, and then proceed to reform that person thus solving in their marriage a problem the parents could not solve.

Marriage also is a means of completing oneself. Partners are chosen because they represent a quality that we lack or supply a resource that meets a need we experience. This self completion perspective is a deficiency-oriented process. Partners are selected to provide security for an insecure person or to provide the love that was never received in their family of origin. Sometimes this deficiency is too great and excessive pressure is placed on the partner which rapidly drains their resources and creates a dependency that is unhealthy for the relationship. On the other hand, choosing a mate who makes you feel a sense of wholeness is also a very positive experience especially when the experience is mutual.

Both of these "unfinished business" factors merit your consideration when choosing a mate because they will certainly surface after marriage. In the first case you may realize the hard way "why" your parents were never able to solve their problem when you can't solve it in your marriage either. Second, most marriages that ultimately fail involve an element where one or both partners feel unfulfilled (uncompleted) as persons and perceive the marriage to be the obstacle to that fulfillment. If your choice of a partner is based on either of these factors, make sure you are aware of it and that you are in the role of choosing rather than being a pawn directed by forces beyond your control because you refuse to acknowledge them.

Marriage as Conformity

The expectation to marry is such an intrinsic part of the world around us that whole volumes have been written to document it. In our "couple oriented" society, family, friends, and work environment send us messages that marrying is the thing to do. Most of the adult world that surrounds us is filled with people who are or have been married. As soon as we hit the marrying age, which is any time after our late teens, we get the message.

Families are the biggest pushers. "Don't you think it's about time you settle down?" which when translated means "Get married!" is a common statement we hear from parents and relatives. Sometimes the message is more oblique: "You know, Dad and I don't want to be so old that we can't enjoy our grandchildren.'' When addressed to a single son or daughter the implication is hard to miss that something (like marriage) should transpire to make giving them grandchildren a reality.

Peers also do their part. As the circle of our single friends begins to narrow, the norm of being married is set and pressure in the form of kindly ribbing sends the message that you better get on the ball. Even if couched in the context of "misery loves company," we are still drawn into the web of marital bliss.

The work place also is frought with pressures and expectations related to marriage. One young woman who worked for a large insurance company said she felt that getting married and pregnant was part of the job description. The company's policy was to hire girls right out of high school and employ them for an average duration of five to six years at which time the girls usually would terminate employment in order to start a family. She stated that "if you weren't married after five years, people thought something was wrong with you." The big social events of office life were "getting your diamond," the company sponsored wedding shower, and the company sponsored baby shower. These events seemed to mark each girl's career path through the company.

All of these environmental influences coupled with our own physiological and social development account for the most prominent reason people get married—"the right time." One woman astutely recognized this phenomenon: "I was ready and it scared me because I knew that whoever asked was likely to get a yes."

Social expectations and "the right time" are certainly realities and part of the facts of life. However, choosing a partner on that basis only is like playing Russian roulette with three of the six barrels loaded. Taking whoever comes along at the right time may work out, but it may also flop. When you get into the right time, make the effort also to make a right choice. Doing so takes work rather than simply going with the flow. Although your marriage may enable you to conform, conformity should not be the reason you marry.

Marriage as a Tool

Marriage as a means to an end has long been an acceptable reason for couples to solidify their relationship. In fact, a legitimate reason for marriage is to form an economic contract that will pool your resources as a means of attaining goals you hold in common. However, when a partner is selected simply to acquire wealth, prestige, or social position, marriage is being used as a tool. Many people believe that if you are going to fall in love anyway, you might as well fall in love with someone who is rich, famous, or has any number of other prestigious qualities. For example, marriage has often been used as a vehicle for moving up the social ladder.

Practicality is another aspect of the marriage as a tool perspective. Many men enter marriage because it is the practical thing to do given their life goals and plans. Many messages in the career game intimate that marriage is a stabilizer that must be in place before advancement can occur. Consequently, men often seek a spouse as a prerequisite to their move up the corporate ladder of success. President Harry S. Truman once poked fun at this practice by commenting that behind every successful man is a good wife and a surprised mother-in-law.

Although marriage has been and will continue to be used for acquisition purposes, certain drawbacks are built-in. One partner or the other may feel used. When stress enters the marriage, allegations will be made that you married "for" something rather than marrying the person. Some of the most painful realizations we have witnessed in marriages have been where one partner gets a confirmation from the other that the real reason for marriage was to obtain a more desirable status or asset (e.g., wealth). No more devastating blow can be delivered to a person's self-esteem than to be told that you were a means to an end. It also generates deep bitterness and resentment.

Marriage always will bring together assets of the individuals involved which may be quite different in value. Marriage also will open opportunities which were not available before. But the choice of a partner should not be solely on the basis of acquisition. To do so violates the integrity of the human bond as well as betrays the dignity of the person you are choosing. In doing so, you also undermine your own integrity and sense of self-worth. Such is not the foundation that produces a growth oriented and personally fulfilling marriage relationship.

**Marriage as a
Response to Crises**

The most common crisis that propels a couple to the marriage altar is pregnancy. Many couples admit later that had it not been for the pregnancy they may not have ended up with each other. A marital choice based on pregnancy will almost always raise complications in the marriage. It is a fact that must be recognized throughout the marriage and the subsequent life of the child. Even under the best conditions a "forced" marriage tends to be perceived as tainted by the partners themselves and may be an embarrassment to the resulting child and the extended family.

Marriage due to pregnancy is not a cure-all. It escalates the problems of marriage because the couple not only has to learn to relate to each other as husband and wife but very quickly must learn to be parents. Consequently, the relationship has little time to form before it has to be reorganized to accept the third party. Additionally, if the partners are young (teens to mid-twenties), they are catapulted into obligations and responsibilities of full adulthood without benefit of the transition years which make handling those pressures easier. Marriages that occur before one or both partners are "grown up" often short circuit the individuals' work on their personal identities because they must slip quickly into "the grid of obligations to act as spouses and parents" (Sheehy, 1976, p. 91). Both may later feel robbed of their youth and wish they could have stretched their wings a bit before having to fly. We have worked with many couples in which one partner wanted out of the marriage because he/she felt denied the "right to youth" and wanted to recycle his/her single years by leaving the marriage.

We also have worked with couples where either the man or the woman had failed to take precautions to prevent pregnancy as a way to force the marriage issue. Such tactics are bound to engender bitterness and reprisal no matter how much you want to be married to that person.

Premarital pregnancy is an undeniable fact of life. Approximately one in six children are born to unwed mothers (Saxton, 1983). Estimates on the number of abortions vary but are increasing, and no statistics exits on how many marriages occur in which the woman is already pregnant. Such being the case, pregnancy may well emerge as a significant factor during courtship. While the preference is for pregnancy not to be a factor during courtship, when it is, be sure to take into account those other elements we have addressed rather than making your decision solely on the pregnancy issue. Doing so is the responsible course of action which will have both short-term and long-term benefits.

Another common crisis factor in marital choice is referred to as the "jailbreak" phenomenon. Marriage is entered into as an escape mechanism even though it may be considered the lesser of two evils. When the life of a young person in their parents' home becomes intolerable, he/she begins to search for a relationship that permits escape. Females are more prone than males to utilize the jailbreak approach. The woman seeks out an older, more autonomous male and then exchanges the undesirable child-in-the-home status for that of being a wife and quite often a mother as well.

Jailbreak marriages have a very poor prognosis for several reasons. First of all, the person is not prepared to make adjustments that are necessary to cope with the new adult status and responsibilities. Second, usually he/she finds that no more autonomy exists in the marriage than was in the family. These two reasons result in the person eventually feeling overwhelmed, trapped, and wanting to get out again.

The real achilles heel of a jailbreak marriage is not that the person tends to be young and immature or even that he/she can't cope with the pressures. It is the fact that he/she starts a pattern where marriage is used successfully as an escape. Consequently, when feeling trapped or overwhelmed again, a new relationship is found which helps him/her extricate him/herself but continues the jailbreak pattern. This tendency to use a relationship to get out makes jailbreak marriages unstable. The person never gains any degree of independence and finds difficulty in coping with life in any other way.

Example

> *The Jailbreak Phenomenon. An example of the jailbreak pattern is a couple who came for therapy because their relationship was deteriorating. The marriage was her third and his first. She had married at age eighteen to get out of the house. At twenty-four, she found a lover to get out of her marriage. She married him and at age twenty-seven became disgruntled with him as well. Then she had an affair with another man which broke up the marriage. After living with this man for two years, they married. At the point of therapy, she was again discouraged, but did not want to repeat the pattern of breaking out again. Her story is not unusual and in some sense personifies what might typically be expected if the jailbreak approach is used as the method of choice in courtship.*

Our intentions here are to be realistic, not negative. Every marriage has the potential to succeed regardless of its impetus. The two participants can and will determine whether that potential is realized. Some marriages that result in response to crisis factors do succeed, but the odds are harder to overcome. Pregnancy and the jailbreak methods are choices that generally can be avoided. If they are not, you will make the already difficult process of being married even more difficult.

Marriage as Impulse or Evolution

Two other factors that explain why people marry may seem quite incongruent at first glance. However, marriage on impulse and by evolution have a common base—little serious thinking, evaluation or testing go into the process of deciding. Some people marry on a whim, popping the question, agreeing to marry, and saying their vows before any intrusion of reality can enter the picture to slow down the process. In some places like Nevada and Mexico, the business of marrying people who do so on a lark is quite well established. Such an impulsive move means that all of the work we have been discussing thus far in this book will have to be done after the fact. Also hidden in this style of choosing a partner is the impulse to leave the relationship when things get tough or when something better comes along.

Example

The Impulsive Marrier. One man reported he was making progress after three marriages. All had been entered into after very short courtships, one of which was only three days. He was currently living with a fourth woman and said this time he wasn't going to make the mistake of marrying. He was a construction worker whose job took him all around the country. This mobility fed into his impulsiveness in his relationships with women resulting in a trail of heartaches and children to testify that he had been there.

With the advent of the "living together" relationship that is gaining popularity in our society, another causal factor in marriage has emerged. Evolution from live-in partners to spouses seems to occur as a result of a combination of forces that are woven together in a nondistinguishable tapestry of emotional pressure. Parents are accepting the live together style but are sending the message they would be more comfortable if their children were married instead of living together. We have talked to many parents who heaved a sigh of relief when their child finally married the live-in partner.

The partners themselves by mutual agreement never raise the issue of marriage because that would be unsophisticated and indicative of immaturity or inability to cope. The couple holds each other up under the guise of pseudo-openness until some moment when the time is right, and they take the plunge.

Some of these couples do go through intense and careful discussion before deciding on marriage. But, more often than not, they report that the decision was a rather simple one. That admission for us is a red flag that indicates they really haven't come to grips with the issue of marriage. One couple reported that they had lived together for two years in relative bliss and all their problems started when they got married. The idealism of their live-in experience quickly eroded when the realities of marriage surfaced. No matter how you explain living together, an undeniable difference exists between living together and being married. Don't get caught in the mental delusion that they are the same.

Living together is conceived as a trial marriage—a test to see if partners are compatible. Statistically the incidence of "unmarried couple households" significantly increased during the 1970s but the amount of growth in the 1980s has been comparatively small (U.S. Bureau of the Census, 1984). Researchers have indicated that couples who live together before marriage have no less tendency to divorce or greater likelihood of being happily married than those who don't (Macklin, 1978). The testing that is important is not that of physical compatibility but the other dimensions we have been describing. Although trial marriages may be a reality, there is no such thing as a trial child. The one thing that tends to tip the balance toward marriage for live-in couples is children. Either because pregnancy occurs or because the couple does not want to have a child out of wedlock, they decide to marry. Although indicative of a responsible attitude, basing the choice to marry on the prospect of a child is not a solid foundation for a healthy marriage.

Awareness and acknowledgement of the various factors we have just discussed will constructively assist you in your selection of a marital partner. If one or more of the factors apply, discuss them with your partner as part of your courting process. The benefits of doing so will be that communication channels will be opened that you didn't know existed. Second, these discussions will reduce the chances that the negative, manipulative aspects will surface to threaten your marriage later. Mutual recognition of these factors will give you a greater sense of respect for each other as persons and a deeper valuing of marriage as a relational experience of choice.

CONCLUSION

Two basic factors are essential to dating and courtship experiences. The first is openness and the second is responsibility. We have emphasized the importance of knowing yourself in Chapter 2 and the importance of sharing that knowledge openly in relationships in Chapter 3. In other chapters we have stressed knowing yourself in different contexts. As intimacy develops, sharing that knowledge in an open, honest, and genuine manner is imperative. Courtship is the arena for that type of sharing.

You cannot think of everything before marriage, and you and your partner always will be in the process of changing. In time you will discover things about yourself and your partner that you did not know or realize. However, you are only kidding yourself if you are playing a role, disguising your real self, and afraid to confront issues that you know are a point of conflict. Bach and Wyden (1968), authors of *The Intimate Enemy,* believed that couples should have some fights before marriage in order for reality to emerge and to give partners a more complete view of each other.

If you are afraid to reveal yourself during courtship because you feel it is too soon, or you don't know each other well enough, or you think it will hurt the relationship, wait until you can reveal yourself before even considering the question of marriage. We also realize that when you become emotionally involved with someone, you have difficulty and/or lack the courage to follow a path of openness, self disclosure, and confrontation. However, we advocate and applaud that courage. Openness is not to be construed as a destructive force involving obligatory revelations that damage your own sense of self esteem or test your partner's level of acceptance. Rather openness is a permission that gives you and your partner the freedom to express your real selves to each other. Certainly risk is involved but when you share your unique selves, benefits will vastly enrich your relationship.

Responsibility is the counterpart to openness that keeps it in check. Responsibility in intimate relating means being able to move into as well as out of a relationship without creating or leaving scars that will impede or jeopardize the growth and fulfillment of yourself or your partner in future relationships. We surely will have painful experiences in our search for intimacy, but if partners act responsibly, these painful experiences need not devastate us. Rather those painful experiences can be learning experiences that will translate into positive qualities in other relational experiences. Responsibility implies a sincere concern for the other person, an unwillingness to exploit or manipulate the other for one's own benefit and a certain amount of determination to act in the other person's best interest in spite of your own feelings and desires.

In some ways the whole purpose of courtship is to seek and share the answer to the question "What does marriage mean to me, personally?" The more elements that are explored and shared between partners, the better the basis for deciding on whether to continue the relationship into marriage. When asked this question many couples respond rather vaguely, resorting to clichés and pat answers to assuage the fears of each other and any interested third party. However, the question requires concrete responses which emerge out of the considerations we have reviewed in this and preceding chapters. A general rule of thumb is "no specifics—no marriage."

When a relationship reaches the point where partners know each other as persons, are clear about and have expressed their feelings for and expectations of each other, and when the elements of merging their lives together have been seriously considered, the courtship is completed and marriage is the next stop. How long this should take is a matter of great debate. At some point you may have to make a decision to continue courtship before making a far reaching decision such as to either break it off or make the commitment to grow together under the marriage contract. The relationship may need to be explored more deeply first.

The consequences of marrying too soon have been addressed, but the consequences of waiting too long are also serious. Not deciding is also an irresponsible course to follow. Waiting too long may usurp a sizable chunk of your and your partner's life leaving bitterness and regret as scars that will cause problems whether you finally marry or not.

No set timetable or checklist exists that you can use to make your decision. The decision is the most personal and complex one you will ever face, but it is also the most important. Take the time and effort to grow together and know together that you are meant for each other and then "go for it."

REFERENCES

Bach, G. R., & Wyden, P. (1968). *The intimate enemy: How to fight fair in love and marriage.* New York: Avon Books.

Framo, J.L. (1982). *Explorations in marital and family therapy: Selected papers of James Framo.* New York: Springer.

Hendrick, C., & Hendrick, S. (1983). *Liking, loving and relating.* Monterey, CA: Brooks/Cole.

Lauer, J., & Lauer, R. (1985, June). Marriages made to last. *Psychology Today,* 22-26.

Lederer, W., & Jackson, D.D. (1968). *The mirages of marriage.* New York: W.W. Norton.

Macklin, E.D. (1978, March-April). Non-marital heterosexual cohabitation. *Marriage and Family Review,* 1-12.

Rathus, S.A. (1984). *Psychology* (2nd ed.). New York: Holt, Rinehart, and Winston.

Saxton, L. (1983). *The individual, marriage, and the family.* Belmont, CA: Wadsworth.

Sheehy, G. (1976). *Passages.* New York: C.P. Dutton.

Short, R.E. (1978). *Sex, love, or infatuation: How can I really know?* Minneapolis: Augsburg Publishing.

U.S. Bureau of the Census (1984). Current Population Reports, Series P-20, No. 389. *Marital Status and Living Arrangements: March 1983.* Washington, DC: US Government Printing Office.

THERE'S LIFE AFTER MARRIAGE:
YOUR WEDDING AND BEYOND

The meaning and experience of marriage is addressed. The concept of commitment and the importance of love and respect are stressed. The typical issues, problems, and crises of marriage are described and several models for effective marital growth are presented. The role of sex in marriage and issues related to money, individual interests, and lifestyle are discussed.

Then Almitra spoke again and said,
And what of Marriage, master?
And he answered saying:
You were born together and together
you shall be forevermore.
You shall be together when the white
wings of death scatter your days.

*Ay you shall be together even in the
silent memory of God.*
　　*But let there be spaces in your
togetherness.*
　　*And let the winds of the heavens
dance between you.*
　　*Love one another, but make not a
bond of love.*
　　*Let it rather be a moving sea between
the shores of your souls.*
　　*Fill each other's cups but drink not from
one cup.*
　　*Give one another your bread but eat
not of the same loaf.*
　　*Sing and dance together and be joyous,
but let each one of you be alone,*
　　*Even as the strings of a lute are alone
though they quiver with the same music.*
　　*Give your hearts, but not into each other's
keeping.*
　　*For only the hand of Life can contain
your hearts.*
　　*And stand together yet not too near
together:*
　　*For the pillars of the Temple stand
apart,*
　　*And the oak tree and the cypress grow not in
each other's shadow.*

—*The Prophet* by Kahlil Gibran 1951, pp. 15-16

These eloquent lines by the poet Kahlil Gibran capture the beauty,
essence, and character of marriage and, as such, supply a fitting
backdrop for this chapter on the meaning and experience of marriage.
We have chosen to include the words of Gibran "on marriage" in their
entirety because both elements, togetherness and separateness, contribute to a meaningful and fulfilling marriage.

Since many books and articles have been published on marriage, we will confine ourselves to those elements that we have found to typify marital experience and contribute to making marriage work. Our purpose is not to paint a rosy picture of marriage but, rather a realistic one which has both anticipatory merit for those of you who are not married and practical merit for those of you who are.

We will start with the nature, implication, and meaning of the marriage ceremony as a lead-in to the reality of life after marriage. We will consider marriage as a crisis, review the various aspects of the marriage relationship, and identify the dynamics which give the relationship security and growth. The essential ingredients that form the glue in marriage will lead us into a consideration of male and female relating in marriage. A model for the "working marriage" will be reviewed, followed by discussion of the functions of sex in marriage. Finally, we will point out typical areas of marital conflict and conclude with a summary that identifies essential elements of a healthy marriage.

Our major purpose continues to be getting you to think and consider, not to give "pat" answers. Marriage is a process, not a mold. In marriage, you have the unusual opportunity to create the experience you want and "what you create is what you live."

In your reading and performing of activities in the previous six chapters on preparation for marriage, you have scrutinized yourself, your relationships, and your family of origin. You have courted and decided to take this man/woman to be your wedded husband/wife. You have decided to legalize and solemnize your relationship in a marriage ceremony and, as such, create for yourselves what Haley (1963) identified as the perennial dilemma of all married couples: Are you now staying together because you *want to* or *have to?*

You have been warned repeatedly, maybe even by your parents, "Wait until you're married, everything changes." Even couples who have lived together for some time have acknowledged this transformation.

"Is there something magical about saying 'I do?'" "Is there really life after marriage?" "Can we do anything to make ours a good marriage?" The answer to all three questions is *yes*. However, the first thing that must be realized is that marriage is a commitment, not for a year, or five years, or twenty-five, but for life. Marriage is not a commitment to a lifestyle, a house, a career, or even some idealized vision of a marriage, but to a relationship with the other person, your spouse. Almost all of the persons we have seen in counseling for whatever reason have said they made that commitment. In fact, most of the people getting married would stress commitment. Yet, one of three first marriages ends in divorce. Granted, some marriages are intolerable, but in our view those are far less than one in three. Commitment can mean many things to many people, but it is the bottom line in a relationship, the one thing that differentiates marriage from living together and sustains a marriage through the hard times. This theme of commitment is implicit in all our discussions of marriage and family life.

THE MARRIAGE CEREMONY

The marriage ceremony, in whatever form it takes, is a commencement, not an accomplishment. The ceremony is the beginning of a committed life together, not the end of a courtship. Weddings are meant to be transition rituals that "shift the relationship from a private coupling to a formal joining of two families" (McGoldrick, 1980, p. 97). When a man and woman leave their fathers and mothers to join their lives together in marriage, they do not automatically become one. Rather, the marriage ceremony is a signal of their intent to *become* one, a process which requires a lifelong effort.

Going about the business of saying "I do" has many variations. Traditions, mores, customs, and cultural factors affect how the ceremony is handled. Changing societal patterns and expectations impact upon the marriage rite. The importance of the marriage ceremony has waxed and waned over the years. During World War II many couples married in informal ceremonies often on very short notice because time did not permit planning large nuptial affairs. During the late sixties and early seventies, young people were seriously questioning the values and traditions of their families and society in general. As a result, couples began creating their own unique marriage ceremonies, often marrying in unorthodox environments, as opposed to marrying in a church or a courtroom. They created original vows rather than repeating the standard phrases used over the years. Recently, a return has been made to the more lavish wedding ceremony with many of the ideas of the sixties incorporated to make even the most traditional affairs unique and personal to the couple.

The marriage ceremony is a special and significant event. The ceremony is a rite of passage that has meaning to the individuals marrying, their families, and the audience. In some sense the wedding ceremony is a symbolic event that leaves an indelible mark on all of the participants.

For the individuals, the ceremony represents a coming to fruition of their hopes, dreams, and fantasies about marriage. Images with which each has grown up, cultivated by romantic notions derived from observing other people getting married, come to the fore in planning a ceremony. In some respects how the wedding is planned and put together by the couple is a prototype of how the marriage will go. In fact, many couples have their first serious premarital quarrels over planning their wedding. The ceremony should incorporate elements that have meaning for each partner. We can't count the number of times in therapy where one spouse said to the other, "Even our wedding ceremony was all your way." Do not discount the impact of your view of how a marriage rite should be.

Example

Am I Really Married? One woman after 13 years of marriage and three children began having recurring dreams that she and her husband had never really married. Upon discussion, a discovery was made that throughout her childhood she had dreamed of getting married in her family's church with all of the traditions and ceremony associated with weddings in her home town. She had discarded these dreams to marry her husband in a neutral setting without any of these notions incorporated. As a result, her subconscious was still telling her she was never "really" married. Consequently, this couple considered redoing their marriage ceremony as a rededication of themselves to the marriage and to complete the unfinished business of her childhood dreams.

The wedding is also significant to the families of the marrying pair. The ceremony symbolically represents a letting-go and a letting-in. Each set of parents must let go of the child they have reared, weaning them from their family milieu, while at the same time making room for the entrance of their child's spouse into the family network. Here again expectations of the family come into play in planning the marriage ceremony. Often a couple will heave a sigh of relief when the wedding is finally over because of the turmoil created in trying to please both families by what happens the day of the marriage. In this regard McGoldrick (1980) pointed out that "the more responsibility the couple can take for arranging a wedding that reflects their shifting position in their families and the joining of two systems, the more auspicious for their future relationship" (p. 110). We often advise prospective spouses to avoid asking their parents what kind of wedding they should have or turning the responsibility for the wedding over to one's family or one of the two partners (usually the woman). Rather we suggest they ask their parents, family, and friends what has impressed them about weddings, including their own. After garnering that information, the couple can then sit down and decide what they want, combining outside input with their own ideas. This approach avoids some of the pressure of having to please everyone which inevitably results in somebody being disappointed and the couple being stressed.

The audience also plays a significant role in a wedding. In fact, one of the predictors of difficult marital adjustment is when a wedding occurs without family or friends present (McGoldrick, 1980). The audience represents society's recognition of the marriage and the changing status of the two individuals involved. The congregation adds its confirmation to the vows and celebrates the change with the couple. For the audience, the wedding serves to remind those already married of their own commitment. The ceremony recalls to married couples' memory their own ceremony and often the effect is a rededication. Next time you attend a wedding, notice how many people are emotionally moved by the ceremony. For those unmarried, the wedding serves as a stimulus creating images and ideas that may eventually affect the planning of their own weddings.

The marriage ceremony plays an important role in helping the couple embark upon their task of melding their different personalities and backgrounds into their own unique family. A central aspect of that ceremony and that process is represented in the marriage vows.

The dictionary definition of vow is: "A solemn promise, especially one made to God or to some deity; an act by which one consecrates or devotes himself/herself to some act, service, or condition; a promise of fidelity or constancy as, for example, a marriage vow." Note that the marriage vow is selected as typifying the meaning of a vow. Vows by their very nature, reflect an anticipation of permanence. A man and woman look at each other and promise before God and man:

To have and to hold, from this day forward, for better or worse, for richer, for poorer, in sickness and in health, to love and to cherish forsaking all others, as long as we both shall live.

The exclusivity and weight of such promises are sufficient to make even the most resolute quiver and quake if they take serious note of what is being said. And the point is that many people enter marriage repeating their vows without taking them to heart. Many times people have heard the vows often enough to know them by heart, like the Pledge of Allegiance. Yet, the meaning is missing. One important result of the contemporary practice of writing your own marriage vows is that the couple must actually come to grips with what they intend to pledge to one another. Even if you opt for the traditional vows because of their ritualistic meaning and beauty, sit down with your prospective spouse and ask yourselves two questions: (1) What does each phrase mean? and (2) Does that meaning convey the intent of my commitment? Doing so will result in the surfacing of expectations for the marriage and a realization of the meaning of commitment. Some couples formalize the process even further by writing marriage contracts which state their expectations, obligations, and commitment. Coming to grips with that to which you are committing yourself is a giant first step toward marital adjustment and satisfaction. One note of caution: when creating and/or reviewing your marriage vows, be realistic in your idealism.

Example

> *Realistic Vows. One couple in therapy brought in their marriage vows on which they had worked meticulously and had written in poetic verse. In their ceremony they had memorized and recited their vows to each other. Their greatest pain in therapy was the realization of how far they were from what they had vowed to be. Another couple whose vows took them twenty minutes to recite got a reaction from one observer that there "weren't enough years in a lifetime to do everything they had pledged to do."*

Remember that the basic message of your vows is a statement of commitment to each other and a dedication to work toward a realization of all the elements to which you pledge yourselves. While commitment is a necessity, avoid generating standards which place undue pressure on the marriage. Sufficient stress is built into marriage, naturally, as we will note in the next section; you need not add the strain of unattainable idealism by your promises. Plan a meaningful ceremony, enjoy it to the extent you are able, and then get on with the business of being married.

THE CRISIS OF MARRIAGE

The reality of actual life after marriage has been captured in humor and wit. Ambrose Bierce (O'Neill & O'Neill, 1972) once defined marriage as "a community consisting of a master and a mistress and two slaves, making in all, two" (p.15). One young man approached us after a recent presentation on marriage and asked why we didn't mention the three rings of marriage. Since we had no idea what the three rings were, we asked him to elaborate. He promptly informed us the three rings are "the engagement ring, the wedding ring, and the suffering." Another view of life after marriage is reflected in the comment, "A man isn't completed until he marries and then he's finished."

Although these perceptions may sound humorous, they emphasize the fact that adjusting to marriage is not all that easy. Minuchin (1974) pointed out that the marriage itself is a crisis. When two people commit marriage, they are immediately faced with the consequences of their act. They must figure out a way to deal with the basic tasks of what is known as the establishment period of the family life cycle (Walsh, 1982). These tasks include: (1) learning to relate to each other, (2) learning to relate to their extended families, (3) developing their own style of coupleness, and (4) addressing the prospect of having children.

Typically referred to as the honeymoon period, the first year or two of the marriage is extremely crucial. In Old Testament law, a soldier could not be sent into battle for one year after marriage. Contemporary society has reduced that time frame to one or two weeks, depending on how much time off one or both can get from their respective places of employment. The point, however, is well taken because often during the honeymoon couples first begin to realize how difficult marriage is. McGoldrick and Carter (1982) maintained that "becoming a couple is one of the most complex and difficult transitions in the family life cycle" (p. 178). Marriage requires a renegotiation of a myriad of personal issues that previously had been defined by the individuals themselves or by their parents. Eating, sleeping, having sex, fighting, celebrating holidays, squeezing the toothpaste, working, spending vacations, paying the bills, and simply living, all must be renegotiated.

These negotiations are encumbered by two factors. First is the fact that the marriage does not simply bring together two persons with different personalities but marriage also brings together two family systems and two family legacies. These elements alone make the negotiations complex. The second factor is time. All these issues must be settled before the intrusion of a third party in the form of a child. During this initial period, patterns, roles, and expectations are set which chart the course of the marriage. It is the only time in the life of the couple when they can use *innovation*. All subsequent changes involve *renovation*.

The process of renegotiation also goes beyond the couple themselves. They must renegotiate their relationships with parents, siblings, friends, and relatives. The biggest problem in this area is usually in-laws. Haley (1963) has noted that having in-laws is the major distinguishing characteristic between man and all other forms of life. The importance of this area tends to be overlooked by the couple as they struggle with what they perceive to be differences in each other. Seldom will a newly married couple present for counseling with specific in-law complaints. Usually they think their problems are the result of how the other person is. Only after much serious consideration do they realize that extended family traits and differences are at the bottom of their issues.

Given the consideration just described, you might not be surprised to discover that newly married couples become discouraged or find themselves beginning to consider divorce as a viable alternative to the hassle of negotiating seemingly unresolvable differences. Marital adjustment is simply not an easy thing to accomplish. In fact, a number of factors have been identified by Carter and McGoldrick (1980) as making marital adjustment difficult. If one, a few, or many of these factors apply in your case, that does not mean you are doomed. Rather, we present these factors to help you realize the explanation for difficulties and a means of getting direction for resolving them.

Researchers have indicated that the following factors make marital adjustment difficult:

1. The couple meets and marries after a significant loss.

2. One or both partners wish to distance themselves from family of origin.

3. Family backgrounds of each spouse are significantly different (religion, education, social class, ethnicity, age, and so forth).

4. The couple has incompatible sibling constellations (Toman, 1976).

5. The couple is dependent on either extended family financially, physically, or emotionally.

6. The couple resides either extremely close to or at a great distance from either family.

7. The couple marries before 20 or after 30.

8. The couple marries after an acquaintanceship of less than 6 months or after more than 3 years of engagement.

9. The wedding occurs without family or friends present.

10. Either spouse has a poor relationship with his/her siblings or parents.

11. The wife becomes pregnant before or within the first year of marriage.

12. Either spouse considers his/her childhood or adolescence as unhappy.

13. Marital patterns in either extended family were unstable (Carter & McGoldrick, 1982, p. 179).

ACTIVITY: Springboard for Discussion

Despite the ominous innuendoes associated with the number thirteen, within each of these factors is a positive course of action that can compensate or overcome the difficulty, as well as explain it. Space does not permit elaboration, but use the list as a springboard for discussing where you seem to be hitting snags in your relationship. During your discussion increase your understanding of each other and suggest solutions. Decide upon a plan of action to help overcome obstacles and increase probability of success for your marriage. You also may note that most of these factors already have been addressed in the previous chapters. If you need to do so, review those parts that may be helpful at this point in your discussions.

PRINCIPLES FACILITATING MARRIAGE

Four basic principles have been observed that facilitate effectively dealing with the tasks of the establishment stage of the marriage.

1. **Retain an awareness of each other's specialness with respect to personhood and privacy.**

   Sometimes marriage is viewed as a ticket to encroach on one another's lives. The healthy sense of respect and sensitivity to the other person's privacy that characterized courtship also must be retained in marriage. One man commented that he knew the honeymoon was over when his wife walked in while he was shaving and went to the bathroom. To keep a sense of awe and mystique alive as long as you can is very useful while you form your relationship.

2. **Pay attention to developing your coupleness, don't just let it happen.**

   In working out your coupleness, becoming a couple is important rather than simply being two individuals who now live together. To do so, quantity time *and* quality time both must be spent together. Patterns and roles need to be noticed and discussed so that you do not become victims of dynamics set in motion by unspoken expectations and/or unconscious forces.

3. **Give your marriage the first priority;** after all, it is the one relationship that must stand the tests of time, change, and family.

4. **Be aware of the impact and importance of extended family ties in the marriage.**

   Together resolve to do the following:

   a. Clearly define your marital boundaries, rather than displacing negative emotions on the extended family;

b. Treat extended families as "created equal" and despite differences, do not treat one family as better than the other. Neither spouse should reject his/her family of origin transferring loyalty and affection to the in-laws, nor should one spouse pressure the other to do so.

c. Be supportive at least 51% of the time when your spouse is dealing with issues related to his/her own family of origin. Rather than place your partner in the middle, the nonrelated spouse can serve as a valued resource by supporting the family of origin work of the other with benefits that will strengthen the marriage.

With these guidelines in mind, let us now turn our attention to the various experiential elements that form the nature of the marriage relationship.

THE MARRIAGE RELATIONSHIP:
COMPONENT PARTS

The marriage relationship tends to be construed as a singular entity when in fact it is a composite of several components that gives both stability and the potential for growth. The stability aspects are called *togetherness* and *apartness,* and the growth aspects include *pushing-resisting* and *leading-supporting.* Each of these elements will be briefly discussed.

Stability Aspect

Togetherness. The time spent together as a couple is a very significant aspect of marriage. Togetherness is symbolically represented in Figure 7.1. At the beginning of the marriage, togetherness is the whole of marriage, the reason for being married. The transition from time spent together in courtship to time spent together in marriage is easy to make. The transition appears at first to be simply a matter of "more of a good thing." Yet togetherness has its drawbacks. First of all, it is the easiest aspect of the relationship to set aside when the responsibilities of life begin to wear away the energy and enthusiasm of the partners. Whereas, in courtship, time was always made for each other, in marriage time together begins to be put on hold because of pressing responsibilities in other areas. One of the first signs of eroding togetherness is when the couple begins to talk about spending "quality time together" because they don't have as much time for each other. The quality time principle is a facade. The reality is that quantity time makes quality time possible. We have talked with many couples who have tried to remedy their lack of togetherness by planning quality time weekends (and even splurging financially) to reconnect, only to end up having a miserable time. The consequence of this band-aid approach is that they move farther apart.

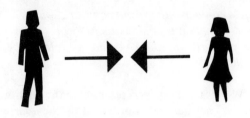

Figure 7.1. Togetherness.

Togetherness may take a back seat temporarily at different stages of life, but it should never be relinquished. Often when children come on the scene the marriage gets put on the back burner. Sometimes couples complain to us that they can't find time for themselves because of the kids. Our remedy for that ailment is a dose of DDT (**D**oing **D**ishes **T**ogether). We have the couple tell the children that they will do the dishes if the children leave the kitchen and do not create a situation demanding their parents' attention. The children also are told that if they come in the kitchen or cause a ruckus, they will have to do the dishes. We have yet to see this technique fail. The parents have uninterrupted time almost every day to talk and be together, and the children know enough not to ruin a good thing. Sometimes men balk at the idea of doing dishes but a little poem by Christopher Morley lends credence to the technique. It goes:

> The man who never in his life
> has washed the dishes with his wife
> Or polished up the silver late—
> He still is largely celibate.

Giving togetherness a back seat for any length of time is dangerous because you may have difficulty revitalizing it, and you may lose it altogether.

The second problem with togetherness is suffocation. Too much of each other, especially in conditions of exclusivity, can lead to boredom and a sense of being trapped.

Example

Being Everything to Each Other. One couple in therapy described their relationship as taking place almost entirely in their home. The husband would go to work and come home. The wife's contact with the outside world was primarily through television and her husband. When they presented themselves for therapy, the husband said he could not tolerate being her whole life any longer.

Apartness. While togetherness is essential in the relationship, it must be kept in balance. That balance is provided by the *apartness* aspect of the marriage (see Figure 7.2).

Figure 7.2. Apartness.

Apartness represents what the individual partners do separate from each other. Work, individual interests, recreationally or avocationally, friendships, group memberships, or any number of activities they do alone fall into this category. Apartness is important because it affirms each partner's individuality and in many ways stimulates the excitement of getting back together. Often apartness is put on hold during courtship and during the early phase of married life. Slowly, individualistic activities and pursuits begin to reassert themselves. This may create jitters in the relationship because one or the other is not prepared for doing things alone or begins to think their partner is losing interest in them.

Basically, doing things apart is healthy for the relationship but a couple of guiding principles need to be followed. First whatever is done apart must not detract from or jeopardize the relationship (particularly the togetherness aspect). For example, if one partner becomes overcommitted to his/her career or has an affair, apartness then becomes a detrimental factor in the marriage. Some individuals in marriage let their personal interests go, thinking they are doing so in the best interests of the marriage or because that's the way marriage is.

Example

Individual Interests and Marriage. A striking example of the importance of maintaining individual interests was a man who during the early years of the marriage had been physically active as a runner. He was in the military as a career and could work in a daily regimen of exercise as part of his workday. When he retired and took a civilian job, he stopped running because of his work situation and experienced considerable weight gain. He began criticizing his wife for her individual interests, one of which was aerobic dancing, and very often he would come home from work in a negative mood. In a sense, his loss of his military identity and his exercise coupled with his added weight generated a negative self-image that he projected at home by being critical and moody. When this was recognized, his wife instituted a plan of having his running clothes ready instead of his dinner, when he came home from work. He started a running routine, lost weight, and he and his wife began to fix dinner together after he finished his exercise and showered. In this case, taking care of himself resulted in a more positive self-image which spilled over into more satisfying relations with his wife.

A second principle is that apartness activities must be negotiated for the benefit of togetherness when such activities become a problem. Getting wrapped up in your own pursuits is very easy to do, even when the activity has no intrinsic characteristics that threaten the relationship. Each spouse must have the permission of the other to raise apartness activities for purposes of negotiation if they appear to be detracting from togetherness time. One common complaint of mothers is that fathers still seem to manage to do their individual things while the mothers' time gets totally engulfed by the children. Oftentimes the entire course of counseling is renegotiating a better balance in apartness time between the spouses in order to make togetherness time more positive.

Growth Aspect

Togetherness and apartness in balance form the foundation of the marriage and give it stability. The next two aspects of the relationship give the marriage its dynamic thrust and make growth and excitement possible.

Pushing-Resisting. This pertains to the process involved in molding your differences to fit together (see Figure 7.3).

Figure 7.3. Pushing-resisting.

Pushing each other to change and in turn resisting that push is an inevitable part of every marriage. As spouses face each other on a day-to-day basis, habits, idiosyncrasies, traits, and attitudes in each other's personality begin to rub the wrong way. Usually the little things bring this aspect of the relationship to the fore. How you squeeze the toothpaste, whether you close the door on the medicine cabinet, how the toilet paper should be put in the holder, and a million other little things generate irritations and angry flare-ups. Even how you take your socks off can become a focus of major debate.

Example

A Right Way to Take off Your Socks. One day about four years after we were married, Toni rather casually mentioned to Jim that she would be pleased if he would turn his socks right side out when he took them off. Jim, just as casually, said fine and proceeded to forget all about the request. A week later when Toni again raised the request, Jim asked her why she was bugging him. She explained how turning the socks right side out would be time efficient when she folded the clothes. Jim understood and again forgot. Toni in her persistence raised the request again, to which Jim responded with righteous indignation that he had been taking off his socks the same way for twenty-seven years, and she was just trying to change him. Well, the die was cast and a full blown argument ensued. At one point Toni angrily asked Jim if he would like her to show him how to take off his socks. Jim just as angrily retorted, yes, he would. For those of you who do not know how to take off your socks, you slip the top of the sock down over your heel, grab the toe of the sock and pull. It comes off right side out every time provided, of course, you have it on correctly in the first place.

After telling this story to a class one day, a student sent us the following poem.

Model Mate

The perfect mate, the one to hitch to,
The ideal guy a girl should switch to,
Is the fellow who, without a pout,
Will turn his soiled socks right side out.

Colleen Stanley Bare

The pushing-resisting element of the marriage functions on the friction principle: *rub together until the rough edges are smoothed all the while lubricating with love.* This aspect of marriage is the source of tension in marital relating. Pushing-resisting also is the arena which produces the data to prove that marriage changes a person. When the pushing-resisting is balanced, that is, both spouses participate in both ways to a relative degree of equality, the pace of adjusting to each other and forming a suitable fit is expedited. When the pressure is all one-sided, when one partner absolutely refuses to budge, when one person refuses to push, or when both abdicate, the marriage runs into trouble.

Most couples who divorce and many who come for counseling have their greatest difficulty with this aspect of the relationship. Some have already given up trying to either change the other or please the other by changing. In situations where the changing is all one-sided, bitterness results. One woman explained her feelings in this regard by stating to her husband, "Somehow you always end up doing what you want to do, and somehow I end up doing what I don't want to do." Such a situation over time will erode the relationship.

Example

The Little Things Count. Sometimes the little differences around which the pushing-resisting evolves are indicative of bigger differences. One couple came in for counseling after one year of marriage complaining that all they did was fight and argue. When asked by the counselor for an example of what they fought about, the husband sheepishly said, "Which way the toilet paper should come out of the holder." She thought the toilet paper should come over the top so you could control the flow, and he thought it should come out from the bottom so you could easily reroll it if you got too much. They described a game they played when traveling in which they bet on the way the toilet paper would be installed in their motel room. However, this along with many other "minor" differences had escalated the tension between them to intolerable levels. Both spouses were university professors who had put marriage off until their careers were established. Consequently, they married in their early thirties after extensive experience as autonomous individuals. Each had become set in their ways, and the pushing-resisting was reflective of their inability to accommodate to each other or be flexible enough to work out a compromise.

Pushing-resisting dynamics are necessary for coupleness to emerge. Resistance to change is a natural part of human nature and can be expected, especially after the enamored aspect of the relationship wears thin. Courage and willingness to push will counteract complacency. Continued efforts to change each other will keep the element of risk alive in the relationship and prevent the couple from stopping the process of becoming one prematurely.

Leading-Supporting. The balance to pushing-resisting is provided by the *leading-supporting* dimension of the relationship (see Figure 7.4).

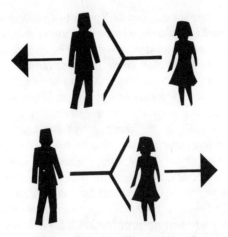

Figure 7.4. Leading-supporting.

Leading-supporting refers to that aspect of the relationship in which each partner takes the initiative knowing that the other will support his/her efforts. Leading-supporting provides the means by which the identity of each person is preserved in the context of the relationship. Again, a balance is necessary. A relationship in which one person does all the leading and the other all the supporting will eventually create a problem. When a man does all the leading, the woman ends up submerging her identity in his. Women who live out their lives in that manner find difficulty surviving once they lose their husband. Other women are finding out how painful losing their identity in marriage is. When a woman does all the leading, the man's self-esteem is eroded to such a point that even his children no longer respect his judgment or person.

The leading-supporting element of the relationship builds a reservoir of caring because it solidifies the practice of putting the other first. In balance it is highly correlated with productivity, excitement, and a high level of self-esteem in both spouses. Combined with pushing-resisting, leading-supporting produces a growth-oriented marriage experience that is intrinsically fulfilling and beneficial to the marital pair as a couple and as individuals.

Example

Case of Tom, Carol, and Jennifer. Consider the following case example which demonstrates how an unresolved issue affects all the aspects of the marriage relationship just described.

*The family consists of Tom (27) who is a skilled worker, Carol
(24) who works part-time outside the home, and their three and
one-half year old daughter, Jennifer. The couple had been married five years when they came for counseling. The main issue
for her was his drinking, and for him the issue was her lack of
affection (primarily sexual) toward him. Tom was a ritualistic
drinker, stopping with the boys after work and drinking on
weekends, usually in the company of his softball teammates.
Early in the marriage she would accompany him weekends and
would even go down to the bar to meet him after work. When
their child was born, she began to make demands that he come
straight home from work and cut back on the softball. When he
resisted, she began to consider his drinking the problem. He, of
course, felt there was no problem with his drinking and accused
her of being cold and bitchy even when he wasn't drinking. As
the couple went round and round on this issue, they developed
hostility and distance until finally the wife demanded they go to
counseling or else she would leave. Consequently, he consented
to counseling.*

Let's look at the situation presented in the case of Tom, Carol, and
Jennifer in terms of the various aspects of the relationship. As the issue
remained unresolved, their *togetherness* time became characterized by
tension. Time together always ended up focusing on the drinking issue,
and they had fewer and fewer moments of positive time together. Even
though both at various times would decide to try to make the time
together good, something always triggered the negative feelings. Consequently, *apartness* time not only increased but was more attractive than
the time together. She began developing a circle of friends separate from
him, often discussing his drinking with them, and he reverted to more
and more time drinking with the boys. The *pushing-resisting* became
totally one-sided. He began avoiding going home because he knew she
was home getting ready to lower the boom as soon as he walked in the
door. He stopped pushing her because she could always one-up his
demands by zeroing in on the drinking. The *leading-supporting* aspect of
the relationship became narrowly defined. Until he stopped drinking, she
would not support him in anything. He also withdrew from her, leaving
her with the full responsibility of their child. Gradually the *leading-
supporting* component translated into *withdrawing-pursuing*. She would
pursue him about his drinking and he would withdraw. He would pursue
her about sex and she would withdraw. Consequently, the relationship
reached an impasse where neither person was willing to change and
where both were extremely angry and unhappy.

You might be tempted to say, "Well, that's it for that relationship, divorce is the only answer." Let's go back and see where changes could be made that would reverse the negative spiral in the marriage. First of all, their togetherness was undermined because of a question neither could objectively answer: Does he have a drinking problem? They can argue forever but since neither is expert enough to make that assessment; the problem continues. The intervention here would be to get them to agree to an evaluation by a chemical dependency expert with the stipulation that both accept the result. Consequently, if the evaluation determined he had a drinking problem and treatment was necessary, he could get the help he needed and she could support him through the process. If, on the other hand, the evaluation determined he did not have a drinking problem, the couple could turn their attention to renegotiating their apartness time, setting aside the drinking issue. As the issue of drinking dissolves, the couple can reconnect in other areas allowing the expression of caring and affection that had been put on hold to flow again. *Togetherness* time becomes more positive and *apartness* time is in better balance. *Pushing-resisting* can focus on other areas where the issues raised are not so one-sided and the withdrawing-pursuing can transfer back into *leading-supporting*. Consequently, the stability of the relationship (togetherness and apartness) is reestablished and the growth dynamics (pushing-resisting and leading-supporting) are remobilized.

LOVE AND RESPECT:
THE ESSENTIAL INGREDIENTS IN MARRIAGE

In spite of all the factors we have discussed and all the aspects of the marriage relationship, two essential ingredients appear to account for marriages succeeding. They are *love* and *respect*. Interestingly enough, one or the other on its own merit cannot secure the marriage. They must co-exist in essential balance for their bonding power to work. They are much like the two tubes of material that are required to make epoxy glue. Either tube applied alone results in a failure to bond. But if you mix the two ingredients together in equal proportions and then apply, an almost unbreakable bond is created. The same is true with love and respect in marriage.

Most complaints about the lack of fulfillment or satisfaction in a marriage relationship are couched in terms of one of these ingredients. As we worked with couples over the years, we noticed a distinct tendency for wives to tender their dissatisfactions about husbands in terms of lack of love, caring, and sensitivity. Husbands, on the other hand, have tended to express their complaints in terms of lack of respect. Wives feel unloved and yet are criticized by their husbands for not showing them affection. Husbands feel their wives no longer respect them and yet are criticized by their wives for not valuing them or treating them as a person. A woman is more likely to say, "He doesn't show his feelings" or "If he would only let me know he loves me . . ." A man tends to say, "She doesn't value or respect me enough" or "I never get any credit for what I do."

Gerald Zuk (1981), eminent family therapist and originator of triadic-based family therapy, documented the previously noted tendencies and categorized them as "continuity values" and "discontinuity values." He observed that in therapy males tended to project discontinuity values which stress order, authority, reason, systematic functioning, compartmentalization of life, efficiency, schedules, and *respect*. Females, on the other hand, tended to project continuity values which stressed the goodness of expressiveness, warmth, nurturance, disclosure of emotions, exceptions to rules, egalitarianism, viewing life as a whole, and *love*. As such, most conflicts between husbands and wives are values conflicts emanating from the dominant perspective each holds with respect to each other and the world. For example, husbands say, "I can't talk to her when she gets emotional" or "If she would only use her head instead of her feelings, we would be able to solve our problems." Wives say, "He never shows his feelings" or "If he would just loosen up and let me know what's going on inside, we would be fine."

Consequently, when issues arise in marriage, love and respect tend to become opponents instead of teammates. When either partner is all one way, the result is inevitably an impasse. Both have the capacity to express love and respect and both sets of values. The fact that one set of values predominates is likely a result of the "complex interaction of genetic heritage, societal, and cultural norms, family orientation, and environmental circumstances" (Trotzer, 1981, p. 45). In some sense a biblical guideline was established long ago with regard to love and respect. The Apostle Paul directed husbands to "Love your wives" and wives to "reverence your husbands" (Ephesians 5:33). The meaning of these directives is that husbands are supposed to be lovers (in the broadest sense) or leaders in love, and wives are to be leaders in respect. As each takes responsibility to do so, a reciprocal reaction occurs: love begets love and respect begets respect. In healthy marriages we find these dynamics operating whether the couple knows about the biblical dictates or not.

In all our marital work, we always assess the balance of love and respect in the relationship. Whenever the balance is disproportionate or when one or the other is lacking, we strive to help the couple attain an equilibrium between the two ingredients. Keeping your finger on the pulse of the love-respect interaction is an accurate barometer of the health and strength of your marriage relationship.

MALE AND FEMALE
RELATING IN MARRIAGE

Even though Chapter 2 stresses the importance of coming to grips with your sexual identity as a prerequisite to marriage, the implications of the last section reflect the reality that relating to each other as male and female will still be an issue in marriage. A marriage has not existed in which the couple did not struggle at some level with effectively joining maleness and femaleness in a compatible manner. In many ways, with respect to sex differences, the issue becomes "never the twain shall meet" rather than "we two shall become one." Developmentally, the story is more a matter of the two sexes crossing paths than walking along the same path.

The story starts long before marriage. Females develop and mature emotionally, physically, and intellectually sooner than males. Girls notice boys earlier than boys notice girls. Girls date older males in adolescence and boys date younger females. In the early to mid-twenties, both reach the same point and paths cross resulting in the pull toward intimacy and marriage.

Once married, the couple travels arm in arm for a distance until the pull toward family, the woman's biological time clock, and other factors route her path toward the home and family. The male certainly applauds her route but typically extricates himself to pursue life outside the home as the "provider." The female is now in the home as primary child care worker and the husband moves in and out of her life as her "token adult." However, once the issue of children is settled and the children are on their way to school and/or heading out of the home, the female changes course and heads once again for the career or workplace she may have left behind. Interestingly enough, the male who is now well established outside the home also changes course and begins to look toward home for meaning and the investment of his time. Consequently, they meet at the door. Just as she is leaving, he is coming home. She is seeing a good twenty-plus years of fulfilling career ahead while he is looking to start to enjoy life. Finally, about retirement time, they once again cross paths, and link up arm in arm to walk out into the sunset—together at last. But even then their paths diverge. Since life expectancy for males is less than females, the woman may find herself viewing that sunset alone.

The scenario just described is fraught with loopholes and exceptions, but hopefully the point is clear. The first area where male-female differences emerge is in the area of communication. Relating to each other as male and female will require your attention, and differences will manifest themselves in your communication, fighting styles, and fighting patterns. The woman is likely to be the talker; she wants the man to tell her his feelings. The man discovers whenever he does express himself, the woman gets upset, so he avoids talking and withdraws. He also gets confused because she accuses him of not telling her his feeling when he tells her what he thinks. In return, he accuses her of being too emotional and uses that as an excuse not to talk at all.

The fight pattern that typically follows goes something like this. She pressures him to express himself which he avoids and resists. She persists to a point where he explodes, saying things that hurt her. She then withdraws from him, resulting in a period of little or no contact between the two. This is resolved either by time, i.e., things go back to normal on their own, or he apologizes. Then the cycle starts all over again.

Even in starting over, there tends to be a difference. He wants to wipe the slate clean and start fresh. She has a good memory and takes a historical view—"We have to settle the past before we can get to the present." He wants to forget the past and focus only on the present. So the battle continues.

Example

Getting Along in Retirement. The male-female relating dilemma was evident in a retired couple who came for counseling. Her agenda was to rehash and resolve all the pains incurred in the course of their relating before she could be open to their developing a friendly retirement lifestyle. He wanted to simply apologize and turn over a new leaf so they could get on with the business of enjoying their retirement years together.

One of the most useful ways of resolving the differences we have been describing is to *learn each other's language.* So often in counseling we see couples who have developed language and perspectives that are so different, they need a translator (the therapist) to communicate. For example, one ground rule to deal with the think-feel controversy is to treat the words think and feel as synonymous. If the man says what he thinks it represents what he feels, and if the woman states what she feels it represents what she thinks. By dropping the distinction, communication can flow unencumbered. After learning each other's language, *work toward developing a common language.* This goal does not mean adopting one or the other's language. It means creating a language to which both contribute. That language thus becomes your direct channel of communication. Finally, *practice your language skills with each other.* Practice makes perfect and you will discover that being tri-lingual is exciting: speaking your own language, your spouse's language, and your common language.

A second area where male-female differences emerge is in the area of sex. Our clinical experience indicates that men are more able and willing to separate sex from the status of the relationship than women. Wives cannot understand why after and even in the middle of a fight, their husbands can come to bed and even think about sex, much less engage in it. Husbands can not understand why wives let their feelings interfere with their sex life. When matters concern sex, men tend to function from a need, enjoyment, and quantity perspective, while women tend to stress intimacy, romance, and quality. We will speak more directly to this issue when we address the function of sex in marriage later in the chapter.

The third aspect of male-female relating we will address here has to do with the current shift in the woman's role in marriage precipitated by the women's movement and other contemporary societal forces. McGoldrick (1980) noted that "when women used to fall automatically into the adaptive role in marriage, the likelihood of divorce was much lower" (p. 110). Although role battles have been fought in every marriage from time immemorial, the context of contemporary society has opened more options for that struggle to encompass. We have discovered that the transition is just as painful for a traditional couple to negotiate a shift in domestic roles from a 90 - 10 split to an 80 - 20 split as it is for a more contemporary couple to negotiate a 50 - 50 status. The full extent of the changing women's role remains to be seen, but it does affect each and every couple in some way. One gentleman tacitly acknowledged this impact when he walked through our door for the first marital counseling session and said, "Look, Doc, I know why I'm here—I gotta do more around the house. But tell me this! How come now it takes two people twice as long to do the same thing one person did in half the time?" We do not have the answer to this dilemma, but several guidelines have been helpful to couples who are in the throes of negotiating their respective sex roles.

First of all, recognize the fact that role changes do not tend to occur in a conversion-like manner. Work toward changes in moderate steps, acknowledging where you are before setting goals as to where you are going. Second, avoid the use of red flag words in your negotiations. Words such as chauvinist, feminist, or liberated have a tendency to conjure up emotion-laden images and connotations that interfere with communication. Third, be aware that answers found in the world outside your relationship pose as much a threat to the relationship as a resource. Try to keep negotiations in the context of your relating as much as possible. You can get ideas from the outside but they will only be helpful if you can make them your own. The key is not how others have settled the issues or how others tell you they should be settled, but how you settle the issues that counts.

The impact of the changing status of women in marriage is certainly worrisome and deserving of a wary eye. McGoldrick (1980) took the opportunity to state that "achieving marital adjustment in our time, when we are moving toward the equality of the sexes (educationally and occupationally) may be extraordinarily difficult" (p. 110). Do not become discouraged but do treat your own sex role negotiations with all due seriousness.

THE WORKING MARRIAGE*

* Information in this section is credited to Charles Jaekle and the Marriage Enrichment Center of Washington, D.C. and was obtained from a workshop presented at the 1978 APGA National Convention in Washington, D.C.

The working marriage is based on the recognition and acceptance of several basic propositions.

1. The working marriage requires growth.

2. In a working marriage, partners experience being married to many different people, not because of changing partners but because of change in your partner.

3. In a working marriage, partners fall in and out of love (marry and divorce) many times, all in the context of one relationship.

4. In a working marriage, both partners' individuality is nourished in the context of the relationship.

5. Working on the marriage relationship is a necessity requiring the efforts of both partners.

These constructs portray the reality that marriage must account for changes over time that inevitably occur in each individual, accommodate to the emotional vascillation of relating patterns, respect the worth and dignity of each partner and be a dynamic rather than a static process. When such is the case, the marriage will not only be working but exciting.

Companionship

The core of the working marriage is *marital companionship*. Being companions is the umbrella under which all other aspects of relating fall. Companionship is the one element that maintains from beginning to end, from youth to old age, from the wedding day "till death do us part." It provides the vehicle through which partners nurture each other psychologically and physically. Witmer (1985) stated that "physical strokes" (touching), especially from a person whom we love, are just as important as "psychological strokes" which affirm our value as a person. Deprivation in either domain can do damage to the well-being of those individuals involved. Companionship enables us to experience the physical strokes as well as the psychological ones and is maintained by the dynamic activities of working, playing, negotiating, and exchanging.

Working

That aspect of the relationship entitled working is where partners pool their assets and manage their resources to achieve common goals. Working taps the achievement motivation of the couple, generating a team effort that provides satisfaction in both striving together toward and attaining their goals. Sometimes couples lose track of each other over time and forget how well they worked together in the early days of their marriage. When couples are just starting out and things are tough, energy is mobilized. Later in life the "tough" days are often remembered as the golden era of the relationship. Sometimes in counseling we have to give couples projects on which to work to get them back in touch with the working aspect of their relating. The major drawbacks to working for couples starting out are the lack of clear goals or the lack of common goals. Two people "working" together who don't know where they are going, or who are going in different directions quickly become disgruntled.

Playing

The counterpart to working is playing which is the element of companionship where partners engage in mutually satisfying and enjoyable leisure activities together. This aspect of the relationship was likely fully developed in courtship and should be given no less vital place in marriage. Problems enter when working squeezes out playing and vice versa. If one finds a lack of common interests or if one or the other is unwilling to put common interests above individual interests, the playing aspect of the relationship will suffer. Playing is not one person going along with the other to play. It is finding a common ground where not only the activity is enjoyed, but doing it with your partner is enjoyable.

Negotiating

This is the interactive component of the relationship where differences between the two individuals are worked out. The goal is to seek mutuality and find ways to account for and accommodate to differences without damaging the relationship. We have discussed this aspect of the relationship in many different ways already, and it should be clear that inflexibility and unwillingness to compromise will interfere with the negotiating function.

Exchanging

Exchanging is the contributive aspect of the relationship. It involves each partner giving to the other from the unique resources each brings to the marriage, thus accentuating the other's life. It is that part of the relationship where each partner acquires something from the other. Exchanging is the experience of growing because of what the other person has given to you and vice versa. The essence of exchanging is captured effectively in the following lines of poetry:

> I love you not only for what you are
> But for what I am when I am with you.
> I love you not only for what you have
>   made of yourself
> But for what you are making of me.
>   (author, date, & source unknown)

Exchanging is a positive contribution to each other's individuality. Problems arise when the exchanging is unbalanced or when what one or the other has to contribute is devalued.

Principles of a Working Marriage

The four dynamic components of marital companionship are held in place by the four basic principles of the working marriage.

Principle 1: Fighting—I know you to be both lover and adversary.

This principle recognizes the fact that the same person can be your most intimate partner at one point and your most bitter opponent at another. Some couples develop a mistaken idea that effective marriages are marriages in which no fighting occurs. Some parents go so far as to make sure they never fight in front of their children, thinking that such a practice demonstrates their togetherness. Such is not the case. Not fighting in front of the children simply teaches them not to fight. Consequently, they never learn what to do when they encounter differences they cannot resolve. We generally tell parents that they can fight about almost anything except the children in front of their children. The important element of such encounters is not the fighting, but the result. Children need to see differences are resolved. Being able to move from lover to adversary to lover in the course of your relating presents a much healthier and realistic picture than simply creating an ironclad rule of no fighting.

Principle 2: Intimacy—I can be close to give and to get.

Intimacy has many faces including the intellectual, sexual, spiritual, and emotional aspects of a person's life. Some of these aspects can be sought outside the marriage. A typical example is intellectual intimacy where one partner may meet intellectual needs in work or associations specifically tailored to their intellectual interests. Other aspects such as sexual (physical) intimacy are reserved for the marriage relationship alone.

Intimacy implies equality because it is difficult to become truly intimate with someone who is in a controlling position. Consequently, intimacy also involves vulnerability. Many individuals find the most difficult part of marriage is becoming intimate. They come face to face with the question, "How can I control if I show vulnerability?" Therefore, they choose not to get emotionally involved, thus restricting marital growth. In a working marriage, partners risk vulnerability for closeness in which they can give and receive without restriction.

Principle 3: Communication—I know and signal what I need and want from you.

When couples get stuck, more often than not they describe their difficulties as a communication problem. The fact should be evident by now that communication is the backbone of the marriage. However, communicating takes effort and it also involves skills (see Chapter 2). Sometimes the problem is in the "knowing." One or both do not know themselves well enough to be able to frame their wants, needs, and desires to their partner. If such is the case, a crash course in self-awareness may be necessary to unstick the communication process. Other times the problem is in the "signaling." The couple may be afraid or not know how to express what they know. If fear is the barrier, the problems usually are elsewhere and not in the communication. If the problem is a matter of not knowing how to communicate, a communication skills program (e.g., couple's communication) may be helpful. In any case, effective communication is contingent on staying in touch with yourself and each other and using all the tools of the trade (Miller, Nunnally, & Wackman, 1975).

Principle 4: Commitment—I belong with you (not to you).

The bottom line of the working marriage is commitment. If the intention is to stay together, then any fighting is only a transitional phase in the relationship. The nature of fighting also changes because no underlying agenda exists which says "I can leave the relationship if things don't go my way." The relationship itself cannot be used as a bargaining tool. So we have come full circle to the point made at the very beginning of our chapter on marriage—making marriages succeed is a matter of commitment.

FUNCTIONS OF SEX IN MARRIAGE

Sex in marriage is the second most difficult topic to address briefly in a book of this nature (love is the first). A case can certainly be made for sex being everything that marriage is, when broadly construed with all the ramifications in the relationship considered. Sex also can be viewed as only a part of marriage, an important part, but not the whole of marriage. We have already pointed out that differences will occur in the way sex is viewed in the male-female dimension of the marriage. These differences tend to emerge later rather than earlier, giving rise to accusations in arguments about sex couched in terms of "You never used to . . ." or "You always used to . . . before." We are not going to try to resolve the issue of whether sex is all or part. Nor are we going to set a criteria or standard that will enable you to measure whether your sex life is good or not. Each couple must work that out, just as they work out the other aspects of their relationship. We are, however, going to address the various functions of sex in marriage and suggest a prioritization of those functions that tend to be associated with a healthy and satisfying sex life for both partners.

Intimacy

The first function of sex in marriage is *intimacy*. The sexual act symbolically and physically expresses the coming together of the marital pair at the very deepest level. The act is the consummation of the marriage, the experience where maleness and femaleness are physically joined to become one. The intimacy aspect of sex houses the expression of love, caring, warmth, and closeness. Intimacy is where partners share a mutual vulnerability without risk of hurt or rejection. Intimacy is the function of sex that supercedes all other aspects. It is what makes sex more than simply a physical act, an interpersonal obligation, or a tool to make a family. As such, sex deepens and strengthens the relationship and opens a channel of communication that is private and special to the couple and to which no other person has access. The real "joy of sex" comes from the intimacy level, as does the real pain of infidelity. The intimacy aspect of sex stays alive throughout the marriage regardless of physical changes that occur with age. One of the most exciting and enlightening discoveries of sex research has been the documentation of the various forms of sexual activity among the elderly, all of which have been linked directly to the expression of intimacy (Starr & Weiner, 1981). Knowing "you are never too old" to experience the intimacy that accrues from sexual relating is an encouraging fact of life.

Procreation

The second function of sex in marriage is *procreation*. This aspect of sexual relating has certainly become more complicated. Before the advent of birth control and the expansion of role options, procreation was rather straightforward. Given the mutual physical ability to have children, your options were essentially three: (1) have sex, have children; (2) don't have sex, don't have children; and (3) have sex and take whatever comes.

In contemporary society the reproductive aspect of sex has shifted from the domain of chance to the domain of choice. You can choose when to start having children and when to stop. You can decide who will be physically responsible for starting and stopping via birth control options and surgical procedures. In some ways the proliferation of options has not done married couples any favors. Sometimes choosing the method of birth control is a more difficult decision than deciding when to have children. With the "choice" dimension being added to procreation, a mandatory fact is that couples need to communicate and negotiate honestly with one another. A sure way to generate resentment in your partner is to have and carry out a hidden agenda with respect to having or not having children. This very issue is one in which many of the couples we see have become embroiled. How the controversy is settled has far-reaching ramifications not only for the marriage, but also for the children that may be born.

Need

The third function of sex in marriage is *need*. Because of the difficulty in effectively differentiating between physical need and psychological need, we are treating them as synonymous in the interests of brevity. One of the realities about marriage is that seldom do spouses have exactly the same sexual needs. Their needs may be compatible during certain phases of the marriage or even during certain times during the menstrual cycle of the woman. Inevitably, however, the likelihood of needs being out of sync will occur. From our counseling experience we have found that differences in each person's need for sex has a direct impact on their ability to count. A common occurrence is for a couple to come in, sit down, and argue about how many times "it" happened during the last week or month. Since presumably they were both involved together with each other, we are amazed at how often they disagree numerically.

If couples can recognize and accept the reality of differing needs for sex, a heavy load of pressure will be lifted from their sexual encounters. Such recognition also will facilitate choosing to become involved sexually even when one or the other isn't in the mood. Differing needs generate a sense of obligation relative to sex. As each partner seeks to fulfill their pledges to meet each other's needs emotionally, psychologically, and physically, a time comes when you set aside your own feelings for the sake of your partner. Consequently, a feeling of obligation arises with bittersweet overtones. While one person's need has been met the experience varies because there is a difference between "wanting to" and "having to" (obligation). Many couples find their enjoyment of sex eroded because they are engaging each other out of obligation. This feeling creates a drawback to approaching sex solely on a need basis. If partners can accept the need differences and credit their partner for responding to meet their need rather than hold it against them, not only will needs be met but enjoyment will be enhanced. The fact of the matter is that sometimes persons who think they are not interested find themselves very interested once they get into the act.

Pleasure

The fourth function of sex in marriage is *pleasure*. This aspect is certainly the most fickle of our sexual experiences. Pleasure tends to vascillate between all and none with so many variations in between, they are impossible to count. Enjoyment, excitement, arousal, stimulation, and a multitude of other words could be used in our attempt to describe the pleasure aspect of sex. All would fail in some sense because most of the time the sense of pleasure is determined by one's own emotional and perceptual state. Physically, what is pleasurable for one person may not be for the other. Sexual images corresponding to what constitutes sexual pleasure may be different. As couples discover each other sexually, pleasurable activities may not develop until there has been lots of practice. Pleasure is greatly associated with getting to know one another's likes and dislikes and experimenting to find those sexual practices which are mutually pleasurable. *Pleasure is a companion of sexual activity, not a goal.* Seeking sexual contact purely for the sake of pleasure will produce short-term gratification and generate a tendency to become dissatisfied with one's partner. Over time, if pleasure is used as a criteria for sexual success, disappointment is assured which, in turn, may lead to thoughts and actions that pull one or the other away from sexual activity in the marriage. Sexual pleasure is the frosting on the cake. Pleasure comes with the package but if you try to eat the frosting without the cake, your taste for it will quickly dissipate.

The key to an exciting and satisfying sex life, just like every other aspect of married life, is communication. You need to let each other know what you think and feel, what you like and dislike, what you need and want. Sex in itself is an act of communication. Sex uses a physical means to send messages between the two of you that leave their marks long after the sexual act is over. Researchers indicate that the typical sexual encounter lasts only five to eight minutes including foreplay, climax, and afterglow. Typical couples engage in sex two to four times a week. That's about 32 minutes out of a week at best. A moot question is, if you marry for sex, what are you going to do with the rest of the time? Ray Short (1978) told the story of a sophomore boy who when asked the question sheepishly said, "Think about the next 8 minutes."

Communication provides the connector and facilitates fulfillment in your sexual experience. If you place intimacy as your first priority in relating sexually, then your individual needs will be met, pleasure will be experienced, and procreation will occur in a healthy manner.

AREAS OF MARITAL CONFLICT

If you have stuck with this book thus far, you could be thinking we are trying to scare you off. So many things can go wrong and so many problems could crop up. But if you are like most of us, you are still going to or already have leaped into marriage. (Even when fully prepared, the step of marriage is still a leap.) So you roll up your sleeves and say, "O.K., where can I expect trouble?"

In Figure 7.5 is illustrated a general overview of basic conflict areas in marital relating. Relating to each other (personality clashes), relating to extended family (legacy clashes), relating to children (parent/child clashes), and relating to society (lifestyle clashes) are typical areas in which conflicts occur. Some specific sources of conflict determined by research and clinical practice are (1) money, (2) sex, (3) roles, (4) extended family, and (5) lifestyle.

Money

A major area for marital conflict is money. Who's in charge of the money? How is it spent? Who's responsible for getting it? Whose money is it? How is it valued? Who pays the bills? Who holds the checkbook? These are but a few of a million money-related issues. Couples can find ways of integrating almost every other aspect of life into their quarrels about money. Families of origin, values, religion, personality traits, sex, ethnicity, power, and children can be woven into a good fight over money by a skillful couple. Whether you have money or not conflicts over fiscal issues emerge. Money conflicts transcend all socio-economic class boundaries.

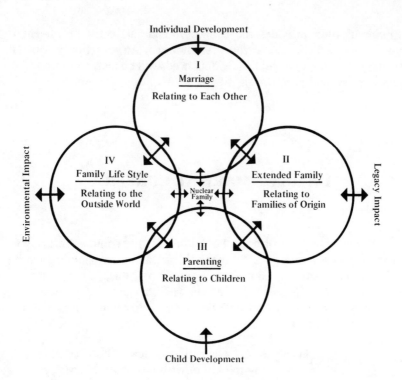

Figure 7.5. Basic areas of marital conflict.

Sex

The category almost as comprehensive as money is sex. We already have alluded to sex problems in the last section, but questions of when, where, how, how often, what is enough, who is in charge of birth control, when should we have children, should we have children, how many children should we have, when have we had enough children, and many others are struggled over in the course of a marriage. Sometimes the fact that people enjoy sex at all is a miracle. One couple in therapy told us that everything in the marriage was in turmoil except their sex life. We informed them that we certainly didn't want to interfere with that area and advised them to go to bed whenever the pressures from the rest of their life got too heavy.

Roles

Negotiating roles and role reciprocity is a continual struggle for couples because of the natural tendency for circumstances and individuals to change. Roles always involve complementary parts and function according to rules and priorities. The "battle of the sexes" is essentially a roles struggle. Haley (Seagraves, 1982) has described a satisfactory marriage as a process of working out shared agreements (rules), largely undiscussed, between two people. Consequently, marital conflict can emerge on any of three levels: (1) over the rules themselves, (2) over who makes the rules, and (3) over enforcement of incompatible rules or ambiguous communication about rules. Sager (1976) stated that all couples develop a marriage contract which contains agreements (rules) that are (1) conscious and verbalized, (2) conscious and not verbalized, and (3) unconscious. Any or all of these areas can cause trouble in negotiating roles.

Extended Family

Issues related to extended family are always with the couple, sometimes dormant, sometimes camouflaged, sometimes obvious, but always there. That's the reason we included a whole chapter (5) on your family of origin.

Lifestyle

The large catchall category of marital conflict entitled lifestyle encompasses all the areas not previously mentioned. This may sound like a cop-out but it really isn't. Lifestyle essentially relates to how a couple chooses to use their time and resources to create the kind of life they want. Struggles in this area emerge from individual differences in interests, values, and expectations of marriage and family life. Couples who do not have lifestyle conflicts do not develop a couple lifestyle. Since no two individuals are exactly alike (clones disqualified), lifestyle conflicts are not only inevitable but healthy for the marriage.

THE HEALTHY MARRIAGE

The healthy marriage is a process and a product. No set recipe can be found, but essential ingredients are available. The process starts with commitment as the bottom line. Communication and willingness to work on the marriage are necessary. The realization that marriage is a lifelong process of becoming a couple must be grasped. Saxton (1983) has concluded that a successful marriage is built upon three fundamental factors:

> congruence of role perception, reciprocity of role interaction and equivalence of role function; that is, each of the couple must agree reasonably closely about their mutual expectations. They must also interact in a way that fulfills each other's important expectations. And, the satisfaction provided by each, for the other, must be of relative equivalence. (p. 243)

Mace and Mace (1977) added three more ingredients to a happy marriage. They are (1) commitment to growth, (2) an effective communication system, and (3) the creative use of conflict.

These six items sound like a big order and they are. Remember as you go into the next chapter, the marriage is the key. Nourish it, keep it growing, and do not let it slip into obscurity as the other facets of life impose themselves upon you. The marriage is what must stand the test of time and is your support system for coping with life's eventualities. Marriage is also the key to your family. For as we say in the family therapy business, "As goes the marriage, so goes the family."

REFERENCES

Carter, E.A., & McGoldrick, M. (Eds.). (1980). *The family life cycle: A framework for family therapy.* New York: Gardner Press.

Gibran, K. (1951). *The prophet.* New York: Alfred A. Knopf.

Haley, J. (1963). Marriage therapy. *Archives of General Psychiatry, 8,* 213-34.

Mace, D., & Mace, V. (1977). *How to have a happy marriage.* Nashville: Abingdon Press.

McGoldrick, M. (1980). The joining of families through marriage. In E.A. Carter and M. McGoldrick (Eds.), *The family life cycle: A framework for family therapy.* New York: Gardner Press, 93-119.

McGoldrick, M., & Carter, E.A. (1982). The family life cycle. In F. Walsh, (Ed.). *Normal family processes,* 167-195. New York: The Guilford Press.

Miller, S., Nunnally, E.W., & Wackman, D.B. (1975). *Alive and aware: Improving communication in relationships.* Minneapolis, MN: Interpersonal communications programs.

Minuchin, S. (1974). *Families and family therapy.* Cambridge, MA: Harvard University Press.

O'Neill, N. & O'Neill, G. (1972). *Open marriage: A new life style for couples.* New York: Evans.

Sager, C.J. (1976). *Marriage contracts and couple therapy.* New York: Brunner/Mazel.

Saxton, L. (1983). *The individual, marriage, and the family.* Belmont, CA: Wadsworth Publishing.

Seagraves, R.T. (1982). *marital therapy: A combined psychodynamic behavioral approach.* New York: Plenum Medical Book.

Short, R. E. (1978). *Sex, love, or infatuation: How can I really know?* Minneapolis: Augsburg Publishing House.

Starr, B.D., & Weiner, M.B. (1981). *Sex and sexuality in the mature years.* New York: Stein and Day.

Toman, W. (1976). *Family constellation: Its effects on personality and social behavior.* New York: Springer.

Trotzer, J.P. (1981). The centrality of values in families and family therapy. *International Journal of Family Therapy,* 42-55.

Walsh, F. (1982). *Normal family processes.* New York: The Guilford Press.

Witmer, J.M. (1985). *Pathways to personal growth.* Muncie, IN: Accelerated Development, Publishers.

Zuk, G. (1981). *Family therapy: A triadic based approach* (rev. ed.). New York: Human Sciences Press.

AND THEN THE FAMILY

The family as a system is discussed. Concepts such as generational boundaries, communication, and roles are presented. Parenting (mothering and fathering), parent-child relations, and sibling rivalry are discussed. The family life cycle is traced along with typical developmental crises and tasks that occur in each stage. The impact of family life experiences on identity development of children is addressed.

WHAT is a family?

What IS a family?

What is A family?

What is a FAMILY?

The answer to that question "What is a family?" could fill volumes and present many contradictory perspectives. The only way to insure your sanity, if you really wanted to know the answer, is to throw up your hands, throw away the books, and make up your own. In some ways this chapter may be viewed as simply adding to the plethora of perspectives on the family. However, the fact is that both contemplation of marriage and occurrence of marriage automatically raise the prospect of family as a real dimension of the marital experience even though initially it is only a matter of potential. Whether by choice or by chance, a family in some form is a product of a marriage. Even couples who cannot or choose not to have children carve out some form of family domain.

We recently talked with a man and his wife who were celebrating their 45th wedding anniversary. They had not had any children but they ran a little restaurant together and in their eyes their customers constituted their family.

However, our focus in this chapter is on family experiences that involve children. Our purpose is to acquaint and remind the reader of the various elements that constitute family life. Whether you are anticipating or already in a family, we want to provide a context of concepts and ideas against which your perspective of family experience can be compared. Our intent is to attribute predictability to family life which can provide a sense of normalcy even though actual family experiences may still be difficult to cope with or adjust to. We will point out some of the typical places where families get stuck or have problems, and provide guidelines and suggestions to help you prevent problems and ferret out solutions when they occur. Finally, we want to present the family as a growth experience which has a dynamic influence on every one of the participants and is the vital reason for individuals and couples to be "better ready than not" when the family experience emerges.

Our chapter will begin by addressing the various definitions of a family leading to the view of a family as a system. The various dynamic forces in the family system will be discussed, and the purposes of the family with respect to children will be raised. The parenting process, including mothering, fathering, and the parental dyad, will be presented. Finally, the family life cycle and its various stages will be described including the characteristics, basic developmental tasks, and typical problem areas that pertain to each stage. Our conclusion will present a listing of traits that have been defined as indicative of a healthy family.

DEFINING THE FAMILY

Concepts for this section were drawn from a lecture by Dr. David Keith, of the Family Psychiatry Department at the University of Wisconsin.

Our purpose here is not to present a definitive definition of the family but rather to provide a sampling of the various perspectives that depict what a family is. One view is that a family is a group of humans with a biological linkage. This definition is the basis of the old adage "blood runs thicker than water" and depicts the essence of family as being passed from one generation to the next via heredity. Boszormenyi-Nagy and Spark (1973) have accentuated this view of family by ascribing the term "invisible loyalties" to relationships that have blood ties. Although this view has personal, clinical, and theoretical validity, it does not provide a broad enough base to contain all of family experiencing. For example, the view does not deal adequately with families that are created via adoption or through the merging of two or more biological families as in the case of remarried or blended families. Yet as was noted in Chapter 5, biological family ties are a key dimension of family life.

Another view of family is that it is a network of stresses which emanate out of emotional ties between the relating parties who conceive themselves to be a family. Carl Whitaker, eminent family therapist, uses the question "What's cookin?" to obtain a sense of the family. His view is that the nature of the family's stresses determines the family and defines its experience. If no stress is present, no family exists. Consequently, if you are feeling distraught because of tension or stress between yourself and other family members, you can be assured that you *are* in a family. That's another way of saying that stress is an accompanying trait of a family—it comes with the package.

A family is also a group of people traveling through the life cycle together with each person at a different stage. When you think about this definition you may come to the conclusion that a family is really a creative miracle. The fact that no two individuals, parents and children included, are ever at the same point in their individual development lays the groundwork for all kinds of potential hassles and misunderstandings. Yet families seem to overcome and accommodate to these differences in spite of the obvious variabilities in their individual members. This definition certainly affirms the resiliency and resourcefulness of families and raises the overall concept that differentness need not be a barrier to togetherness.

A corollary to the definition of family posed in the last paragraph is that a family is a mass of contradictions in which children are reared. We often ask clients if their parents ever contradicted themselves. This question usually produces a long list of parental discrepancies, inconsistencies, and hypocrisies that were experienced in the process of growing up. Yet most of us survive such injustices and when we become parents actually are thankful that our parents weren't perfect when we find ourselves being just as flawed as we rear our children. This definition surfaces the fact that individual acts do not make a family. If such were the case, our individual egos would be quite fragile and vulnerable; instead the overall character of the family solidifies its impact on the lives of the individual members. Also, families leave lots of room for error before they become detrimental to offspring.

Another definition of family is provided by the family in which you grew up. In that sense, all families are normal and normalizing. What I have experienced in my family is what family is to a greater or lesser degree. We certainly compare "our" family to other families and can modify what we don't like, but in many respects our personal family definition will be the one by which we live. We have found that family therapy is often a process of helping a family discover what their own definition is and once that is clear, they can act to live the definition or revise it to the benefit of family members.

Family is forever. This view of family sometimes feels like a burden that is too heavy to bear. This point means I am inextricably connected to my family despite any efforts I make to distance myself from them. This connection is almost as if a brand signifying our family of origin is inscribed on our foreheads at birth so no question can be made about our family connection. This view presents the indelible impact of our family emotionally and psychologically on us as persons, and emphasizes the seriousness of family as a force that cannot and should not be taken lightly. Consequently, going about my family business as responsibly and capably as I possibly can becomes imperative.

All families are both *for* the culture and *against* the culture (Minuchin, 1974). This definition places the family unit in a context and ascribes two counteracting dynamics which preserve the family's identity while being responsible for inducting its members into society at large. The family in one sense defines itself by differentiating its members from society, but at the same time teaches the family members how to be a part of society and to carry on the mores, norms, and values to which the society at large subscribes. This definition adds the element of a societal connection to the family. Families do not exist in a vacuum. They are influenced by the world around them and in return influence that world by sending individuals out to make that world what it is.

Finally, every family is unique. This idea may be obvious, but we have yet to talk with two families that are exactly alike. Some families are similar but never identical. Each family has its own combination of dynamics (pressures and tensions), relationships (alliances and coalitions), communication patterns (family language), roles, rules, history, memories, and values. Just coming to grips with the role of these elements in a family is a life-long process. Consequently, what you see in a family, your own or someone else's, is only a mere reflection of what the family is. So much more always can be found. This constant discovery is what makes families so exciting and scary at the same time. One of the things we often do is have each family member make a sculpture or picture of how he/she sees the family. Inevitably, every family member sees it differently. As this occurs, the family gets many views of itself from within, begins to realize its own identity, and creates its own answer to the question "What is a family."

THE FAMILY AS A SYSTEM

When two individuals choose to unite their lives in marriage, they create the foundation that family therapists call the nuclear family system. Their joining, referred to as the "crisis of marriage," requires that the two persons reorganize their individual lives in such a way that a two-person unit emerges. The more successful they are in doing so the more likely the result will be satisfaction in the marriage and ultimately in the family. Consequently, the marriage sets in motion a relational process that will be carried forward throughout the life of the family. That process is one of reorganizing in response to increasing complexity during the expanding years of the family experience and reorganizing in response to losses during the contracting years. This view of family is based on the definition of the family as a system.

Family therapists and family therapy in general have been responsible for applying a systems perspective to family life. The family is viewed as a number of parts related to each other in such a way that a change in one part affects all other parts. Translated into family dynamics that means families are confronted with reorganizing whenever parts are added as in the cases of marriage and the birth of children or when individual parts change as in the cases of spouses growing older and children growing up. Also, when parts are subtracted or lost, as in the case of family members dying or leaving home, changes occur in the family. For example, when a child is born, a two person system must reorganize itself into a three person system. Such reorganization is not always easy because child-birth is another system's crisis. The same holds true for each additional child that comes into the family. The family must change to accommodate or problems will ultimately arise. Such also is the case as children grow up. The family organization when children are babies is much different than when those babies are teenagers. What accounts for the family's ability to make these changes while still maintaining its overall identity and consistency as a family?

Homeostasis

The family system operates on the basis of two dynamic forces which alternately surface as dominant, counteracting each other in ways that enable a family (1) to accommodate to change without disintegrating, and (2) to prevent unwarranted or harmful changes from disrupting the family. The first force is called *homeostasis*. Homeostasis is the force within the family which acts to keep it from changing. Homeostasis functions to maintain the status quo and operates according to the *principle of equifinality*. Equifinality essentially means that whatever is introduced into the system is accomodated in such a way that the system itself does not have to change. A typical example of the homeostatic force that many of us have experienced is returning home after becoming an adult. Even after years away from the family and having independent lifestyles quite different from our parents, we find ourselves acting the same way we used to act when with our family. We sit in the same places around the dinner table and rely on mom to do the wash and iron for us. Many people bemoan the fact that they just don't act like themselves around their family. A likely explanation for that is the homeostatic mechanism.

Homeostasis is generally the dominant force in a family and accounts for the tendency for families not to change. In fact, we have a family therapy adage that says "if you want to know if a family exists, try to change it." The positive side of homeostasis is that it gives a family stability, security, and consistency. Homeostasis is the element that pulls families together in crisis and helps it weather the storms of change without falling apart. However, unchecked homeostasis also can be a damaging force creating rigidity in the family and preventing the family from having the necessary flexibility and elasticity to deal with the addition of or changes within family members. Consequently, a second force is necessary as a check and balance. That force is the dynamic of *morphogenesis*.

Morphogenesis

Morphogenesis is the force in the family which pushes a family to change. It is the dynamic which enables families to reorganize to accommodate to differences that occur throughout the life cycle of the family. In one sense families are continually changing and morphogenesis translates that changing into growth. Morphogenesis provides the elasticity necessary for individual differences to emerge in the family, but it also has a dangerous side. If left unchecked (change simply for the sake of change), chaos results. Families sometimes appear so disrupted and disorganized in counseling that the question of "Who's in charge here?" is very appropriate. Such families have become victimized by the morphogenetic force which enabled everyone to do their own thing without any consideration of the other family members. Homeostasis provides the check and balance to morphogenesis.

When these two forces work together in balance the family functions well. Homeostasis gives way to morphogenesis when change becomes necessary and then reasserts itself to translate the change into the status quo. Often times families have their most difficulty in the transition, that is either they have a hard time loosening up to let the change process occur or they have had a hard time stabilizing because change is occurring too rapidly. Other times families appear to be changing when they really aren't.

Example

> *Change But No Change. One family came for counseling because the oldest daughter could not adjust to the high school in the town to which the family had moved. She was pressuring her parents to allow her to attend a private school as the solution. In the course of working with this family, the fact became apparent that although the family appeared to be changing due to relocating geographically and the daughter going into high school, the actual organization of the family was such that the daughter was still being treated as a child. Her lack of adjustment to the high school and request to go away to school was her signal to her parents that she wanted their permission to grow up. This family had trapped the daughter in a childhood mode which was held in place by the homeostatic force in spite of superficial physical changes.*

In contrast to families that have difficulty changing are families that are in a constant state of flux. They have problems producing feelings of safety, security, belongingness, and rootedness. One of the hypotheses submitted in explanation of the rash of teenage suicides in Plano, Texas had to do with the high rate of transiency among the corporate families who populated that community (Gelman, 1983). Due to extensive mobility, children were unable to establish strong friendships, a sense of identity among peers, or a sense of roots. These families live by a morphogenetic norm that mobility is necessary for advancement but pay a steep price in terms of forming roots in a community network that gives sufficient depth to combat feelings of isolation and loneliness under duress.

Sub-Systems

Each family system is composed of sub-systems once children arrive on the scene. Essentially, two sub-systems exist although any combination of two or more parts within the family could be construed as a sub-system. However, most families have at least two: the adult sub-system (AS) and the sibling sub-system (SS). The AS is basically composed of the marital pair as parents and any other adults that play a significant role in the affairs of the family. The SS is composed of the children. While the adults essentially must carve out their roles as spouses in relation to each other and parents in relation to the children, the children must carve out their roles in relation to the parents and to each other. Hence, dynamics emerge which are referred to as *sibling rivalry*. Each child faces the task of differentiating from the others and must figure out how to garner the attention of the parents in his/her own special way. The children are assisted in their work by the dynamics of their birth order and sex which we have already described in our discussion of family constellation in Chapter 5. The product of sibling rivalry is the individual identity of each child as a person first in the family and later in the world outside the family.

As the struggle for role definition occurs in each of the two sub-systems, the natural inclination emerges to drag members from the other sub-system onto your side to increase your clout. For example, one parent will try to use a child or the children to persuade the other parent to do or not to do something. Children will try to get a parent to take their side in a quarrel with a sibling. Such movements (i.e., parents into the sibling sub-system and children into the adult sub-system) are quite common. However, if not kept in check, the whole system can become upset and disoriented with children inappropriately functioning as adults and adults inappropriately acting as children. In counseling, we view the tendency of the sibling sub-system to form a coalition against the adult sub-system as a healthy sign of closeness among siblings and parents respectively representing,a clear differentiation of children from adults.

The process of drawing a third family member into the interaction between two family members is called *triangulation*. When triangles become the basic unit of family functioning the family is usually in trouble. The most likely member of the family to be triangulated either by choice or by being chosen is mother. A common complaint of many mothers is that they feel like a switchboard in the family through which all other members communicate. Certainly the keys to effective family functioning are to keep the adult and sibling sub-systems clearly differentiated and to avoid using the triangle as a basic relating pattern.

Super-System

One other system needs mentioning at this point and that is the super-system. The super-system refers to the world outside the family system. Every family exists in an environment which impacts upon the family and with which members of the family must interact. Family members move out of the family system and into the super-system and back again. Work, school, neighborhood, church, community organizations, and so forth all compose the super-system. As each family member leaves and returns, the family is affected. How the family chooses to relate to the super-system as a unit is also crucial. In any case a continual interaction exists between the two which affects family life and functioning. How that interaction occurs and how sub-systems relate to one another have to do with family *boundaries*.

BOUNDARIES AND FAMILIES

Boundaries define the nature of interaction in families. They determine who relates to whom and how. Boundaries are important because of their relational implications. On the positive side they facilitate contact, protect family members from intrusion, and provide a basis for security and predictability in the family. On the negative side boundaries can create obstacles and interfere with contact and communication, directly creating either distancing phenomena or overinvolvement. Boundaries are essentially the rules, expectations, patterns, guidelines and roles by which a family functions. Such boundaries may be either spoken and explicit (verbally stated in the family) or unspoken and implicit (never verbalized but fully recognized as the way things are done in the family). Most families have both spoken and unspoken rules, but some families have more of one than the other. For example, families which rely extensively on spoken rules may have a high level of communication but also may overwhelm family members by the sheer number of rules to which members must adhere. In contrast, families which live by unspoken rules manifest considerable family loyalty (only family members know) but develop an indirect communication style that interferes with forming direct and intimate contact between family members.

Types of Boundaries

Three types of boundaries apply to families. The first is *clear* boundary depicted graphically in Figure 8.1. In relationships with clear boundary channels of communicaiton are established and clearly understood. Relating parties know how to gain access to one another and are welcomed in doing so. But also areas of designated privacy are respected and not intruded upon. Consequently access is available but so is separateness.

Figure 8.1. Clear boundary.

The second type of boundary is referred to as the *enmeshed* boundary (Figure 8.2). In enmeshed relationships, no distinctions are made. The atmosphere is almost as if no restriction exists between relating parties in their access to one another. All boundaries are diffused, everything is open, and fusion with its corresponding loss of individuality results. Although relating parties are inseparable, giving a sense of belonging and support, no privacy is present. Over time, for one to function without the other becomes impossible.

Figure 8.2. Enmeshed boundary.

The third type of boundary depicted in Figure 8.3 is the *disengaged* boundary. In disengaged relationships all channels of communication are cut off. Access is restricted and no avenue of contact is available. Relating is characterized by distance, and walls are built psychologically between relating parties. Over time total loss of contact occurs signalling the demise of the relationship.

Figure 8.3. Disengaged boundary.

Family Organizational Patterns

Using these boundary concepts we can then describe a sample of family organizational patterns that emerge over time. The most healthy family pattern is the family with clear boundaries (Figure 8.4). In these families freedom of movement and communication can be found. Members can move in and out of contact with one another and in and out of the family without creating tension, disruption, or confusion. Children have access to parents and vice versa and anytime an emergency arises access to one another is obtained without difficulty. Because the family has clear boundaries within and between itself and the super-system, it maintains a clear identity while still interacting effectively in the surrounding world. Parents can go about their business of being adults (going to work or socializing) and children can go to school or develop peer relationships without jeopardizing the family. Balance of time in the family and out of the family is valued as not only meaningful but necessary. A six year old can go to school or a teenager to college causing some stress or requiring readjustment but the individuals still feel a sense of support and belonging.

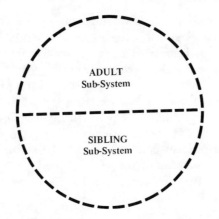

Figure 8.4. Family with clear boundary.

Some families organize themselves utilizing enmeshed boundaries. They place a premium on togetherness and view any movement away from or out of the family as a threat to the family's well-being. These *families naturally coalesce into what Murray Bowen (1966) called an un-differentiated ego mass* in which no one individual stands out, only the family. Because these families are so threatened by anyone moving out of the family, they tend to place a disengaged boundary around themselves, thus isolating themselves from interacting with the super-system. Figure 8.5 illustrates this point.

Figure 8.5. The enmeshed family.

When children are young, a natural tendency to become enmeshed is present because babies and toddlers need the watchful eye and care of parents. Parents experience motivating and magnetizing pulls toward the child because of the joy and excitement he/she represents. These pulls usually dissipate, however, as the child begins to flex his/her autonomy muscles and pushes for independence. However, if the enmeshed state becomes the norm, the child will have difficulty leaving the family to go to school. If continued further, the family will experience an even greater crisis when the adolescent child attempts to strike out away from the family. In an enmeshed family, usually only dad is given permission to leave. He may go off to his work place but then must scurry home immediately afterward. All other exits are blocked.

The enmeshed family provides an intensive experience of togetherness but little individuation is encouraged. The sad result is that when children grow up they are faced with essentially only two choices: either bolt and be cut off from the family or sacrifice their individuality to the altar of family conformity. However, internal elements do their best to prevent this extensive enmeshment from occurring. First, the natural growth process of children produces pressures on the family to become more flexible since each child ultimately strives for autonomy and independence. Second, the super-system pressures the family to release members to contribute to the larger society. Children must go to school, adults to work, and the family must play its part in the neighborhood or community. Thus, the exaggerated scenario as depicted in this brief description usually does not materialize.

A third type of family organization is the disengaged family (Figure 8.6). In these families communication has broken down to the point where little contact occurs between family members. Home becomes little more than a place to hang your hat. Walls between members become so impenetrable and intimacy is so absent that family members immerse themselves in the world outside the family.

Example

The Disengaged Family. We worked with one family of a disengaged nature where the dad was a workaholic spending up to 70 hours on his job. Mom had taken to drinking and had become an alcoholic. The oldest son was a member of a delinquent gang, and the daughter had gotten pregnant at age 14. The reason the family presented for therapy was because the daughter would not tell anyone who the father of her child was.

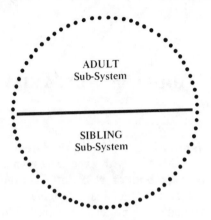

Figure 8.6. The disengaged family.

Disengaged families draw enmeshed boundaries around themselves enabling family members to get outside the family what they cannot get inside the family. Family members manifest extensive autonomy and independence but learn little about developing intimacy and belongingness. Times occur in the family life cycle when families may be more disengaged than other times. For example, parents with teenagers or young adults may feel like they are merely keeping a boarding house with a revolving door. The tendency for everyone to go his/her own way during that phase of family life is strong. Yet, in spite of the strong thrust away from family, a good family time can be had by all when parents have the fortitude to say "We will do (name activity) together on (state time and day)" instead of asking for suggestions and trying to gain consensus. Such a tactic, however, must be used judiciously.

We have given you a brief review of the continuum of polarities relative to types of family organizations. And certainly, all kinds of degrees of organization are found between enmeshed and disengaged. We have also identified the ideal to be strived for in the sense of healthy family relating. Yet families are more than just types of organization. They have a very personal impact upon each new member who is introduced into it. The family is essentially responsible for providing an arena in which each child's identity is formed and developed. Consequently, the type of family system you, as parents, create will determine the nature of the child's experience and ultimately the nature of the child's identity.

THE INDIVIDUAL IN THE FAMILY SYSTEM

When a child is brought into a family the parents acquire the responsibility of providing that child with experiences which can be differentiated into two categories, both of which influence the development of a child's identity. The first category is *belongingness* and the second is *separateness*. Belongingness responds to the need to love and be loved in the child and conveys the message that they are valued for who they are and not what they do. Belongingness is foundational to personality development. Family members realize that no matter what happens they always belong to the family. Belongingness provides protection, security, and a sense of being worthwhile in spite of occurrences outside the family. Some psychologists fear, however, that with the rising divorce rate and the exodus of both parents to the work place, children's belongingness experiences are being eroded. Urie Bronfenbrenner (1977), a noted child psychologist, has stated "the psychological development of the child is brought about through his continuing involvement in progressively more complex patterns of reciprocal activity with persons with whom the child develops a strong and enduring emotional attachment" (p.11). He also said that this bond is an "irrational emotional attachment" which can only be developed by experiencing many interactions with the same person. The loss of quantity time interactions due to the availability of only one parent or because both work can discourage the development of intimacy which in turn will undermine continuity, the link of belonging between those who come before and those who come after in families (Bradt, 1980, p. 126).

As children experience belongingness, they learn to identify with the family unit and develop a sense of loyalty and connectedness. They also develop the capacity to relate effectively with others as well as having their need to love and be loved met. If belongingness experiences are overemphasized in the family, the child loses the opportunity to develop individuality and uniqueness. Over time, the exclusive emphasis on belongingness results in an enmeshed family system with all the negative ramifications already discussed.

Separateness experiences enable a child to develop autonomy, independence and self responsibility. He/she produces an identity that is characterized by self-confidence and the ability to function on the basis of his/her own recognizance. If separateness is over-emphasized, however, the child loses his/her sense of intimacy and closeness, ultimately losing the capability of becoming intimate and functioning cooperatively in a group. Over time, the emphasis on separateness will result in a disengaged family system leading to dispersion of the family into the super-system.

An interesting phenomenon we have observed in marital counseling is that children reared in each of the above described ways tend to find each other in marriage. Like magnets, the person raised on a diet of separateness is attracted to the intimacy and closeness of the person who was force fed on belongingness. The person reared in the enmeshed environment finds the autonomy of the person reared in the disengaged setting attractive. Each appears to have his/her needs met in the other. In marriage, however, they each find themselves reverting to their former patterns, and when each is unable to convert the other, the marriage collapses.

Traditionally, families have tended to emphasize belongingness experiences more for females, providing them with less encouragement to achieve, be assertive, or venture out into the world in a career. In contrast boys were more likely to experience an emphasis in separateness being encouraged to achieve and be career oriented. This tendency has produced need deficits in both men and women. Contemporary parenting needs to create an equitable balance for both male and female children enabling them to fully develop both aspects of their personalities. Consequently, family systems that strike a balance between belongingness and separateness produce the most healthy identity in children. Family members are enabled to be both intimate and autonomous which sets the stage for their creating families in the same vein. Families with clear boundaries generally provide offspring with that balance.

Before leaving the family systems view, we would like to share with you the metaphor of the family as an orchestra as presented by Salvatore Minuchin at a workshop conducted at the Philadelphia Child Guidance

Clinic in March, 1980. Each person in a family is like an instrument in an orchestra which can play the same note or different notes. If all the instruments play the same note all the time, the music will be dull and pedantic. It will be simplistic and unstimulating. If the instruments play different notes, the notes may be either harmonious or discordant. However, if they always play different notes particularly when discordant, the music will be chaotic, tense, and displeasing. Yet when, the instruments play the same notes some of the time and different notes in harmony some of the time, the music will not only be exciting and stimulating but personally and aesthetically pleasing. Total sameness (enmeshment) or total discord (disengagement) are pathological in families. Our hope is that you will strive to develop an orchestra where each instrument is appreciated for its contribution and can play the family melody, at times in unison and at other times in harmony. And that like a conductor, you will treat discord as a signal to work harder to refine your family symphony which when performed will ring with excitement and life resulting in fulfillment to you and your musicians.

PARENTING:
THE BACKBONE OF FAMILY LIFE

No matter how many ways you attempt to define family, the definition usually involves children, and when children are involved, the deduction is that you are a parent. One frustrated father made the comment in a family session that "children wouldn't be so bad if you didn't have to parent them." Little doubt exists that children bring out the best and worst in us and that how we handle the task of parenting to a large degree determines the nature of the family. We need to stress once again, the importance of the marriage to effective parenting. We may call parenting the backbone of family life, but the marriage is the marrow that gives that backbone its strength.

Although you may never have spent extensive amounts of time and energy contemplating the nature of an ideal parent, likely you have visualized yourself as such at some point. Each of us has probably vowed never to do some of the things our parents did. We determined to learn from their mistakes with us or our "spoiled" brothers and sisters. We likely committed ourselves to approach child rearing with the "correct" formulation of love, communication, permissiveness, and discipline. Our children would experience the proper balance between a feeling of belongingness and a sense of accomplished separateness making us proud of their achievements in the super-system. The children would have many experiences of family togetherness as you would congenially play games, read together, and take off on this or that family vacation or outing. If your parents didn't provide you with the travel experiences for which you yearned, you would make certain that your children "saw the world." If your dad was too involved with his work, you would make sure time would be spent throwing the baseball or football, coaching the kids' teams, or watching their games.

All these ideas sound wonderful but the bubble bursts when the real family experience arrives. Why are so many parents frustrated and exasperated by the experience called parenthood? Could we possibly underestimate the power of children to confound even the most consistent, intelligent, firm, and enlightened parents? Has the world changed once again making parenting a whole different ballgame? Now the game of parenting is being played in a domed stadium on astroturf instead of outside on the good old sod. Furthermore, the rules have changed and to top it all off we find ourselves looking and acting more like our parents with each passing day. If your mom screamed at you, and you swore you would never do that to your children, why does your voice produce a piercing sound before you even have a chance to stop it? In some respects parenting is a real enigma because the best laid plans and the sincerest intentions fall by the wayside in the press of family action. Some solace can be found in comments like "a good parent learns to love being hated" or "parents have to endure the pain of parenting in order for children to benefit." But such epithets are hardly sufficient to assuage the frustration.

Yet a balance does exist. Being a parent provides the greatest experiences of love and joy. It gives a sense of fulfillment and always makes life more real. Parenting is the only experience we know where you can go from the height of joy to the depth of despair and back again in less than a minute. In the next few pages we would like to share with you some observations and ideas about the three basic components of parenting: mothering, fathering, and the parental dyad. Before we do that, however, we would like to set the tone for our discussion by having you read Kahlil Gibran's (1951) poem "On Children".

Your children are not your children.
They are the sons and daughters of Life's longing for itself.
They come through you but not from you, and though
    they are with you yet they belong not to you.

You may give them your love but not your thoughts,
    for they have their own thoughts.
You may house their bodies but not their souls,
    for their souls dwell in the house of tomorrow,
    which you cannot visit, not even in your dreams.
You may strive to be like them, but seek not to
    make them like you
For life goes not backward nor tarries with yesterday.

You are the bows from which your children as
    living arrows are sent forth.
The archer sees the mark upon the path of the
    infinite and He bends you with His might that
    His arrows may go swift and far.
Let your bending in the archer's hand be for gladness;
For even as He loves the arrow that flies, so He
    loves also the bow that is stable.

                    (Gibran, 1951, pp.17-18)

Mothering: The Pull Toward Overinvolvement

Motherhood is going through a metamorphosis of sorts. Go to any supermarket where you can observe young mothers shopping with their preschoolers. They will be clad in jeans or jogging suits or will be wearing the attire of a career woman squeezing in a run to the store between office, day care center, and home. These scenes are hardly the images of mothers from years gone by when moms wore housedresses and only dressed up for going out. Contemporary mothers are slim, physically active, and frequently as involved in a career as they are in the home. Have things really changed or has just the uniform changed? Children still need to be reared and that is a tough all-consuming task. Whether working outside the home or not, women are still the center of the family and the emotional barometers of family ups and downs. They feel for and with every other member of the family. They basically run the household. Studies indicate that in spite of the massive reentry of women into the work force, women are still held responsible for the housework (Brozman, 1980). Has anything changed or has more just been added?

Motherhood. The thoughts of motherhood no longer call up the image of a fulfilled woman happily ensconced in her home with her children and an attentive husband who lets her know what a good job she is doing. The fairy tale ending of living happily ever after is now a point of ridicule. A recent interview of high school girls on their feelings about mothers and motherhood indicated that although the girls deeply respected and admired their mothers (some of whom were single parents), they did not want that kind of life for themselves. They did not want to marry until they had established careers, and a surprising number did not want to have children at all (Roisinger, 1984). This attitude is also reflected in current U.S. Census data (U.S. Bureau of the Census, 1984a) on fertility of American women. In 1983, 27% of ever-married women in the 25 to 29 age group were still childless as compared to 16% of that same group in 1970. Looking farther ahead, twice as many women in the 30 to 34 ever-married group were still childless as compared to the 1970 comparable age group. Is information such as this cause for concern or commendation?

On one hand a more realistic appraisal of motherhood and its lifelong commitment is a good sign. Yet, on the other hand, the fact that motherhood is no longer considered an appealing life's calling is very sad. Society has done much to change that. In spite of the fact that men report more satisfaction in their marriages if wives remain at home and many women would choose to do so, the role of housewife and mother is looked down upon by a society that places more value on careers outside the home. If you want to check this out, do a little eavesdropping at any social gathering where people are getting acquainted. Notice how women at home are apologetic for being "just a housewife." Notice how husbands are proud of a wife's unmarried sister who has pursued a career or a Ph.D. but find themselves groping for something to say about their wives who are in the home and the mothers of their children. Notice how women who are at home are impressed by another mother who works or has a career. A regretable commentary on our society is that one of life's hardest jobs gets so little recognition.

ACTIVITY: Considering the Role of Motherhood

As you and your partner think about motherhood and consider the option of the mother remaining at home for some period of time after the birth of children, make a point to talk with women who have made this a positive decision. Find out how they deal with society's attitudes, what resources and networks they have developed, how they meet their need for adult interaction, and what part their husbands play. Share and discuss with your partner your concepts and opinions regarding motherhood. Would your partner like for the wife to stay at home as a convenience, or does your partner consider being a housewife a meaningful life choice? How will the decision to stay home affect the family economic picture? A good suggestion is to get the ramifications of becoming a one income family clear if you have developed a life style that is contingent on two incomes. Preparation for having less before children come is preferable to getting bitter about having less after they arrive.

Overinvolvement. One of the major problems of motherhood is the issue of overinvolvement. Children's demands, the tendency of husbands to disengage from the family and a mother's natural enabling behaviors have left women so strung out that they have no room for personal growth. Children and family can quite easily become a woman's whole life. In fact, the fear of that destiny is one of the deterrents to having children for women today.

Example

Becoming a Mother Is Risky. One young couple who came into therapy because they were battling over when to start their family spent weeks and weeks negotiating the conditions for having children. even creating a written contract with consequences for the husband not following through. He wanted to start a family now, and she wanted to wait, being immersed in a fulfilling careeer and also wanting to complete gradute school before having children. When the time came to sign the contract, she got cold feet. She admitted that the real reason she didn't want to have children was because of her fear that after having a child, her mothering instincts would emerge so strongly that they would wipe out her desires for a career and graduate school, goals which had already consumed the greater portion of her twenty-eight years. She just was not willing to take that chance.

Many women who come to therapy are caught in the throes of trying to achieve a balance between their own personal needs and those of the family members, husbands included. The situation becomes especially tense when adolescent children become critical of their mothers and seem to refute all of the care, training, and emotional investment she has made in them over the years. When she reminds them of their ingratitude or begins pursuit of her own interests sometimes to the exclusion of their needs, both mothers and children begin to take on a negative view of motherhood. This includes younger children in the family who also are being forced into the readjustments of an adolescent family with less mother availability. The following is an example of a family we saw in therapy where the mother went from extreme overinvolvement to extreme underinvolvement.

Example

Mother Flip Flop. The presenting problem was a daughter in junior high, who was acting out in school and had been threatening suicide. The family consisted of seven children, three of whom were grown, one who had been killed in a childhood accident, and three who were still at home. The father was a recovering alcoholic and mother was emotionally bankrupt after having given her all to her husband and the first set of children. Since she had little left to give in the home, she started a career as the owner of a small business, immersing herself fully in the business. When she pulled out of the home, the three teenage children left at home began placing demands on the parents for family involvement (an action that is quite contrary to the stereotypic adolescent). Therapy consisted of reattaching mom to the family in a manner that would prevent a recurrence of motherhood burnout, enabling mother to build herself up outside the family, but still be available to the children during their critical adolescent years.

Mothers will often come to a female therapist in pursuit of a role model while at the same time fearing that therapy will push them toward a career when that is not what they want or need. On the other hand, a push toward career is just what some women want to help them deal with a resistant husband. In this case the therapist legitimizes the woman's inclination to get out of the house. Both of these examples point to the fact that shifting away from being an overinvolved mother is not an easy task.

In working with families where mom has become overinvolved, the problem is not just a matter of getting dad to fill in the spaces being vacated by mom, but also a matter of getting mom to give up her position of sole caretaker, especially when dad is not likely to do things the way she does. A woman's idea of how a home should be run is likely quite established and she finds difficulty in pulling back and letting him do things his way. Husbands who make a serious effort to become more involved tend to give up in sheer frustration. Instead of making "how things are done" another arena of conflict or simply letting things go back to the way they were, work on negotiating clear role expectations considering each other's expertise and perceptions. Cultivate understanding and acceptance rather than criticism which results in resentment and bitterness. On one hand a wife needs to recognize and acknowledge her husband's willingness and efforts to be more active in running the home. On the other hand, a husband needs to accept the wife's expertise in the domestic sphere and not see her efforts to instruct or guide as criticism.

Joys. Despite the above commentary, the joys of motherhood are manifold. Those joys have been captured in poetry, literature, art, and photography. Even fathers who have opted to become househusbands attest to the specialness of being intimately involved with every change, every event, every step of growth and achievement that occurs in the family, being first to see it, hear it, and share it. A vast difference exists between being there and hearing about it second hand in the evening when it is already old news. Being the primary caretaker has its tradeoffs, but also involves emotional experiences that produce intense joy as well as frustration. Some mothers, who choose to be primary caretakers and want to see their children grow up, assume the attitude that they are doing it for themselves and not necessarily "for their children." Motherhood is what they want not what they owe or must do. Consequently, they don't feel cheated when their children forget to express gratitude for mom's great sacrifice. If a woman begins to feel like a pawn instead of a queen in her family, she must be helped to realize she can make any of the moves necessary to survive the onslaughts of forces which may result in her undoing. She must mobilize her own resources and those in her family to insure her own personal fulfillment as she carries out her place in the family in whatever form that might take.

Fathering: It's More Than an Act

A couple years ago Jim was asked to give an address to the Wisconsin State Convention of the American Association of University Women on the topic of fathering. When he informed Toni of the invitation, adding a prideful comment about their wanting an expert on the subject, Toni casually replied, "Then why did they ask you?" Consequently, the first principle that emerged about fathering was that if you want a man to really get serious about his fathering, ask him to give a talk on it. The second major discovery was that if you make a man an expert in public on fathering, his wife will make him accountable in private.

Men have always been eager to get into the act of fathering on the beginning end (i.e., the biblical act of fathering in King James English is so and so "knew" his wife and "begat" so and so), but seem to lose their inspiration once the children arrive. Comments like "I'll wait until my child has a little personality" epitomize the tendency to let mom do the work of child-rearing. All too often by the time that "little personality" is present, dad has created a lifestyle in which children do not conveniently fit.

Images of Father. All of you know something about fathers, having had your own, watching your friends' fathers, and possibly being one yourself. But if you do not have a handle on what fathers are really like, let's look at some of the images presented in the media. Image one is the eager beaver dad who rushes home from work to greet his wife and children with exuberance and an enthusiastic readiness to do things with the kids that are exciting and fun. Forget about the image you have of dad arriving home dead tired and grouchy, mumbling hello, and then grabbing a beer or a martini and the newspaper never to be heard from until supper time. Also forget the household rule about never talking to dad until after supper (when he is supposedly relaxed). Also forget about dad's after supper disappearing act where he magically dematerializes and reemerges in his workshop, study, or out in the yard.

Image two is the dad who works hard during the week to provide for the family but devotes his weekends *entirely* to his family. Forget about the golf, fishing trips, home projects, and lawn care that use his weekend time and in which he engages only occasionally (3 to 4 weekends a month) for his own mental health.

Image three is what we call the "Hallmark father." Recall the commercial where an 18 or 19 year old daughter is leaving for college and Dad hands her a card which she reads, tears welling up in her eyes. She turns to him and says, "Dad, you finally said it." Don't think about questions like "Where was he during the first 18 years of her life?" and "Why didn't he say it before?"

These images raise the question, "What is the real picture of father?" Research and clinical practice have indicated that the typical American family in which two parents are involved is characterized by dads being on the periphery either by choice or because mom wants it that way or both. A study of middle class fathers with newborn infants found that they spent an average of 37.24 seconds per day attending directly to the baby (Howard, 1978, p. 37). Based on these kinds of data, American families have been described as "fatherless" not because of death or divorce but because of father absence.

Dad's Role. The typical life cycle of the American family is that mom raises the kids with dad's blessing while he is off "providing" for the family. (Translated that means he is advancing his career and preserving his own mental health.) However, as things get a little tough with the kids at home, mom calls on dad for support and power. He gets the privilege of becoming the "heavy" and his kids curiously begin to see him not only as distant but as the executioner. They view him as mom's heavy artillery in the parent/child war. Dad begins to wonder why his kids don't like him and why he doesn't experience their love and respect.

From the child's perspective, Dad appears too busy, too distant, too tired, and too dangerous to be approached. One father, made aware of this viewpoint by his child wrote the following verses:

I Wish My Daddy Was A Dog

One day when Bruce was just a lad
First starting out in school,
He came into my workshop
And climbed upon a stool.
I saw him as he entered
But I hadn't time to play.
So I merely nodded to him
And said, "Don't get in the way."

He sat a while just thinking...
As quiet as could be.
Then carefully he got down
And came and stood by me.
He said, "Old Shep, he never works
And he has lots of fun.

He runs around the meadows
And barks up at the sun.

He chases after rabbits
And always scares the cats.
He likes to chew on old shoes
And sometimes mother's hats.
But when we're tired of running
And we sit down on a log,
I sometimes get to thinking...
'I wish my Daddy was a dog.'

Cause then when I come home from school,
He'd run and lick my hand.
And we could jump and holler
And tumble in the sand.
And then I'd be so happy—
As happy as could be,
'Cause we would play the whole day through,
Just my Dad and me.

Now I know you work real hard
To buy us food and clothes.
And you need to get the girls
Those fancy ribbons and bows.
But sometimes when I'm lonesome
I think 'twould be lots of fun,
If my Daddy was a dog,
And all his work was done."
Now when he'd finished speaking,
He looked so lonely there,
I reached my hand out to him
And ruffled up his hair.
And as I turned my head aside
To brush away a tear,
I thought how nice it was
To have my son so near.

I know the Lord didn't mean for man
To toil his whole life through,
"Come on, my son
I'm sure I have some time for you."
You should have seen the joy
And sunlight in his eye,
As we went outside to play—
Just my son and I.

Now, as the years have flown
And youth has slipped away,
I've tried always to remember
To allow some time to play.

When I pause to reminisce
And think of joys and strife,
I carefully turn the pages
Of this wanderer's book of life.

I find the richest entry
Recorded in this daily log,
Is the day that small boy whispered,
"I wish my Daddy was a dog."

Elrod C. Leany
(Reprinted by permission)

Evolution and Revolution of Fathering. The state of fatherhood is changing. In fact, fathering is such a hot topic that a Newsweek article dubbed fathering the "New Family Romance of the 80's" (Langway, 1981). The romance is both evolutionary and revolutionary and extends from pre-natal involvement to grandfathering.

In the evolutionary domain the whole process of having babies is being revised. Our own experience attests to this evolution. When our first child, Traci, was born, Jim went through the "waiting room scene" anxiously awaiting the news. The doctor finally entered the waiting room, gave a hearty handshake, and said "Congratulations, it's a girl and Toni is doing fine." By the time Daniel came around we had a doctor who was caught in the cross-currents of change in the medical profession. He finally consented to allowing Jim to watch the delivery through the door of the delivery room. When Benjamin was born, Jim donned the medical garb and sat next to Toni and had the newborn placed in his arms immediately after birth. Now husband and wife can move into a birthing suite and process the full gamut of the birth experience together. Other couples also are opting for home births facilitated by professional midwifes instead of the hospital/obstetrician scene. Research and our own experience have indicated that the father-child bonding is maximized by increasing dad's involvement from the very start of the child's life.

The revolutionary aspect of the fathering process has to do with the discovery that men can be nurturers. Over the centuries men have always wanted to be and considered themselves to be great lovers, but have had difficulty in doing a great job of loving, particularly when it came to caring for their children. Men are beginning to realize that they can and even want to be more involved with their children at a caring level. Not surprisingly, a major impetus for this shift has come from single parent fathers. More than one million children who live in the United States are currently being reared exclusively by their fathers. A common complaint we hear from divorced mothers is "my ex-husband is a much better father now than when we were married. If he had taken more time with the kids then maybe we wouldn't have had so much trouble." Sometimes the trauma of divorce with its subsequent loss of child contact time awakens the nurturant side of dad.

The movie *Kramer vs. Kramer* emphatically dramatized the fathering dynamics just described. But interestingly enough the need for fathers to be nurturers and involved in rearing their children has long been documented. The Apostle Paul, often criticized for the imprisonment of women in subservient roles wrote, "Fathers, bring your children up in the nurture and admonition of the Lord" (Ephesians, 6:4). The fact appears to be that men have actually erred from this directive in two ways: first turning over the "bringing up" to their wives and also stressing the admonition (discipline) over the nurturing.

Fathers, however, are getting increased assistance in changing their image. Programs such as the Fatherhood Project in New York City have been developed to encourage greater male involvement in childrearing. Courses are being taught such as "Oh Boy-Babies" for pre-adolescent boys, "For Fathers Only" for fathers and their toddlers, and "Father and His Baby" for fathers and their newborns. The idea of fathers being involved in the family is rapidly becoming not only respectable but also the norm.

Studies are beginning to emerge that document the impact of this shift in fathering. One study indicated that children who were frequently cuddled and cared for by their fathers were better able to withstand stress and adapt to outsiders. They also learned more easily. Studies of successful women often indicate that they had strong supportive fathers (Langway, 1981). Gerald Zuk (1975) has summarized the impact of this change as follows:

> While members of the women's liberation movement might not take kindly to my explanation of why father-alienation and father absence cause behavior disturbances in children (i.e., children are poorly prepared for life outside the home) I think they would agree that the society is dominated by male values; that women face a serious handicap competing with men and that there is a deep sense of frustration and antagonism in women. It will be good for children to have their mothers less frustrated and antagonistic toward society when measures are taken to equalize their opportunity. But it will be equally good for

children when the society takes further steps to discourage father alienation, father separation, and father absence. (p. 23)

However, problems with fathers becoming more prominent in the family still remain. For one thing, men still have a tendency to be all talk and no action when the domestic scene is the issue. Studies continue to indicate that although men consider it reasonable and right for fathers to share the tasks of child-rearing and housework, actual doing lags far behind the stated ideal. Dads also are famous for the "quality time cop-out" approach to child-rearing. Because their schedule and responsibilities are so heavy, they resolve to spend quality time with their children. We often challenge fathers to apply that same principle to their work life and their personal interests such as hobbies, exercise, and diet. The fact is, *fathering must be a high enough priority to produce quantity time because quality time is a product of quantity time not its substitute.*

The final obstacle to fathering is mom. Studies and our clinical practice indicate that more often than not working moms opt for the "super-woman" approach (doing it all) rather than negotiating a co-parenting arrangement with dad. Moms who don't work outside the home feel threatened by dad's entry into what they consider their domain fearing that if they give anything up they will lose their place in the family and their sense of self-worth. Consequently, while dad has a problem making himself get involved, mom has a problem letting go. We have come to the conclusion that *just as women need assertiveness training in the workplace, men need assertiveness training at home.*

A common scenario we see in the struggle of getting dad involved in the family occurs as follows: Mom wants dad to be more involved in the home so she can have more time for herself. Dad sees this request as simply making her job easier but under pressure accommodates. When he goes along with doing more, mom either pulls back or ups the ante, either frustrating dad or overwhelming him. So the struggle continues. However, if dad can come to the point of wanting to be involved himself and can realize that mom has a problem letting go, a satisfactory resolution can be attained.

If you are a male, our hope is that you will do your part to carry on this evolution and revolution in fathering. We believe that doing so will not only contribute meaningfully to your children's development but that it will accentuate your marital relationship and give you a deep sense of personal fulfillment.

The Parenting Dyad:
United We Stand, Divided We Fall

We realize that this time honored battle cry was not intended to be a motto for parents, but it certainly applies to the parenting experience. Although we have emphasized the importance of mother and father, the combination of the two is the answer to effective parenting and fulfilling family life. In the age old struggle between parents and children, certain facts exist. For example, in a conflict between one child and one parent, the odds favor the child. In a conflict between two parents and a child, the odds slightly favor the parents. This is the reason that families were intended to have two parents. This is also why children expend inordinate amounts of energy in devising strategies to prevent parents from being together. Children learn quickly that in a conflict between a child and two parents who disagree the advantage goes to the child without question.

One of the biggest obstacles to effective parenting is that parents contribute to their own stress by engaging in conflict over how to parent rather than negotiating a mutual approach and forming a co-parenting team. A number of well known parenting principles exist which most parents know but have difficulty implementing that emphasize the value of the team approach. First of all, a united front provides the most effective means of coping with the stresses of child rearing generated by a child's natural inclination to expand his/her boundaries. Second, a united front prevents the parenting issue from encroaching on the marriage or undermining the bond of caring and respect. Third, a united front, although not desirable in the child's eyes is a source of the child's security. That security emanates not from the parents' love and respect for the child but from the parents' love and respect for each other.

How to attain a united front, however, is the problem. Some parents in their resolve not to appear separated make a rule never to fight in front of their children. As noted in Chapter 7, such a rule is both unrealistic and unhealthy for the children because they never learn how to resolve conflict when it arises. A more appropriate guideline is "you can fight about just about almost anything in front of the children *except* the children." Negotiations relative to child rearing may be conducted within the confines of the marital pair where each can express his/her views when different without providing ammunition to the children. When an agreement is reached then the resolve to stand together is more likely. Negotiating an equitable or satisfactory approach to a child situation in the heat of the battle of wills or upon impulse is difficult to do. A better idea is to have developed mutual guidelines in anticipation of events rather than in reaction to them.

Parents who desire to form a working parental coalition need to learn three simple phrases. The first is "I don't know." Often a child pressures a parent or parents to provide information or explanation on an immediacy basis. If such is lacking, avoid the temptation of shooting from the hip. Instead of appearing to know when you really don't, indicate to your child that you do not know but will find out if you can.

The second phrase that parents have difficulty with is "I was wrong." Since our parental egos tend to be fragile anyway, we have a tendency to try to cover, deny, or rationalize our mistakes. Children tend to be much more responsive (and forgiving) when parents admit (own) their errors. At the same time, children learn to do the same by following the parents' example.

The third phrase has to do with children's requests for an immediate decision. The key phrase here is "I'll check it out and get back to you." Mothers especially need to learn this statement. Because of their greater proximity to children, mothers often get pressured to make decisions when dad is not around and then catch it in the neck from dad for deciding without him. If this phrase is used often enough, children will soon get the picture that the position relative to decisions is going to be a mutual one and urgent requests will lessen. Children also will learn to plan ahead. We realize that following this approach all the time is impossible but, if the "I'll check" rule is the norm, fewer conflicts will evolve.

Finally, given the fact that each of you has been parented differently, start with the basic premise that differences will arise in your approach to raising children. Treat those differences as resources to be molded into a complementary approach rather than as a basis for contention over right versus wrong ways of rearing children. One couple who had battled strenuously over the issue of strictness in dealing with their children finally reframed their differences as complementary rather then oppositional. In recognition of their progress the husband commented tongue in cheek "my wife and I now work together. I teach the children there are rules, and my wife teaches them there are exceptions."

Do not be afraid to seek out resources to assist in parenting. Very few schools offer majors in parenting. The usual education for each of us is our own experience of being parented. However, many books have been published on parenting that are both readable and practical. Although most of you will wait until you are immersed in child rearing to read them, we recommend reading them before marriage or parenthood. Doing so will help you make some decisions as to how you want to be as parents and provide you with viable alternative behaviors and practices before undesirable patterns have emerged that you will want to change. Books we recommend though certainly not exhaustive, are the following classics: Haim Ginott, *Between Parent and Child* (1965) and *Between Parent and Teenager* (1969); Rudolph Dreikurs, *Children the Challenge* (1964); Gordon, *Parent Effectiveness Training* (1970); Dodson, *Dare to Discipline* (1977); Spock and Rothenberg, *Dr. Spock's Baby and Child Care* (1985); and Dodson, *How to Parent* (1970) and *How to Discipline With Love From Crib to College* (1978). Additional books are Faber and Mazlish, *Liberated Parents, Liberated Children* (1974) and *How to Talk so Kids Will Listen and Listen so Kids Will Talk* (1982); Shaeffer, *What is a Family* (1975); York, York, and Wachtel, *Tough Love* (1982); Procaccini and Kiefaber, *P.L.U.S. Parenting: Take Charge of Your Family* (1985); Lewis, *40 Ways to Teach Your Child Values* (1985); Ewy, *Preparation for Parenthood: How to Create a Nurturing Family* (1985); and Canter and Canter, *Lee Canter's Assertive Discipline for Parents* (1985). Parenting classes and parent support groups also provide useful resources in working out effective parenting. However, we recommend that you read these books together and/or go to classes together as the best approach to using these resources to create an effective parenting team.

Permissiveness-Authoritarianism:
The Great Debate in Parenting

One of the issues all parents must face is how firm they should be with their children. Certainly society has already made numerous movements up and down the continuum never seeming to settle in one place for too long. Generally, excess on either end—too permissive or too authoritarian—produces complications in children and of course every child who becomes a parent recalibrates his/her parenting to get just the right balance. In our work with families we operate from the premise that parents are basically in charge of children. A hierarchy should exist in a family with the parents doing the parenting.

Children and adults are certainly equals in terms of worth and value as human beings. However, children do not have the life experiences, cognitive abilities, and emotional maturity to function organizationally as equals in a family. Even in our democratic society children do not obtain the right to vote until they are eighteen and considered capable of making adult judgments. Children deserve to have input into family and personal decisions and should grow up with a sense that their ideas count. Parents need to acknowledge and listen to children's ideas and opinions and be willing to credit them for their viewpoint.

A large part of our job as parents is to train our children to become good decision-makers. They need to grow up with a sense of responsibility and control rather than feeling inept and powerless. However, until children are ready to completely assume the role of adult including responsibilities and privileges, they are the parent's responsibility. One of the changes family therapy has re-introduced is the old-fashioned idea that parents are in charge of children. This idea of authority has certainly been abused as evidenced by the increased incidence of child abuse. However, one of the possible causes of such abuse is the powerlessness parents feel relative to controlling their children in positive, growth producing ways. Children themselves who have been reared in overly permissive environments end up feeling rudderless and become victims of impulses, urges, and whims over which they have learned no control. William Glasser (1969) pointed out that children need both love and discipline in order to grow up as responsible, healthy human beings capable of relating effectively to other human beings in an intimate manner. If parents stress discipline (authoritarianism) without love, children either rebel or develop a conformity that lacks individuality. Also, they never learn how to develop intimate relationships. If parents stress love (permissiveness) without discipline the child develops a narcissistic, self-oriented conception of the world that manifests itself in irresponsible behavior. The combination of love plus discipline (in that order) helps the child develop the capacity to be a responsible adult capable of intimate relating.

Most parents do the best job they can in terms of parenting even though they are buffeted by many conflicting versions of how they should parent. That fact plus the tendency of children to have amazing persistence and resistance in the face of parental dictates often leads to parents becoming unglued. Trotzer (1982) noted that many studies have been made on the effects of parents on children but few on the effects of children on parents. Sometimes the only place parents can find respite, comfort, and encouragement is in each other. Do not be afraid to be each other's mutual support system in rearing children—support is not only a resource; it is a necessity.

Parents always have hopes and dreams for their children. They hope their children will attain certain personal, educational, vocational, and spiritual goals. They want their children to emulate and internalize certain values. For example, even when parents have no particular religious beliefs themselves, they often feel a responsibility to expose their children to religious training. Parents with little formal education may endure great personal sacrifice to ensure a good education for their children.

We were most impressed by a Black mother in Philadelphia who sent her sixth grade daughter to school in another section of the city because that school had a better educational reputation. The girl had to ride the public bus several hours every day. She also had to go to another section of the city for piano lessons her mother could afford. This mother had to make a tradeoff of her fears for her daughter's safety as the child rode the public buses in order to reach the mother's long range goal of helping her daughter break out of the ghetto life style through education.

As parents or prospective parents we urge you to discuss your hopes, expectations, and goals for your children. Use the information we have presented as a springboard for joining together and forming a co-parenting team. In closing this section we would like to point out that the whole of parenting is essentially a process of creating memories. Gibran's poem noted that our "children pass through us" and as they do, they acquire memories which they consciously or unconsciously will seek to recreate or strive to obliterate in their own children. The memories which you create are your legacy to your children. Therefore strive to create memories which they retain and pass on as a monument to your existence and impact on their lives.

FAMILY LIFE CYCLE

Before leaving our discourse on the family, we would like to give you a bird's eye view of the developmental sequence of events you can anticipate while moving through the experience of family life. Like individuals, families go through stages of development, and even though each family member is at a different stage of individual development, the family stages are experienced together. Each developmental stage has its own traits and characteristics and comes with built in problems and tasks that must be addressed if the family is to move effectively from one stage to another. In fact, each stage is in some way preparatory for the next. Therefore, if tasks in one stage are handled capably, movement into and through the next stage is facilitated. However, if problems and tasks are left unattended or unresolved, an accumulation of difficulties occurs which can overwhelm the family.

Knowing what the various stages of family development are and what to expect can provide a sense of security and predictability to family life. Typically, families who are experiencing stress come to believe that what they are confronting is unique. However, when viewed in light of the usual problems of their particular stage of family development they realize that most families in their situation are struggling with many of the same things. This doesn't remove the problems, but it does provide a sense of assurance that what is being experienced is not abnormal.

In our work with families we have found two basic places where family problems arise. One is in recognizing and dealing with the typical tasks and problems associated with the stage of development in which the families are, and two is in making the transition from one stage to another. Knowledge of the family life cycle is a helpful resource in dealing with both of these difficulties. Consequently, each of the stages will be discussed in order of sequence as a means of providing a sense of their flow and nature.

Stage 1: Unattached Young Adult

Carter and McGoldrick (1980) contended that the development of an autonomous single life and dealing with what Erik Erikson called establishment of ego identity as opposed to role diffusion is the first stage of the family life cycle. As the young adult comes to terms with his/her own family of origin and differentiates from it, the stage is set for entry into the family arena. How you handle that transition has a profound impact on who, when, and how you will marry and live out the succeeding stages of the life cycle. Becoming yourself forms the foundation for intimacy and serves as the cornerstone of a new family structure. Chapters 1 through 5 have developed this idea in detail.

Stage 2: Establishment Stage

Eastablisment refers to the period of time from the marriage to the birth of the first child. This is a critical stage because it forms the foundation for the family. We will not elaborate here because we have dealt with this stage extensively in Chapter 7. The primary tasks in this stage are to learn to relate to each other, to establish a sense of coupleness, to develop a differentiated relationship to each spouse's family of origin, and to address the prospect of children. Effective work on each of these tasks paves the way for the next stage of family life.

Stage 3: New Parent Stage

This stage is initiated by the birth of the first child and extends until that child is age three. The primary tasks of this stage are learning to become parents and reorganizing the marriage in a way that accommodates the child into the relationship. Many couples believe that this is the "real" first stage of family life because this is the time that they run into their first experience of heavy stress. Realization of the awesome responsibility of bringing a new life into the world and effectively dividing and distributing responsibilities along with the emotional excitement and pressure can create stress in the marriage. Husbands may feel displaced, and wives may feel unattractive, overwhelmed or irritable, especially during the post-partum depression that often follows giving birth. Expenses may go up while income may go down. The marriage may become dissolved in the family, and couples need to pull themselves together as a twosome so that the pre-eminence of the marriage is not lost. The new child also brings renewed interest in the couple from each spouse's family of origin as they seek to lay claim to their rights as new grandparents. Certainly the togetherness of the marriage is tested and the reorganization of daily life around the needs of the child is a challenge. The baby needs physical care, love, warmth, and nurturance while the parents feel a sense of mission as they get their family off the ground. This stage is a time of enthusiasm and optimism, a time when patience is necessary, and a time to be cherished because before you realize it, the stage is past and the child along with additional siblings flex their muscles and move the family into the next stage. Being a pioneer parent is stressful and exciting, but also short lived.

Stage 4: Pre-School Family

The first child age three to six plus siblings defines the pre-school stage of family life. The primary tasks of this stage relate to development of the first child's personality and reorganizing the family to make room for additional siblings. As the family size increases arithmetically, the complexity of the family increases geometrically. Not only does the marriage have to accommodate to more people but also each child has to learn how to cope with additional family members. Depending on how close in age the children are, child care can become an all consuming task. Parents complain of living in and out of a diaper pail. Children metamorphose from being passive recipients to active contributors forcing parents to mobilize greater energy and locate heretofore unknown resources to cope with their demands. Parents become embroiled in the task of setting limits and teaching children norms that will make for compatibility in the family domicile. Parental roles and practices (including clashes from family of origin sources) get hammered out in the day to day gristmill of family living. Mothers may develop claustrophobia and come to believe that the world is inhabited only by "little people." Not unusual is for adult language patterns to regress to "childrenese" even when talking to adults. Older children regress and the marriage becomes merely a facade as both parents spend most of their time either in the presence of their children or recuperating for the next day.

Yet this stage is stimulating because the foundational core of each child's personality begins to come clear. Once the "no-nos" have been learned, the children add dynamism to family interaction. Their lives and excitement energize their parents, inspiring hopes and dreams for the family and each child. The marriage can become a welcome and fulfilling retreat from the child world and can develop to an even more intimate level as a result of the co-parenting dimension.

Pre-school parents often believe that this stage is the most restrictive of all the stages because the children are "too small" and doing things is "such a hassle." We submit that such thinking is not substantiated and largely a myth or an excuse. In spite of logistical problems which can be worked out, the pre-school stage is a wonderful time for new family experiences. Camping, travel, biking, and other mobile activities have been made possible by the invention of backpacks, buggers, car seats, and other forms of child conveyances. Taking the initiative to do things is essential because children are very adaptable at this age, as long as a substantial parental closeness and positive attitude can be maintained. Establishing family traditions and setting norms and expectations of family activities at this stage pays high dividends in the future when encroachment of outside organized children's activities and friendships tend to erode family togetherness. In addition, children and parents are better prepared for the more active out-of-family experiences that characterize the next stage of family life. Generally speaking, family life at this stage is only as limited as your imagination and resourcefulness.

Stage 5: School Age Family

The school age family stage encompasses the first child age six to twelve plus siblings. The primary task of this stage is introducing the first and succeeding children to the outside world, particularly the school. The key to effective adjustment outside the family is a secure and stable home. Consequently, if the marriage is strong the child faces the new demands of life with confidence and is able to mobilize all his/her energies to cope and adjust. We see many families who are referred because a child is unable to adapt to school. Upon further exploration we find that the child's behavior is directly related to a substantial difficulty in the marriage. *The greatest asset you can give your child for adjusting outside the home is security inside the home.*

During this stage children begin to cut the emotional ties to the home while at the same time making greater demands on the resources of the parents. Caretaking translates into keeping up with and juggling children's commitments outside the home. School activities, scouts, church programs, music lessons, sports, and so forth, create demands of time and scheduling that drive parents crazy.

Example

Overwhelmed. We saw a single parent of two school age boys who was having anxiety attacks. This mother was a well-organized person and kept a month-by-month master schedule of the family activities on the refrigerator. However, she would literally panic when she looked at the schedule, feeling over-whelmed by the pressure of keeping up with the activities of the month.

Parents must develop the ultimate in cooperation during this stage and strive to maintain a balance between their own needs and those of the children. Curran (1983) believed that school age children should be restricted to one activity at a time, and structured activities outside the home should be limited if they interfered with the family's leisure time together. Children need stability, caring, and support as they interact outside the family, but they also need time at home with the family.

An emerging problem in school age families with the contemporary trend of both parents working is all family members become invested in life outside the home and not in the family. Consequently children's allegiance shifts to their peer group. Bradt (1980) pinpointed this problem by asking the question "Are children rearing each other?" Boszormenyi-Nagy and Spark (1973) stated that childhood is a misnomer if a child has no parent in charge. To counter this tendency parents during this stage must not only keep their marriage clearly differentiated and alive but must also maintain a family orientation.

Parents of school age children still have basic control over what the family will do, and children are still heavily invested in the family and not only acquiesce to but enjoy family activities. These assets need to be mobilized and utilized because in retrospect most families look back at the school age years as the golden era of family life. Things have a distinct tendency to change with the advent of junior high and the teenage years.

Stage 6: Adolescent Family

The adolescent family stage encompasses the teen years (13 to 18) for the oldest child and siblings. Adolescence has been described tongue in cheek as a period of rapid change: as children go from thirteen to nineteen, parents age twenty years. The primary tasks of this stage are accepting the issue of adolescence and allowing clear generational boundaries to emerge. A generation gap is a necessity for a teenager. Without a distance between the two generations, a child is deprived of experiencing his/her own separateness and emerging identity.

Adolescence is a time when the parents more than ever need a strong marriage. If any serious difficulties occur in the marriage, the tension and stress of raising adolescents are sure to accentuate them. In fact, parents often contribute to the stress by not having their marriage (particularly communication) in good shape. During adolescence parents must learn to accept the "pain of parenting." Some parents attempt to circumvent the pain by changing their lifestyle in an effort to join their adolescent children. This creates the illusion of togetherness, postpones the separation conflict, and creates confusion in the lives of the children. Other parents get fed up with adolescence and abdicate parental responsibility. This relieves the tension but forces the adolescent to seek boundaries and limits elsewhere. However, finding them in their peer group or in society (laws) often leads to greater pain rather than resolution. Adolescents do need boundaries off which to rebound and these boundaries are best provided by the family.

Many parents do a flip-flop when their children reach adolescence. All during the pre-school and school age years they teach their children to be autonomous and make their own decisions. However, when adolescence hits they want to either recycle childhood or start making the rules (taking the autonomy they taught their children away). This behavior frustrates the children and generates rebellion. As one teenager explained in therapy, "They (his parents) let me walk all over town, ride my bike all over the country, but they won't let me drive the car around the block." Part of the problem is that parents' memories of their own adolescence are still too fresh. They remember what they did and what they wanted to do and are scared to death that their children might be considering and/or doing the same things.

The adolescent stage also tends to be complicated by the parents' own identity crisis as they hit the mid-life panic button. Consequently, while their adolescent children are asking the question "What do I want to be when I grow up?" for the first time, the parents are asking that same question for the last time. In addition, roles may be changing. Mom who is losing her job at home starts looking for one outside the home. Dad starts thinking about coming home and meets his wife and children at the door as they are on the way out. Both spouses may be dealing with the complications raised by the aging of their own parents. This puts the marital pair directly in the middle of what is known as the "sandwich generation." Adolescence tests the metal and fiber of the person and the marriage. As the children test to find out *what* their stock is, the parents are tested to find out *how strong* their stock is.

Families do survive the adolescence stage and even thrive. If parents are willing to set boundaries, revise them to meet changing conditions, and negotiate with teenagers (communication), the family will succeed. If parents can support each other and provide boundaries plus caring to their children, both the children and the marriage will become stronger. The adolescent family stage too will pass and most of the time all participants emerge intact.

Stage 7: Family With The Young Adult

This stage of family life varies in length but generally refers to the time period between leaving school and leaving home by the first child (age eighteen to early twenties). This stage is a bit difficult to delineate because the young adult may engage in a psuedo-home leaving process such as going to college or moving in and out as their financial situation dictates. This stage of family life has been called the "revolving door syndrome" and the young adults involved have been referred to as "nesters" (O'Kane, 1981). The main charateristic is that a young adult is still primarily living under his/her parents' roof. The incidence of young adults between the ages of 18 and 24 living at home has become quite a phenomenon in our society. According to U.S. Bureau of the Census (1984b) statistics, 54.4% of this age group lives at home, an increase of 78% from 1970.

The basic tasks of the family with a young adult are facilitating experimentation with independence and developing new response patterns between the parents and the young adult. Parents and children alike struggle with extrication from the parent-child relationship. Parents allowing privacy for the young adult and the young adult honoring the rules of the parents' home are precarious and volatile conditions to implement. Parents must learn to let their children make their own decisions and children must learn to respect their parents' values even if the children may not accept these values as their own. Often during this time frame emotional reactions become the motivating factors in family life. As wills and lifestyles clash, a point emerges where tension propels a separation. However, *Living With Adult Children* painted a very positive view of this stage of family life and we recommend reading it. This transition stage if handled poorly can leave deep scars that take a long time to heal, but, if handled constructively, provides a solid basis for extended family relating.

Stage 8: Family As a Launching Pad

This stage of family life extends from the departure of the first child to the departure of the last child. The basic tasks of this stage are accepting the adult status of *each* child and reorganizing the family as it contracts in size. This stage may occur rapidly or be extended over a long period of time depending on the ages and circumstances of the children. A common experience is for parents to look at each other one day and realize they are all *alone together*.

During this stage the parents must come to grips with their changing status in their children's lives. They are not as needed any longer especially in the sense of their physical presence. In the marriage a process of recourting is often necessary and exciting as the parents reignite the marital fires and begin to do more as a couple and less as a family. This process is accentuated by economic factors of greater income and less expenses. Sometimes parents become a bit disoriented as they have more and need less.

The biggest problem is that of letting go, especially when the last child heads out the door. A last minute panic may occur in which parents catch themselves figuring out ways of keeping the kids around instead of supporting their flight. Once again the marriage is crucial because now, just as in the beginning, the couple is left with each other. At this point you get some clear data which tells you how effective you were in choosing your life's partner.

Stage 9: Parental Middle Years

This stage extends from the last child leaving home to retirement. The basic tasks of this stage are for the marital pair to get to know each other again and to develop a couple lifestyle that is mutually satisfying. Partners discover they have changed a great deal and must get reacquainted. Now they have time for one another that is unencumbered by children. They also may be introduced to the world of grandparenting as their own children begin to have children. This stage can be the golden era in the marriage because they can still physically do things they want to do and have the financial wherewithal to do so. They can claim their rights as part-time lovers to their grandchildren and then send the children home to the parents.

Whereas child rearing used to encompass the largest segment of the family life cycle and fathers would often die within two years of the marriage of their youngest child (McGoldrick & Carter, 1982), this stage has now become the longest (as much as twenty or more years). Consequently, your choice of a marital partner becomes all the more important. A scary statistic is that many marriages dissolve around the twenty year mark. Such a fate is both a sad waste of your investment in marriage and a warning to make your choice of a life's partner seriously and carefully.

The question becomes "Where will the marriage go from here?" Will you as a husband support your wife's involvement in a career or other individual pursuit? Will you as a wife have plans and provision to accommodate to the empty nest? Will you as a couple strike out together for new horizons? Will you be able to resolve or set aside grudges and bitter feelings to strike a new course? Sheehy (1981) reported in *Pathfinders* that the "freestyle fifties" emerge as a time of renewal and happiness when men and women (husbands and wives) can arrive at the place where they can say "I am who I am." When that occurs both the individuals and the marriage prosper. In fact, the whole family benefits because children and grand-children are responsive to contact with these positive persons who have achieved the inner satisfaction of being themselves.

Stage 10: Aging Family

This stage extends from retirement to death. The basic tasks of this stage are accepting retirement and developing mutuality as both partners face and go through the process of dealing with loss. The marital pair must adjust to more extensive time together and deal with the tensions produced by intrusions into one another's life created by the exodus from career and the work world. Partners must face and deal with a decrease in energy and physical capability. Income often stabilizes and/or decreases due to eroding economic factors that chip away at fixed incomes. The prospect of death and dealing with loss of one's peer group and spouse are part of this stage, and the frustration and emotional discomfort of having to be cared for emerges. Children now reemerge as the caretakers of parents and the difficult process of working out a mutually satisfactory relationship between adult children with their own families and aging parents must be addressed.

The key to effectively coping with tasks of this stage is developing interests and activities that result in self esteem and feelings of fulfillment. Preserving and passing on the family legacy can be a special part of this stage of family life. We often encourage families to make tape recordings of their aging parents asking them to give an oral accounting of their own and their family's history. Old people lose their capacity to reminisce last and while they may not remember things on a day to day basis, they have a clear recollection of the past. Make use of this capacity. Grandchildren and great grandchildren will value their stories and the aging parents will glean a sense of self esteem.

This is only a capsule summary of the family life cycle. Many variations can be found and you will carve out your own unique version of these stages. Hopefully now that you know the sequence, you can compare your own experience to it and chart your course accordingly. Most of all realize that much of the stress and turmoil in each stage of family life is normal and each stage has its own benefits and satisfactions. Move through each one facing the problems and claiming the joys and then move onward for like a river, family life continues to flow.

HEALTHY FAMILY TRAITS

Even though we have packed a great deal of information on the family into this chapter, the answer to the question "What is a family?" still remains for you to determine. No one absolute definition of family life exists and your answer is the one that is most important. But some indicators of family health can be identified. Curran (1983) compiled a list of "traits of a healthy family" which we include for your consideration:

1. The healthy family communicates and listens.

2. The healthy family affirms and supports one another.

3. The healthy family teaches respect for others.

4. The healthy family develops a sense of trust.

5. The healthy family has a sense of play and humor.

6. The healthy family exhibits a sense of shared responsibility.

7. The healthy family teaches a sense of right and wrong.

8. The healthy family has a strong sense of family in which rituals and traditions abound.

9. The healthy family has a balance of interaction among members.

10. The healthy family has a shared religious core.

11. The healthy family respects the privacy of one another.

12. The healthy family values service to others.

13. The healthy family fosters table time and conversation.

14. The healthy family shares leisure time.

15. The healthy family admits to and seeks help with problems. (pp. 23-24)

Any list sounds awesome when presented all at once, but take time to look at it and think about each component. This list is not an evaluation instrument nor an ideal standard. It is intended to be thought provoking and action generating as you create your own family.

In spite of all the problems and cautionary considerations, the family is one of the most rewarding and fulfilling enterprises in which we can engage. In fact, the family is the essence of human fulfillment. Andre Malroux once stated "Without a family, man, alone in the world, trembles with cold" (O'Kane, 1981, p.1). Family life takes a lot of work and a continual processing of where you are at and where you are going. But if you work at it you will never be left alone and cold. We encourage and applaud your efforts to make the most of your family experience.

REFERENCES

Boszormenyi-Nagy, I., & Spark, G.M. (1973). *Invisible loyalties: Reciprocity in intergenerational family therapy.* Hagerstown, MD: Medical Department, Harper & Row.

Bowen, M. (1966). The use of family theory in clinical practice. *Comprehensive Psychiatry, 7,* 345-374.

Bradt, J.O. (1980). The family with young children. In E. Carter and M. McGoldrick (Eds.), *The family life cycle, 121-146.* New York: Gardner Press.

Bronfenbrenner, U. (1977, September 29-30). *Who needs parent education?* Working Conference on Parent Education, Flint, MI.

Brozman, N. (1980). Men and housework. Reprinted in *Family Therapy News,* July, 1981, *12*(4), 1 & 16.

Canter, L., & Canter, M. (1985). *Lee Canter's assertive discipline for parents.* Santa Monica, CA: Canter & Associates, Distributed by Harper & Row.

Carter, E.A., & McGoldrick, M. (Eds.). (1980). *The family life cycle: A framework for family therapy.* New York: Gardner Press.

Curran, D. (1983). *Traits of a healthy family.* Minneapolis: Winston Press.

Dobson, J. (1977). *Dare to discipline.* New York: Bantam Books.

Dodson, F. (1970). *How to parent.* New York: A Signet Book, The New American Library.

Dodson, F. (1978). *How to discipline with love from crib to college.* New York: A Signet Book, The New American Library.

Dreikurs, R. (1964). *Children: The challenge.* Des Moines, IA: Meredity Press (Duell, Sloan and Pearce).

Ewy, D. (1985). *Preparation for parenthood, how to create a nurturing family.* New York: A Plume Book, New American Library.

Faber, A., & Mazlish, E. (1974). *Liberated parents, liberated children.* New York: Avon Books.

Faber, A., & Mazlish, E. (1982). *How to talk so kids will listen & listen so kids will talk.* New York: Avon Books.

Gelman, D. (1983, August 15). Teenage suicide in the sun belt (Plano, Texas). *Newsweek,* 102: 70 .

Gibran, K. (1951). *The prophet.* New York: Alfred A. Knopf.

Ginott, H. (1965). *Between parent and child.* New York: Macmillan.

Ginott, H. (1969). *Between parent and teenager.* New York: Macmillan.

Glasser, W. (1969). *Schools without failure.* New York: Harper & Row.

Gordon, T. (1970). *Parent effectiveness training.* New York: Plume.

Howard, J. (1978). *Families.* New York: Simon & Schuster.

Langway, L. (1981, November 30). A new kind of life with father. *Newsweek,* 93-99.

Leany, E.C. (1965). *I wish my daddy was a dog.* Bluewater, NM: Box 218.

Lewis, P. (1985). *40 ways to teach your child values.* Wheaton, IL: Tyndale House Publisher.

McGoldrick, M., & Carter, E.A. (1982). The family life cycle. In F. Walsh (Ed.), *Normal family processes.* New York: The Guilford Press, 167-195.

Minuchin, S. (1974). *Families and family therapy.* Cambridge, MA: Harvard University Press.

O'Kane, M.L. (1981). *Living with adult children.* St. Paul, MN: Diction Books.

Procaccini, J., & Kiefaber, M.W. (1985). *P.L.U.S. parenting, Take charge of your family.* New York: Doubleday.

Roisinger, M. (1984, May 13). Tomorrow's mothers learn today's lessons. *The Portsmouth Herald,* 1-C.

Shaeffer, E. (1975). *What is a family?* Old Tappan, NJ: Fleming H. Revell.

Sheehy, G. (1981). *Pathfinders.* New York: Bantam Books.

Spock, B., & Rothenberg, M.B. (1985). *Dr. Spock's baby and child care.* New York: Pocket Books, Simon & Schuster.

Trotzer, J.P. (1982). *Attitudes of children towards parents and parenting: A cross cultural comparison of Japanese and United States students in Grades 3-9.* University of Wisconsin-River Falls.

U.S. Bureau of the Census (1984a). Current population reports, Series P-20, No. 395, *Fertility of American Women: June 1983.* Washington DC: U.S. Government Printing Office.

U.S. Bureau of the Census (1984b). Current population reports, Series P-20, No. 389, *Marital status and living arrangements: March 1983.* Washington, DC: U.S. Government Printing Office.

York, P., York, D., & Wachtel, T. (1982). *Tough love.* New York: Doubleday.

Zuk, G. (1975). *Process and practice in family therapy.* Haverford, PA: Psychiatry and Behavioral Science Books.

REMARRIAGE:
THE FRONTIER OF FAMILY LIVING

The special issues and problems of a remarried family are addressed. Dynamics of healthy family functioning that account for forming an effective new unit while honoring legacy connections of past relationships are stressed. The roles of step-parents and step-children are addressed and the importance of effective communication and clear relational boundaries are emphasized. Also addressed is the special situation of a marriage being formed in a family context.

> *In view of the fact that the divorce rate appears to be steadily rising and considering that the marjority of divorced subsequently remarry, it is probable that the reconstituted family may become the predominant family form of the future.*

> —Wolper-Zun and Bross, 1982, p. 114

Ch 9   Remarriage: The Frontier of Family Living   *239*

The astonishing prediction noted in the above quote is based on data that 75% of divorced people remarry and that in 3 of 4 cases the initial divorces occurred in families with children. So prominent is the incidence of divorce and remarriage in which children are involved that Katz and Stein (1983) labeled *stepfamilies* along with *nuclear families* and *single parent families* as the three major forms of family organization in the western world. Consequently, not only are significant numbers of adults leaving one marriage and becoming involved in another, but an astoundingly large number of children also will experience life in a single parent family and a reconstituted or blended family.

The impact of the divorce rate is such that children born in 1977 or thereafter face a 45% chance of spending part of their lives in a single parent family (Cantor & Drake, 1983, p. 2). At the current rate of divorce the number of single parent families are multiplying seven times faster than two parent families. While remarriage often turns a single parent family into a two parent family, the resulting unit is not the same as an intact first family. As such, persons who enter a marriage following a divorce are likely faced with not only choosing a compatible partner and developing a fulfilling relationship, but also must address the complexities created by merging two existing nuclear family systems into a functional step-family unit.

The problem with preparing for remarriage is not that such preparation is unrecognized as a necessity but rather little established evidence exists as to the most effective way of doing it. Preparation is difficult when little reliable or valid data or specific training is available. Beal (1980) noted that "there exist virtually no rituals or rules of passage to assist families with difficulties inherent in the process of divorce" (p. 241). Cherlin (1978) pointed out that "persons who are remarried after a divorce and have children from a previous marriage face problems unlike those encountered in first marriages" (p. 634). The institution of family provides no standard solutions to many of these problems. Visher and Visher (1982) confirm that not only is remarriage more complex, but it is more stressful.

Society does not yet have guidelines or defined roles or relationships for remarried families. Labels and language that positively and constructively identify newly acquired kin are virtually nonexistent (McGoldrick & Carter, 1980). This makes even the simplest of everyday functions such as filling out forms and celebrating holidays embarrassing and painful. However, in recent years serious effort has been given to studying and identifying constructive means of coping with and effectively working through the unique problems of remarriage. Society is beginning to treat divorce, remarriage, and stepfamilies as fact rather than fiction. That recognition is partly our reason for including a chapter on remarriage in this book. We also realize that the sheer force of statistical data is in itself a contributing factor in the dissolution of some marriages. Statistics support the idea that "everybody's doing it," making divorce a norm. Comments like "all my friends are divorced" lay claim to social acceptability resulting in a Catch-22 from our perspective. We do not wish to chastise or make life difficult for those who choose to divorce, yet we do not want to normalize divorce to the point where people getting married are inwardly saying "oh well, if it doesn't work out, we can always divorce" while they stand at the altar and outwardly pledge "til death do us part." Therefore, our purpose is to present information that will be instructive in nature enhancing awareness as a preventive measure to repetition of marital and family breakdowns. We wish to encourage very serious preparation for remarriage and present a hopeful view of reconstituted family life by sharing with you the most current thinking from research and clinical practice.

Our chapter is organized sequentially, tracing the usual development of separation/divorce to family reconstruction. Our intent is not to dwell on detail but rather to highlight key issues and suggest guidelines for effectively moving through each stage. We will start with an overview of the stages and then deal specifically with separation and divorce, the post divorce family, remarriage and finally the reconstituted family.

FROM NUCLEAR FAMILY
TO RECONSTITUTED FAMILY

Wolpert-Zun and Bross (1982) have described three general stages through which families go when a marriage dissolves, initiating a process that leads to a reconstituted family unit. Stage I is the period from marriage dissolution through separation and divorce to a single parent or post divorce family unit. The key theme of this phase is recovery from the loss of the marital relationship. For the parent the tasks are to disengage from the marital relationship and redefine boundaries around a co-parenting relationship. For children Stage I involves a gradual acceptance that parents will not get back together, and that as children they must go about the business of establishing separate relationships with each parent, particularly the non-custodial parent.

Stage II is establishment of a new intimate relationship to remarriage. The main focus of this phase is on the development of a relationship that materializes into a marriage. The couple must simultaneously work out their marital and parental relationships and contemplate not only marital compatibility but forming a family unit as well. The three goals of Stage II are (1) to develop solidarity and cohesion in the marital relationship, (2) to evolve an interactional style that permits negotiating differences and flexibility in simultaneously undertaking marital and parental relationships, and (3) creation of marital boundaries that are not too close or too tight (Wolpert-Zun & Bross, 1982, pp. 116-117). A major problem in Stage II is the tendency to develop a couple relationship that is psuedo-mutual (making it look like no differences can be found between the partners). Because the partners fear failing again, they deny the existence of difficulties or differences which impedes negotiation and resolution of conflict.

Stage III is family reconstruction. This stage is initiated with the remarriage and involves clarification and redefinition of family boundaries. The main task is that of blending two systems which have different histories, rules, roles, memories, and values. Developing boundaries that are more permeable than intact nuclear families and which allow family members to move from one household to another is a necessity. Children need to be accorded dual membership in two family systems thus accounting for affiliation and affect with the non-custodial parent while recognizing the child's membership in the new household.

Neither family system should demand or be given total loyalty. The goal is for the child to have an independent relationship with each system. With this overview in mind, let us turn our attention to key issues and dynamics in each stage that must be accounted for to make effective transition and reduce the obstacles to effective marital and family interaction.

COPING WITH DIVORCE:
TURNING PAIN INTO GAIN

One of the most common questions we are asked by divorcing persons is "How does a person go through divorce constructively?" or, as one of our clients stated "Divorce wouldn't be so bad if it weren't for my emotions." No matter how you rationalize the fact, divorce is a loss and as such a recovery process is necessary. Just as with any other form of loss, how you handle it will affect your later adjustments. You must realize that recovery takes time. The grieving process is estimated to take at least two years and is characterized by the same stages of grief that are associated with death. The only problem is that the person for whom you are grieving is still very much alive and may be very active in your life especially if you have children.

Most divorced persons describe their reaction to divorce in terms of the Kubler-Ross (1969) grief stages: denial, anger, bargaining, acceptance, and growth. Just as in the case of a death, the emotional ties linger on long after the legal knot has been untied. While the court may seal the death of the marriage by decree, the emotional disentanglement still faces those persons involved. Consequently, for the divorced person the most important task is to let go of the marital relationship. This is much easier said than done particularly if you happen to be the one who wanted to hold on to the marriage. The inability to let go is probably the most detrimental obstacle to getting on with your life in the family and in the context of other relationships.

Example

A Coping with Divorce Report Card. A divorced mother brought her 11 year old son to therapy because he was doing poorly in school and was often emotionally distraught to the point of not wanting to leave his mother for fear something would happen to her. The problem was that he was the youngest of three and served as mom's emotional barometer. Although her divorce had been finalized for more than a year, she was still claiming an unrelenting love for her ex-husband. This claim kept alive the pain of the loss as well as fanned the children's hope of a reconciliation. Mom had completely shut herself off from the outside world and her son was doing the same thing in school. When his grades declined to all D's and F's she became concerned and motivated to try to help him. In order to help them both a report card was constructed for mom composed of subjects such as letting go, developing adult relationships, expanding activities, taking care of herself, letting children grow, and participating in physical exercise (P.E.). Her grades were determined to be as low as her son's academic grades and both were put on a program to improve their standing. As mom's grades went up so did her son's.

As an ex-spouse you can choose to either "go" through the divorce or "grow" through the divorce. In order to grow without being totally inundated in the emotional aftermath we have found several guidelines to be helpful to assist in recovery from and coping with divorce. First is the realization that recovery is not a matter of what happens to you but how you respond that determines adjustment. Often a decision not to wallow in self pity or a counteracting effort to act positively when feelings are negative can help turn the corner.

Divorced persons need to learn how to be good to themselves and not exacerbate their situation by imposing guilt trips on themselves. A commitment to give yourself enough time to heal is also necessary so you do not end up in a rebound relationship or become victim to the "tyranny of the temporary." Give yourself the time (general rule of thumb is 2 years) to get better and refrain from berating yourself for slow progress.

Remember that the best gift you can give a future spouse is "no unfinished business" with a former spouse. Take the time to become emotionally detached from your "ex" before becoming emotionally attached to a new intimate partner.

MINIMIZING THE IMPACT OF DIVORCE ON CHILDREN

When spouses are embroiled in separation and divorce, often children are left to their own devices to adjust and cope. The emotionality of the marital conflagration can completely overshadow the needs and pains of the children. A key admonition of parents who are divorcing is *"Don't forget the children."* In fact, if divorcing parents can maintain amiable relations during the course of their divorce and afterward, not only will the detriment to children be less but the parents will experience less intensity in their own experience of loss (Beal, 1980).

For children, maintaining an intact, functioning parent-child relationship is a necessity during and after dissolution of the marriage.

Children of divorce function best if they are able to maintain satisfactory contact with *both* parents (McGoldrick & Carter, 1980). However, more typical is for children to be either ignored or caught up as go-betweens in the marital struggle. In order to circumvent these problems Cantor and Drake (1983) listed seven guidelines to minimize negative effects of divorce on children:

1. Parents need to talk to children about the divorce.

2. Children need to be allowed to express their feelings.

3. Avoid involving children in a divorce triangle.

4. Keep interparental hostility in check.

5. Encourage visitation by the non-custodial parent.

6. Foster sameness (i.e., if possible keep child in the same environment—house, school, neighborhood, friends, relatives).

7. Secure additional help in the form of professional counseling. (p. 166)

Parents tend to overlook changes in their children's behavior that may be directly related to the divorce. Doing so portends future adjustment problems because feelings will either become internalized and inaccessible or translated into acting out behaviors that get the child in trouble. Divorcing parents need to observe their children closely and make conscientious efforts to communicate the following basic messages:

1. The separation/divorce is *not* the child's fault.

2. The children remain loved by both parents.

3. The parents will continue to be involved with their children.

4. Their lives will change.

5. There is nothing they can do to change the situation. (Cantor & Drake, 1983, pp. 74-75)

If the divorcing pair can disengage emotionally without excessive anger, bitterness, or grudges and can redefine their relationship as amicable and supportive co-parents, the best interests of their children and themselves will be served. The stage will be set for more effective relating in the post-divorce family, and the pathway will be cleared for re-engaging in the process of intimacy. Once the grieving process is complete, the door to new relationships will swing open more easily.

SINGLE PARENT FAMILIES

We need to make some distinctions between the general types of single parent families at the outset. The first type is the family where joint custody and cooperative co-parenting is conducted by the divorced parents. In this case the label "single parent family" is a misnomer because the two biological parents are still actively and supportively parenting their children. Goldsmith (1982) called this type of family the "post divorce family," the implication being that parents have successfully extricated themselves from each other as marital partners and have worked out a constructive co-parenting relationship that is in the best interests of the children.

The second type of single parent family is that in which one parent is primarily responsible with little or no help from the non-custodial parent. Statistically these families are predominantly headed by mothers. Only 3% of households are headed by single parent fathers (U.S. Bureau of the Census, 1985a). Although joint custody is becoming more prominent, in only 10% of divorce cases is custody awarded to the father (Saxton, 1983). This type of single parent family is appropriately labeled and presents problems that differ significantly from the post divorce family. Whereas in the first type, problems revolve around communication and cooperation relative to parenting the children, at least more parental resources are available to be tapped. In the second case, the parental resources are less, creating problems first of finding sufficient adult resources to assist in child rearing, and then figuring out how to mobilize them.

The third type of single parent family is that in which wrangling over custody and/or inconsistent availability on the part of one or both parents is still present. This type of single parent family generally comes into therapy as a multi-problem family. Unresolved marital business, children that are alternately triangulated and neglected, children struggling in school, parent irresponsibility and inconsistency, parent sabotage, and a whole host of other dynamics usually attend this family.

Based on these brief descriptions the organization of choice for the single parent phase is the post-divorce mode with the least desirable being the erratic type mentioned in the preceding paragraph. However, problems abound for this fastest growing of family lifestyles regardless of the form it takes.

Making Ends Meet

Single parent families tend to suffer from a lack of or restriction in financial resources. In fact, government economists have become particularly concerned about the feminization of poverty because of women's low pay scales and the fact that women head most single parent families. One of the biggest problems courts, law enforcement, and social service agencies face today is the nonpayment of child support. So critical has this problem become that some counties have organized massive roundups of men who are delinquent in their child support payments.

Saxton (1983) has noted that female-headed single parent families can only expect to make one dollar for every two that a two parent family can earn. Based on the 1979 census figures, the average income for 12 million working men between ages 25 and 34 was $17,967 and for 8 million men between 45 and 54 was $23,002. In contrast the full time average income for women between 25 and 70 was $12,000 (Sheehy, 1981). In spite of the escalating divorce rate and the growing re-entry of women into the work force, women's pay scales have continued to be considerably lower than men's. One in three female headed single parent households is below the poverty line (U.S. Bureau of the Census, 1985b) as compared to a one in ten poverty rate for all families. Efforts are being made at present to devise equivalency scales for traditionally female jobs which would equate them with traditionally male dominated jobs. However, resolution of this problem remains to be seen.

Even if the previous problems do not apply in your case, the fact that financial resources must be stretched to cover two households in itself becomes an economic burden. Having to do with less and extra worry about making ends meet are usual compromises of the single parent family experience.

Task Overload

Single parent families must continue with the same functions, roles, and responsibilities as the married family with one less adult to share the load. Single parents feel they must be both mother and father to their children and immerse themselves in supporting the family, running the household, rearing the children, moving forward with their own activities, and if possible, forming new social relationships, and having some time to themselves. Such an awesome job description can become quite overwhelming and anxiety producing. This overload is often transmitted to children who must pick up more of the responsibility for family functioning. Children sometimes unconsciously take on the emotional stress of the parent and seek to acquire help for the overburdened parent by becoming a "problem" that gets the attention of an outside agency such as the school or social services. Many of our contacts with single parent families have been the result of a child being identified and referred as having some type of adjustment problem in school. Attention in the form of family therapy is acquired in which not only the child receives attention but also resources are mobilized to assist the overloaded single parent.

The task overload phenomenon does have positive side effects as well. Many women (and men) report finding resources in themselves they never knew existed. Children learn to become more responsible and self-sufficient, taking more responsibility in family functioning rather than having to be told and monitored as is often the case in intact families. A typical scenario after divorce is for mom to go back to school to get or finish her degree or earn an advanced degree while the children pull together to pick up the slack and give her time to study. She begins to look more attractive, gains a sense of self-confidence she never had during the marriage, and acquires a sense of self-esteem as she finds herself capable of holding down a job and effectively running a home. The outcome is a positive self image and a metamorphosis that makes her a "new person." Unfortunately these changes are initiated via the pain of divorce instead of in the context of a marriage with a supportive husband resulting in two self-fulfilled people working together and getting on with the job of rearing a family.

Overextending Children's Resources

A common problem of the single parent family is the tendency to get from children that which was lost when the spouse exited the family. This phenomenon referred to variously as the *parental child, spousal child,* or *parentification* may result from children assuming too much responsibility in an effort to help out or the parent displacing need fulfillment from the ex-spouse to the child.

Sometimes one child takes over the parental role in relation to the other children and may even function in some ways as the parent to the parent. Although children must expect to do more in single parent families, care must be taken not to depend on them for emotional needs that are appropriately met by an adult either in the form of a spouse or spouse surrogate (adult family members, friends, and so forth). A key indicator that this may be happening in a single parent family is when one or more children stop engaging in age appropriate activities and substitute activities that are more adult-like in nature.

Example

The Parental Child. An example of a "parental child" is a single parent family that came to us because the youngest child, a 13 year-old boy, had been acting out in school, getting poor grades, and generally being overtly disrespectful to his teachers and school authorities. The family consisted of the mother, a 15 year-old daughter, and the son. The mother wanted her male friend to be present in the sessions until the fact became apparent that the children did not want him there and that he was only marginally interested in the family. In therapy, the counselors discovered that the daughter had been given and/or taken the role of the boy's mother. For several years she made supper for him, got him off to school, and agonized over his behavior in school and in the neighborhood. She tried to train and discipline him and was hurt when now at age 13 he was not appreciative and often rebelled against her. Mom worked long hours and pursued her social relationships after work to the point where the daughter often waited up at night worrying until her mother came home.

The course of therapy was to get mother back into the role as head of the family and to take back the responsibility of parenting her children. In addition, the daughter who did well in school but was socially inactive was encouraged to engage in age appropriate behaviors. The daughter managed to extricate herself from the parental role when she took a summer job away from home. That physical separation assisted the family in reconstructing itself with appropriate generational boundaries and roles. The mother moved back into her adult/parent role, the daughter began to act more like a teenager, and the son's behavior toward authority figures improved.

The "spousal child" refers to a child who fills the role of the missing spouse for the parent. The parent and child become confidantes, spend exclusionary time together, and sometimes the child is given favored treatment and privileged status in comparison to the other children. This can be especially problematic in a three member family because one member of the sibling sub-system is either left out or ganged up on. On the other hand, a spousal child can also become the victim of negative transference where the parent's antagonistic feelings are unloaded in statements like "You're just like your father." The antidote to the spousal child is to cultivate relationships with other adults who can fill in the vacated space of the ex-spouse. Such efforts are often difficult but pay big dividends when a significant other does materialize on the scene. Less resistance and chaos will be created because displacement will not have to occur. A misleading idea is to think that you can use your child temporarily as an emotional leaning post. Once there, the child resents being dislodged causing greater anguish down the line.

Erratic Non-custodial Parent

Research and clinical data strongly indicate that the degree to which both parents can work out an amicable, cooperative, and consistent co-parenting relationship determines the degree to which children attain positive post-divorce adjustment. One of the hardest things with which children have to cope is an erratic, non-custodial parent. When a parent doesn't show up or arrives late without explanation, arrives on the scene unannounced, forgets special events like birthdays and holidays, and makes promises that are not kept, children's emotions are damaged. Such actions also fuel the fires of antagonism between ex-spouses. As such, everyone loses and future positive relationships are severely jeopardized. Make every effort to "put the children first" developing a contact pattern that you can sustain rather than setting up plans that either never materialize or have to be changed.

Child Spies

A final dangerous practice we want to warn against is the child spy. When ex-spouses have difficulty severing their emotional ties to each other, the temptation is present to use the children to collect data to justify one's feelings of vindictiveness. Placing pressure directly or indirectly on a child to be a conveyor of information about the other spouse is both unfair and unhealthy. Creating a boundary for yourself (preferably one that is honored by both parents) to abstain from collecting information about your ex-spouse from your child is a must. This assists the child in forming an individual relationship with each parent and helps you to further disengage emotionally from your ex-spouse.

Summary Regarding Single Parent Families

In summary, the keys to effective adjustment in the post-divorce family are an effective co-parenting relationship, resolution of emotional attachment to the ex-spouse, and helping the children accept the divorce and develop independent relationships with each parent. In terms of family functioning, consistent, cooperative parenting is essential and filling the ex-spouse's vacated space with adults, not children, is mandatory. Although the single parent family may not be considered the preferable family lifestyle, studies have borne out the fact that intact families in which the parents become disengaged and chronically unhappy create more problems for children than divorce. Consequently, organizing a post-divorce family as previously noted will not only facilitate effective post-divorce adjustment for all concerned, but also will set the stage for the remarriage phase of development should that materialize.

REMARRIAGE:
MORE REASONS TO BE PREPARED

When the prospect of remarriage develops, certainly all of the information from previous chapters applies. In fact, if you have already been through a marriage, that information may make a lot more sense and have a great deal more face validity. So we will not spend extensive time on remarriage as a choice but rather point out a few key dimensions for you to consider. In addition, we will more comprehensively discuss the remarriage choice in the context of our discussion on the remarried family.

We reiterate that leftover business from a previous relationship can only cause problems and even jeopardize a new relationship. McGoldrick and Carter (1980) found that "to the extent that each spouse can work to resolve his or her own emotional issues with significant people from the past, the new relationship can proceed on its own merit" (p. 269). Make sure you have given yourself enough time to detach, heal, and forgive yourself and your ex-spouse. Starting over too soon can present more difficulties than you had before. Beal (1980) noted that "marriages established in the context of significant losses such as death of a parent or after a disappointing love affair or marriage are more likely to be unstable" (p. 247). Consequently, we suggest you give yourself time to start on your own and give your new relationship time to evolve before making the choice to remarry.

Negative motivators that persons considering remarriage fail to recognize are the "rebound" and the "anti-choice." In the rebound arena, emotional pain and the desire for release from it propel us into intimacy. This results in a sense of immediate gratification much like the infatuation phase in the courting process. Give that experience time to pass rather than using it as a reason to marry. Moving too rapidly tends to result in choosing a partner who has the same traits as your previous spouse and ends up creating a repetition of the same type of relationship. We have counseled many couples in their second marriages whose chief complaint is that their spouse "is just like my first husband/wife." A common occurrence is for a wife to leave a marriage because of her husband's drinking problem only to marry another with the same problem or a similar addictive personality. When you or your intimate partner just "can't wait" to marry it is usually a signal to move cautiously. This impatience most likely means one or both cannot tolerate delayed gratification and increases the likelihood of repeating the same mistakes.

The "anti-choice" refers to choosing a new partner because he/she is the opposite of your previous spouse. This choice also appears sound on the surface because an obvious difference exists. The problem may be that you have as much difficulty with the flip side of the same coin. One woman told us she married her second husband because in contrast to her first, he was quiet, stable, and dependable. When they came for therapy she was going bananas because no excitement could be found in their relationship. Although the need to learn from your previous marriage is important, using it as a sole criteria to choose a new partner is unwise. Again, take time to get to know your partner as "a person in his/her own right" rather than as an anti-type of a previous spouse.

Sager, Brown, Crohn, Engel, Rodstein, and Walker (1983) have noted several common motivators for remarriage. Each has merits and drawbacks. We identify them here as a check list to gauge your own impetus for remarriage.

Motivators for Remarriage

1. The promise of a loving and caring relationship.

2. Utopian dreams of marriage and family life (in contrast to the horrors to a previous relationship).

3. Desire to have and be in a family.

4. Desire to be revitalized by a partner.

5. Escape from a parental home (i.e., marrying an older divorced person to get you out of the house or marrying because you returned home after divorce and want to get out again).

6. Acquisition of help with family burdens (financial, parenting children, and so forth). (Sager et al., 1983, pp. 61-62)

Although these motivations may be partially valid in each case, make sure you have thought through all your reasons for remarrying making a conscious rather than a reactive decision.

A final note regarding remarriage. Sager et al. (1983) identified the optimum time for remarriage to be 3-5 years after the initial separation. This time frame allows the grief process to do its work and gives the person some time on his/her own but does not forge a single lifestyle that is rigid and inflexible making accommodation to a life together difficult. We concur with this view. We have worked with remarried couples who married too soon and with some who waited too long.

REMARRIED FAMILY:
FACING FACTS AND DEBUNKING FICTIONS

First the Facts

Remarried families are not an endangered species. One-fifth of all families in the United States are stepfamilies making them an integral part of our society (Sager et al., 1983). Although stepfamilies are common, they also are different from intact nuclear failies. This fact is sometimes difficult to accept by the parents who form the stepfamily by remarriage and would like to se themselves as an "ordinary family." For one thing, stepfamilies are more complex; whereas, intact families develop by a process of synchrony being initiated by a marriage and then developing sequentially through the stages of the family life cycle, stepfamilies emerge on the basis of a developmental clash. Minimally, two processes always occur at once. One is the establishment of the marriage relationship, and the other is the formation of a reconstituted family unit. This dualism is operational at all times and can be further complicated if two family systems are merged in which children are in different stages of the family life cycle (e.g., one family has adolescent children and the other has school age children). Finally, further complexity can emerge if the remarried couple has children of their own. TV versions of the stepfamily such as *The Brady Bunch* or *Eight is Enough* do not even scratch the surface relative to complexity.

Visher and Visher (1982) pointed out that stepfamilies differ from biological families in the following ways:

1. All stepfamily members have experienced important losses.

2. All family members have past family experiences.

3. Parent-child bonds predate the new couple relationship.

4. There is a biological parent elsewhere either living or deceased.

5. Children are often members of two households.

6. No legal relationship exists between stepparent and stepchild. (p. 336)

McGoldrick and Carter (1980) added that remarried families must contend with three sets of emotional baggage while intact nuclear families must deal with only one—the parents' families of origin. Stepfamilies have the added baggage from the first marriage, separation/divorce, and period between marriages. If these issues are not enough, another burden is that stepfamilies tend to be viewed by society as second class family units. Negative referents such as broken homes, failed marriages, stepchild, stepmother, or stepfather cast a pallor of disdain on the stepfamily.

Then the Fictions

To further complicate the process of forming a reconstituted family, remarrying partners tend to hold certain myths that interfere with facing the realities of forming a family. Three of the most common myths are as follows:

1. The Myth of Reconstituting a Nuclear Family, i.e., the remarried couple believes they can form a remarried family patterned after a biological, nuclear family model.

2. The Myth of Instant Love and/or Instant Adjustment, i.e., the remarried couple believes an instantaneous family cohesion that emulates their own togetherness will occur.

3. The Myth of the Wicked Stepmother, i.e., the remarrying couple believes they will not fall into the trap of the nasty stereotypic step person. (Visher & Visher, 1982, p. 333)

To counter these myths, remarrying partners must give up their attachment to the ideal first family structure and replace it with a different conceptual model for a family. Remarrying partners need to cultivate an attitude that accepts the time, space, ambiguity, and difficulty involved in all family members moving toward stepfamily organization (McGoldrick & Carter, 1980). Finally one should realize that the "step" implies a relationship of choice that is a two way street and that the "wicked" is not an inherent trait of a stepparent but a possible product if you are rebuffed by children who choose not to choose you.

Visher and Visher (1982) identified four basic categories of tasks with which stepfamilies must deal to become a fully functioning family unit. These are

1. mourning of losses,

2. negotiation and development of new family traditions,

3. formation of new alliances and preservation of old alliances that are still important, and

4. stepfamily integration.

Each of these categories will be alluded to in our discussion of considerations in forming a remarried family.

REMARRIED FAMILY:
CONSIDERATIONS AND COMMENTARY

Many of the remarried families with whom we have worked have presented themselves when rather normal developmental problems have generated a sense of precariousness in the family. Whether the problem emanated from the marital or family domain or both, the precipitating factor in seeking help was a sensitivity to the unique nature of the step-family and a feeling on the parents' part that they preferred to act too early rather than too late. In most of these cases, the family was actually doing quite well but needed reassurance that they were on the right track and affirmation of their ability to succeed as a family unit. We heartily commend such families because they have the courage not to wait.

The most serious precipitating problem that typically brings a remarried family to therapy is dealing with an adolescent who has pressured the family to the point of considering extrusion. These families generally have reached the proverbial end of the line with the child and are ready to boot him/her out in the interest of preserving the family. A common situation is for one parent to be at a point of saying "It's either him/her or me; one of us has got to go." In between these two extremes are many variations. In order to evaluate stepfamilies we see in counseling, the following criteria are considered. These concepts were presented by Robert Garfield in a Workshop on Stepfamilies at the 1983 AAMFT Convention in Dallas, Texas.

1. How the family has resolved the experiences of loss from the prior family.

2. How the family has established new roles and traditions in the remarried household.

3. How the family has developed and maintained relationships with ex-spouses and ex-spouses' kin.

4. How the family has managed to reestablish ties with the spouse's own family of origin.

Dealing with Losses

Even when couples by choice or chance   wait the prescribed amount of time to mourn their loss, remarriage tends to have some residuals from the grieving process. In fact, while the adults may have fully recovered from their loss, the children may be just beginning to recover.

For children, the remarriage signals the end of their fantasies about their parents getting back together. While the marriage day may be the happiest moment in the parents' life, it may be the saddest in the children's. Consequently, in the early stages of the remarried family, children may need permission to and assistance in grieving the loss of their former family unit.

For the child other losses may occur that are activated by the remarriage. Besides the loss of the reconciliation dream, they may have to move to a new environment, have less contact with the noncustodial parent, and lose their position in the sibling sub-system. The displacement in the sibling hierarchy can be particularly painful if the lost position is that of oldest or youngest. Sometimes these factors are overlooked or given insufficient attention as the family re-forms.

Establishing New Roles and Traditions

While a first marriage is complicated by the fact that it joins two family systems, a remarriage compounds that complication by joining 3, 4, 5, 6, or more families. At least 15 family structures are found in a remarriage if both spouses have children from previous marriages. If the married couple has a child, the possible structures jump to 30. This complexity takes time to organize.

When a remarried family is formed, many "instants" result. Instant family occurs but not instant intimacy. If one spouse has not been a parent before, he/she becomes an "instant parent." Instant siblings and instant step-relatives in various shapes and sizes are added to the family. One ten year-old boy told us that after his mother remarried he found that he had a 3 year-old uncle. Add these to the already existing network of relatives from the previous family and even the best of us will get confused.

The key adjustments to watch are those in the sibling sub-system in which the ordinal positions of the merging siblings are jostled into place. If opposite sex teenagers become relatives through this remarriage, awkward sexual tensions may occur. These tensions also may exist between the teenager and the non-biological parent of the opposite sex. Issues of belonging, propriety, privacy, property, and who should be called what must be ferreted out and then managed constructively.

Name changes and names used when referring to parents (first names, mom, dad, and so forth) should be discussed. Names represent delicate loyalty and identity issues that are important to surface. Running rough shod over any of these areas can create inner turmoil and pain in family members. Also important is the attitude with which these issues are addressed. The "laying down of the law" approach appears to have negative consequences while discussion and letting family members make up their minds over time has more potential for satisfactory resolution.

Many remarried families report good results from weekly family meetings in which these organizational issues are discussed. While initially these meetings facilitate adjustment, if continued they also spur growth and development of the family as a unit.

The adults also may have trouble with developing their roles. A stepparent may feel guilty because he/she is unable to love the spouse's child(ren). This lack of emotional involvement is especially problematic when the stepparent tries to discipline without the love factor, a situation that is accentuated when the child(ren) overtly expresses attachment and loyalty to the natural parents.

Examples

Will the Real Mother Please Stand Up? One remarried family of three came to therapy because the son (age 12) had been experiencing difficulties in school. The father (age 40) had been previously married and had received custody of the son after cause for neglect by the natural mother had been shown. The stepmother (age 26) had not been married previously. Although the wife had cognitively known about the situation she was entering, she was not emotionally, experientially, or maturationally prepared for all the ramifications. She indicated she did not love the boy but felt responsible for maintaining discipline. She also was the primary contact person with the school. She harbored thoughts of having a child of her own, but her husband had unequivocally stated he wanted no more children because he was too old. Consequently she became resentful of the child as well. The husband felt she was too hard on the boy and couldn't understand why she didn't love him. The boy was caught between loyalty to a natural mother he rarely saw, a step-mother who disciplined but couldn't love, and a father who was still emotionally scarred from his previous encounter with marriage.

Stepfamily Complexity. Let's look at one additional example of the complexity stepfamilies represent. The Smith family consisted of mother, father, and three boys. Both parents had been married previously. The father had custody of his two sons, ages 10 and 8. The mother had an 11 year-old son, who was born deaf and lived away from home during the school year but was with the family during vacations, and a son who lived with his natural father. They came to therapy because mom was unable to establish a relationship with the father's oldest boy. During therapy the father, whose former wife had committed suicide, ascertained that neither of the two boys were his biological children. His current wife could have no more children. The 10 year-old son was expressing a strong desire to go and live with his mother's parents and was accelerating tension in the family to that end.

The main theme of this family was extreme pain generated by multiple losses. Dynamically the family was unstable. When the deaf child would come home he would displace the 10 year old as the oldest. Because sign language was necessary for communication, mom would get upset with dad because he had not learned how. Besides numerous family of origin and previous marriage issues for both parents, the father had to deal with the knowledge that he in fact had no natural sons and could not have any by his current wife. In spite of all this adversity and complexity, this family did extremely well in therapy as they untangled the issues of the past, experienced and acknowledged their pain, and addressed the current problems of becoming a family unit.

Ex-connections

The nature of the relationships with ex-spouses and ex-spouses' kin is generally a good indicator of the health, vitality, and stability of a remarried family. If the remarried family can form flexible boundaries that allow freedom of movement between ex-relationships and the new family unit without creating undue tension or antagonism, the family is usually in pretty good shape. On the other hand if such contact represents a threat to the new marriage or the stepfamily, probably unfinished business which needs attention is present.

For example, if contact between ex-spouses results in strain in the marriage, usually incomplete emotional detachment is involved. On the other hand, for the new spouse to serve as a go-between for ex-spouses in matters of working out child care and other interrelational arrangements is not unusual. A key to effective resolution of ex-spouse relating is the level of support that the new spouses can give each other to do so. Antagonism between ex-spouses usually lessens significantly when both have new spouses. In addition effective communication relative to the children will reduce stress in both new family units. One cautionary note, relative to contact between ex-spouses and new spouses: a constructive groundrule governing that contact is not to discuss either the former spouse or the current status of the new relationship. Too many hidden agendas could emerge. One woman who had contact with her ex-husband through their co-parenting arrangement indicated she started feeling closer to her "ex" when her current marriage started having problems. This sent confusing signals to both men resulting in negative reactions in the marriage. However, congenial and cooperative relationships can develop between ex-spouses and their new families.

Example

Effective Ex-connections. The Johnson family came for counseling as a remarried family with adolescent children. Mr. Johnson had four grown children from a previous marriage and Mrs. Johnson had 3 teenage boys who lived with her and her new husband. Her former spouse had remarried a woman who had not been married before, and they were about to have a child. Custody arrangements had the boys visiting their father every other weekend and living with him during summer vacation. The Johnson's came to the counseling session because of relational difficulties between the boys and their mother. Although the boys related effectively to their step-dad, the issues involved permeated both family environments. As a result, both remarried families attended the sessions in order to work out consistent boundaries for the adolescent boys that applied to both domains.

Another vital ex-connection is that between the ex-spouses' parents and their grandchildren. Grandparents do not relish losing contact with their grandchildren. You can save yourself a lot of grief if you make positive efforts to keep that connection alive. Not only will your children benefit, but you will circumvent many obstacles grandparents have been known to invent to make life difficult for you.

Remarriage and The Family of Origin Connection

Remarriage tends to have a significant impact on the spouse's relationship with his/her family of origin. While first marriages may be heavily involved with separation and individuation issues, the second marriage signals a shift to a more adult-to-adult relating posture. When a divorce occurs, parents have a tendency to take their child's marriage failure as a personal criticism of their own parenting. They may be hurt by the divorce more than the divorcing child is aware. Sometimes they recoil and withdraw in disapproval as a self-protective mechanism. Thus, when the second marriage occurs the stigma of being bad parents is lifted and an enthusiastic starting over emerges for all concerned. One father who strongly disapproved of his daughter's first marriage told us he was "pleased as punch" by her second choice. This revitalization when it occurs is a valuable resource to the remarried family.

Other times parents react by becoming overprotective of their divorced child and their now fatherless/motherless grandchildren. Although this reaction may be initially helpful to the divorcing parent, it may raise complications when remarriage occurs. The grandparents may resent being displaced by the new spouse creating tension in the marriage and the family. Consequently, the remarrying couple must be sensitive to the grandparents' feelings conveying gratitude for assistance and establishing effective communication as they engage in re-differentiating themselves as a family unit.

SO YOU WANT TO REMARRY

We realize we have only scratched the surface concerning remarriage, but hopefully you get the message that meaningful preparation is equally important if not more so, the second time around. With respect to remarriage many pitfalls can emerge. Clinically we find (1) the denial of the importance of prior loss, (2) little time between marriages, (3) failure to resolve intense relationship issues in the first family (including extended family), and (4) expectations that remarriage will be rapidly and easily accepted, all portend poor adjustment in a step-family (McGoldrick & Carter, 1980, p. 276).

Take the time to do things constructively. Since at least two years are usually necessary to adjust to losses due to divorce, and another two years are needed for remarried families to stabilize and adjust, set yourself to be patient. Four years, give or take a couple, many seem like a long time, but all good things take time especially with regard to family life. So, if your life path leads you to separation/divorce and then to remarriage and you have become a parent in the process, our final appeal to you is that as you go through both the pain and the joy, *take your time* and *don't forget the children.*

REFERENCES

Beal, E.W. (1980). Separation, divorce, and single parent families. In E.A. Carter and M. McGoldrick (Eds.), *The family life cycle: A framework for family therapy,* 245-264. New York: Gardner Press.

Cantor, D.W., & Drake, E.A. (1983). *Divorced parents and their children.* New York: Springer Publishing.

Cherlin, A. (1978). Remarriage as an incomplete institution. *American Journal of Sociology, 84,* 634-650.

Garfield, R. (1983). Concepts presented in a workshop on *Stepfamilies* at the 1983 AAMFT Convention in Dallas, TX.

Goldsmith, J. (1982). The postdivorce family system. In F. Walsh (Ed.), *Normal family processes,* 297-330. New York: The Guilford Press.

Katz, L., & Stein, S. (1983). Treating Stepfamilies. In B.B. Wolman and G. Stricker (Eds.), *Handbook of family and marital therapy,* 387-420. New York: Plenum Press.

Kubler-Ross, E. (1969). *On death and dying.* New York: Collier Books, Macmillan.

McGoldrick, M., & Carter, E.A. (1980). Forming a remarried family. In E.A. Carter and M. McGoldrick (Eds.), *The family life cycle: A framework for family therapy,* 265-294. New York: Gardner Press.

Sager, C.J., Brown, H.S., Crohn, H., Engel, T., Rodstein, E., & Walker, L. (1983). *Treating the remarried family.* New York: Brunner, Mazel Publishers.

Saxton, L. (1983). *The individual, marriage, and the family.* Belmont, CA: Wadsworth Publishing.

Sheehy, G. (1981). *Pathfinders.* Toronto: Bantam Books.

U.S. Bureau of the Census (1985a). U.S. Department of Commerce, population reports, Series P-20, No. 398 *Household and family characteristics: March, 1984.* Washington, DC: U.S. Printing Office.

U.S. Bureau of the Census (1985b). U.S. Department of Commerce. *U.S. Statistics at a Glance.* Washington, DC: U.S. Printing Office.

Visher, J.S., & Visher, E.B. (1982). Stepfamilies and stepparenting. In F. Walsh (Ed.), *Normal family processes,* 331-353. New York: Guilford Press.

Wolpert-Zun, A., & Bross, A. (1982). The formation of the reconstituted family system: Processes, problems, and treatment goals. In A. Bross (Ed.), *Family therapy: Principles of strategic practice,* 114-127. New York: Guilford Press.

CHAPTER 10

RESOURCES
BEYOND THE FAMILY NETWORK

In this chapter is presented an overview of professional and community resources available to couples and families for purposes of enrichment, support, and remediation. Also, specific information is provided regarding programs to help families in crisis or support families which need additional resources.

Marriage and family have the dubious distinction of being both the most resourceful and the most fragile of all social institutions. On the one hand, couples and families endure, survive, and even thrive under the most difficult of circumstances. On the other, they have a tendency to get stuck, become disoriented, and self-destructive, and create experiences and turmoil that draw the attention and intervention of outside agents to them. The reason for this conundrum is not entirely found within the specific marriage or family involved. In spite of best efforts to prepare for, face realistically, and work constructively with typical and usual developmental difficulties of marriage or family life, couples and families find their resources stretched thin or lacking because support systems outside the family have disintegrated or are inadequate to help the couple or family cope and make healthy adjustments.

Lewis (1980) in reporting on the *White House Conference on Families* observed that in American society the family is working overtime to survive. In other words, no matter how resourceful a family may be, it may need outside assistance in some form to successfully adapt to its life circumstances and realistically to face its problems. Consequently, marriages and families may reach the end of their "copability" rope because of inner forces, outer forces, or a combination of both.

The fact that marriage and family come with problems built into their fabric is not even debatable. An ancient Chinese proverb states, "Nobody's family can hang out the sign, 'Nothing the matter here.'" The question is, what happens when a marriage or family is not able to resolve difficulties or deal with tasks on its own? Curran (1983) studied the traits of a healthy family and found that of the 15 traits that typified health, one was "the healthy family admits to and seeks help with problems" (p. 257). She drew the following conclusion from her research:

> Today's family is healthy because it is able to admit to need and seek help in the early stages of a problem. In fact, it might even be said that the healthier the family today, the sooner it is likely to admit to its weakness and work on it publicly, a direct turnaround from a couple generations ago when the best families were problemless. (p. 258)

The purpose of this chapter is to give an overview of professional and community resources that can be mobilized when couples or families need help. The intent is to identify resources available outside the family network and designate their nature and relevance to marriage and family experience. Categories of resources available will first be discussed and then resources will be delineated in a more specific sense, including brief descriptions of the various services and where to obtain them in a general sense. The underlying premise of the chapter is that it is both a sign of health and a wise decision on the part of couples and families to make use of outside resources whenever they are appropriate and available.

That premise applies to all marriages and families, whether they are in a state of health, struggling with problems, or embroiled in crisis.

TYPES OF HELP
MARRIAGES/FAMILIES NEED

Education

The primary goal of education is to assist couples and families in understanding and constructively working with their current or expected life situations. As such, education serves both a preventive and a preparatory function: preventive in that information is presented to increase awareness, knowledge, and understanding, and preparatory in that skills are taught to facilitate effective application of relevant knowledge. Marriage or family education usually takes the form of classes, workshops, or presentations sponsored by social service agencies, community mental health organizations, churches, schools, private practitioners, nonprofit agencies, and civic groups. Topics and information are usually publicized in the media or available through the sponsoring party.

Growth and Enrichment

A basic premise of *Transactional Analysis (TA)* is that "you don't have to be sick to get better." The same applies to marriage and family. Many times couples and families like the manner in which their relationships are progressing but are motivated to make even more satisfying changes in their lives. They just don't know how to do it. Programs, courses, and retreats sponsored by a host of private and public agencies are available to couples and families who are well but want to pursue a deeper, more enriched, and fuller marital/family experience. These programs are also designed as a stimulus for relationships that are not necessarily in trouble but have stagnated or reached a plateau of complacency. They can ignite the spark that enables growth to materialize again in the marriage or family relationship.

The concept of *wellness* has become especially applicable to marriage and family life. In the past, couples basically took a philosophical position that "if it works, it don't need fixing." They believed that the family would take care of itself and only when major difficulties arose would external assistance be sought. This corrective concept is now being complemented by the wellness emphasis. Corrective measures are certainly very appropriate when needed. However, couples and families are beginning to buy into the idea that health in the marriage and family can be actively sought by building upon strengths in a manner that accelerates growth, prevents problems, and enriches life experiences.

Support

Some couples and families, due to the lack or loss of resources, need support services temporarily or over an extended period of time. Support services are intended to either fill in gaps in the family system or shore up the family resources by providing reinforcement, assistance, and encouragement. Support is supplementary to the marriage or family. It recognizes that the family is essentially responsible, but adds more resources to its operation to increase functionality as a unit or to meet specific needs of a member(s) within that unit. Support services are usually available through social service and community mental health agencies; churches; volunteer, community, or nonprofit organizations; and private individuals.

Marital/Family Counseling and Therapy

Counseling. When couples or families run into problems they cannot seem to resolve or have difficulty dealing with the tasks of a particular developmental stage of the marriage or family, counseling can be useful. In most cases, couples or families come for counseling with rather clearly defined problems that are hampering their functioning and causing discomfort in the relationship. Counseling tends to be short-term, averaging 8 to 12 sessions spread out over several months. Counseling is available from trained professionals working in social service or community mental health organizations, private practice, churches or other settings that are locally recognized as mental health care service providers. Counseling services are usually provided in an out-patient setting.

Therapy. Counseling and therapy can be viewed as synonymous or different, depending on the perspective of the person providing the service. Generally, therapy refers to a process that is of greater intensity and longer duration than counseling. Couples and families who come for therapy tend to be in quite serious dilemmas and in need of major reconstructive change (as opposed to problem resolution). The provider also may be more highly trained. Therapy tends to involve anywhere from 20 to 40 sessions over a period of six months to two years, sometimes longer. Therapy services are provided by professionals in social service and community mental health organizations, individual private practice, or group private practice, churches, and other settings which are recognized as mental health care service providers. Therapy services may be provided on either an out-patient or in-patient basis.

Credentials. Marriage/family counselors and therapists generally have degrees at the master's level and beyond. One guideline, however, is to look for credentialing beyond their degree status. If the counselor/therapist is licensed, that means that some governmental agency has recognized his/her credentials and approved that person's right to practice. If the person is a Clinical Member of the *American Association for Marriage and Family Therapy (AAMFT),* it means that the person has met AAMFT's standards of competence for clinical practice in marriage and family counseling/therapy. Licensing will vary from state to state and from discipline to discipline (counselors, psychologists, social workers, and so forth), but a good idea is to seek out professionals who have been recognized by both an academic institution (degree) *and* a governmental agency (license) or professional organization (credential). In addition, some professionals will hold credentials from recognized marriage and family training programs (e.g., *Philadelphia Child Guidance, Boston Family Institute,* or the *Ackerman Family Institute)* that are not associated with an institution of higher education. Such credentials are also valid.

Crisis Intervention

Crisis intervention is necessary in marriages and families whenever the health and well-being of an individual or the unit itself is in danger. Crisis intervention may be mobilized either from within the marriage or family, or by an outside agent (e.g., police, neighbor, social service agent). Crisis intervention is most often associated with self-destructive or other-destructive actions occurring within the marriage or family. Crises also tend to be related directly to one or more of the abuse modalities: alcohol or drug, physical, sexual, or emotional. They also may be precipitated by grief reactions related to the death of a family member, divorce, or other form of loss (e.g., job or physical disability) that deal a traumatic blow to the family. Most crisis services are provided by community mental health and social service agencies or community-based and supported programs which provide services to a designated crisis population. Most communities have crisis phone lines in addition to the specific services. In the absence of specific information regarding help in crisis, the police and/or the emergency room at the local hospital can be contacted.

Availability of Help

All of the categories of services to couples and families previously described in a general way are available in most communities. Perusing the yellow pages of your phone book or simply mobilizing the communication system of your interpersonal network (friends, neighbors, pastor, teachers, counselors, police, and so forth) will get you in contact with the specific program or service area for which you are looking. However, a useful idea is to know generally the specific kinds of programs you can search out and request.

DELINEATING RESOURCES
TO COUPLES AND FAMILIES

The purpose of this section is to label and briefly describe a wide variety of programs, activities, and services in order to increase the specificity with which you can proceed in getting help.

Education

Marriage and family resources in terms of preparation, prevention, and education come in many varieties.

Preparation for Marriage. Premarital counseling or marriage preparation as David Mace (1972), author of *Getting Ready for Marriage,* preferred to call it, is a general requirement of most clergy and churches. Prospective spouses are required to attend one to three sessions (sometimes more) individually and/or in a class of other couples as a prerequisite to exchanging their nuptial vows. We applaud this practice, and advocate even more extensive pre-marital preparation. We recommend using resources such as *PREPARE* (Olson, Druckman & Fournier, n.d.), Roberts and Wright, *Before You Say I Do: A Marriage Preparation Manual for Couples* (1978) or work with a counselor who will guide you through a well-conceived agenda of premarital considerations in a methodical and helpful manner. Effective premarital counseling will touch on most of the topics covered in this book.

Family Planning. Most community mental health programs and many medical groups offer family planning services. In addition, a variety of other private and/or non-profit organizations can be found to assist you in family planning. These organizations usually provide a wide range of services, including sex education, pregnancy testing, family planning methods, venereal disease detection and treatment, and information and referral. Most of these agencies also have medical staff available or actually provide services. Some of the programs may have names like *Planned Parenthood, Birthright,* or *Natural Family Planning.*

Parenting Classes. A parenting class can be found for just about every phase of parenting. Starting with prenatal classes for both parents, these classes move right up the chronological and developmental ladder with the child. Sample titles include *Caring for Your Newborn, Father and His Baby, Parenting Preschool Children, Parenting School Age Children, Parenting Adolescents, Tough Love,* or *Adolescence: The Time of Life Parents Love to Hate.*

Several standardized and highly regarded parenting programs, such as Gordon's (1970) *Parent Effectiveness Training (P.E.T.)* or Dinkmeyer and McKay's (1976) *Systematic Training for Effective Parenting (S.T.E.P.),* also may be available. Recently, step-parenting classes also have been organized and taught to help parents with the special issues of parenting in a remarried family. In fact, educational programs in the whole area of step-families are being promoted by groups, such as the *Stepfamily Association of America, Inc.* (Visher & Visher, 1979).

Family Education Centers. Most of the larger metropolitan areas have family education centers which sponsor a whole host of educational programs designed to meet family needs. These centers may be private (profit or nonprofit) or supported by the community in some way. For example, in Minneapolis, Chicago, and Washington, DC, the *Alfred Adler Institute* has a Family Education Center. The *YMCA* and *YWCA* also sponsor these kinds of programs, as do the adult education branches of public schools, colleges, and vocational technical schools. Other typical sponsors are religious affiliated agencies, like *Lutheran Social Services, Catholic Charities,* or the *Jewish Community Center.*

Growth and Enrichment

The growth and enrichment category of resources is relatively new on the scene. David and Vera Mace (1977) have been pioneers in the whole area of marriage preparation and marriage enrichment. Mace (1977) has labeled marriage enrichment "The New Frontier." He is a founder of the recently established organization called the *Association of Couples for Marriage Enrichment (ACME)* which is dedicated to conquering the marital enrichment frontier and expanding the process as both a preventive and qualitative contribution to marriage.

Marriage Encounter/Marriage Enrichment. Initiated during the late 1950s by Father Gabriel Calvo and the Catholic Church in Spain, *Marriage Encounter* has become a world-wide program (Mace, 1982). Other religious organizations have developed their own versions of marriage enrichment based on similar purposes and activities. Marriage encounter/marriage enrichment is a mental health care process designed to enrich relationships partners expect to continue. Opportunities to participate in marriage enrichment can be most easily found by contacting the clergy in your church or local area. The typical program involves a weekend retreat with the potential for follow-up sessions as well. An extensive network of past participants and leaders exists, forming a context that supports the program and provides opportunity to get first-hand feedback about the program.

First Year Marriage Counseling. David Mace, at the 1983 AAMFT Convention in Washington, DC, called for the development and implementation of a program for married couples during their first year of marriage. He noted that the first year of marriage is much more important than even the courtship period because patterns and roles are forming that later become ever so difficult to change. During the first year of marriage when partners are still really excited about each other and are eager to work things out together is the time to participate in a marriage growth program. Doing so will help you consciously build the relationship you want with benefits that will be experienced throughout your marriage. If no specific program is available in your area, contact a counselor to do this on your own. A friend of ours, Charles Barnard, co-author of *The Theory and Technique of Family Therapy,* (Barnard & Corrales, 1979) has told us that part of his daughter's wedding gift will be his paying for her and her husband to go to counseling during the first year of their marriage. That is not a bad idea, regardless of who pays for it.

Couples Communication Programs. A wide range of programs is available which brings couples together in workshops or classes to teach them communication skills. The most well-known model of this type is the Minnesota Couples Communication Program (Miller, Nunnally, & Wackman, 1976). The advantage to this type of program is that the couple gets the training together in a learning oriented, experiential setting with other couples who are working on the same thing. Couples communication programs are presented in both intensive workshops and weekly class sessions. The sessions are generally taught by professionals with training in communications skills or trainers who have completed the Minnesota training program or an equivalent course.

Family Enrichment Programs. Programs designed to help families improve their communication and maximize their relating potential are becoming more prevalent. Retreats, classes, and workshops are offered to families under the label of *Family Wellness* or *Family Enrichment.* Specific programs such as *Relationship Enrichment Training (R.E.T.)* (Guerney, 1977) or *Understanding Us* (Carnes, 1981) may be available in your area. Churches, mental health organizations, and private practitioners are becoming more active in promoting programs for families which involve the whole family working together. Such opportunities may be just the key to enhancing your family life.

Family Reunions: Harold Wise, in an article entitled *The Ties That Bind Can Also Heal* (Yates, 1979), described family reunions as a therapeutic and health producing experience for family members. You can even hire professionals who will help you orchestrate a family reunion in order to enhance its overall benefit to those in attendance and to the family as a whole. In most cases, just the realization that family reunions are healthy may be enough to inspire you to not only go but to organize them yourselves.

Marriage Counseling/Therapy

The distinguishing features of examples in this section are that the marital pair are the primary and/or only recipients of the service, and they are involved together. Concerns in marriage counseling/therapy generally are associated with relationship problems, sexual difficulties, or divorce.

Marital Counseling/Therapy. Services of a professional marriage counselor can be obtained to help the marital pair work constructively and together on issues and problems of their relationship. In most cases the couple tacitly acknowledges that the goal is to make the marriage better by resolving their problems so the relationship can continue.

Sex Therapy. Married couples, who experience sexual problems, may opt for sex therapy from professionally trained sex therapists. The goal of sex therapy is amelioration of sexual dysfunction (Kaplan, 1974). Masters and Johnson (1966, 1970) are noted authorities in the field and have trained large numbers of therapists in their approach.

Divorce Counseling/Therapy. The marital pair engages in the divorce counseling/therapy process to (1) effectively disengage from each other, (2) learn from what went wrong as a preventive measure in future relationships, and (3) negotiate any unfinished business. The goal is to separate the couple with the least possible psychological damage to all concerned. Although divorce is usually the stipulated goal, the issue of reconciliation may also be addressed.

Divorce Mediation. Structured mediation in divorce settlement is a process that has been developed to assist divorcing couples in developing an equitable basis for terminating the marital relationship (Coogler, 1983). The concept of mediation is rapidly gaining acceptance as an effective means of settling differences between partners once divorce has been decided as the option of choice. The process essentially mediates the divorce settlement in a structured manner under the auspices of a trained mediator dealing with such issues as (1) property division, (2) terminating dependency on the relationship, and (3) continuing ongoing business initiated by the partnership, e.g., responsibility for the children born to the relationship (Baruth & Huber, 1984). Divorce mediation is a viable alternative to the adversary approach espoused by the legal system.

Family Counseling/Therapy

Although many different approaches to family counseling and therapy can be used, we will distinguish services in this section based on who is being treated and that person's family designation.

Nuclear Family Counseling/Therapy. Nuclear family counseling involves the parents and children in a biological family. Usually both parents and all the children will be involved, although the therapist may bring in parts of the family depending on the topic or area being considered for that session.

Extended Family Counseling/Therapy. The family unit is expanded to include the grandparent generation or other members who live with the family. If extended family members live under the same roof with the nuclear family or are intricately involved in the affairs of the nuclear family, this counseling may be essential.

Family Divorce Counseling/Therapy. Once parents have decided upon divorce, they may come for counseling in order to help the children deal with the divorce and to facilitate the transition from being a family with married parents to a family with divorced parents.

Co-parenting Family Counseling/Therapy. Once the divorce has been finalized, parents may want this type of counseling or therapy in order to develop an effective co-parenting approach to the family. Many of the same issues are addressed as in family divorce counseling; however, the differentiation of the adults as parents and not spouses is clearer.

Single Parent Family Counseling/Therapy. The custodial parent and children are usually involved in this type of therapy, although in some cases the noncustodial parent requests the counseling. Counseling is directed toward helping the family adjust to fewer resources and deal with the special issues associated with being a single parent family.

Blended or Remarried Family Counseling/Therapy. This counseling involves parents, one or both of whom have been previously married, and children from the previous relationships who are now joined into a family unit. The family also may include biological children from the current marriage and children of previous relationships who are only in the family part-time. The focus of the counseling or therapy is on forming a healthy merged family system and resolving special issues associated with being a remarried family (Sager, Brown, Crohn, Engel, Rodstein, & Walker, 1983).

Family of Origin Therapy. Framo (1982) called family of origin therapy the "major surgery of family therapy." This therapy is essentially designed to help adult children confront and deal with the unfinished business of their family of origin. Usually the counseling involves advanced planning and requires the cooperation of the adult child's parents, regardless of the geographical proximity.

Network Family Therapy. Sometimes when a family essentially has exhausted all other channels of therapeutic intervention, a family therapy network will be utilized to generate change in the family (Rueveni, 1979; Speck & Attneave, 1973). The process involves the family mobilizing a group of thirty or more people who are willing to assist them in working on their problems. A Family Therapy team then works with the network to move the family in a health direction.

Marriage and Family Checkups

Although the implication of counseling or therapy is that the couple or family has problems, a good idea is to periodically schedule counseling sessions as a precautionary measure. Just as scheduling medical physicals is a wise preventive health care measure, scheduling marriage and family checkups to examine your relationship and family functioning is propitious. To run your car without regularly scheduled maintenance is highly unadvisable. To let your marriage and family run until problems crop up before you take precautions also is unadvisable. Regular counseling done periodically is advantageous to growth and can be interesting and stimulating as well.

Support Services

Support services come in many forms from many different sources. The examples that follow are certainly not exhaustive but are rather a potpourri of possibilities that couples and families have used to strengthen their lives together.

Role Models for Children. Circumstances in families at times warrant consideration of providing children with an outside the family adult or young adult role model. The loss of one parent due to death or divorce, unavailability of extended family members to fill in, age differences in siblings, or lack of siblings may result in parents turning to organizations such as *Big Brothers/Big Sisters of America* or *Kinship* for assistance. These programs and others like them seek to match children with a suitable person who is willing to spend time with and pay attention to the child. Volunteers are screened and matched with the approval of the family and care is taken to follow each match in order to make sure the best interests of the child and the family are taken into account.

Organizations such as the *Boy Scouts/Girl Scouts of America, Boys Clubs/Girls Clubs, YMCA/YWCA,* and *4-H* also extend opportunities to children, not only for activities, learning, and socialization, but also for contact with adult leaders who can be support persons and role models.

Certainly teachers, school counselors, coaches, and youth leaders in churches and community organizations also play important roles in this regard.

Grandparent Connection. Families in which the grandparents have died or live a great distance away sometimes feel the need for children to have the attention only a grandparent figure can provide. A specialness exists to the connection between people who are distanced by at least one generation, and children are sometimes much more responsive to a grandparent than a parent figure. Parents, who value this kind of experience for their children, seek out stand-in grandparents to fill in the gap created by death or distance. *Foster Grandparent* and *Adopt a Grandparent* programs are springing up in many communities. These programs, often sponsored by senior citizens centers, derive benefit in two directions. The children acquire the valued experience of relating to a grandparent and become sensitive to needs and worth of the elderly, and the elderly volunteers find meaning and self-esteem in contributing to the young person and his/her family's life.

Day Care/Child Care Programs. Most communities have public and private day care programs which play a vital role in assisting parents involved in the work force or other responsibilities which require leaving their children under the auspices of an outside-the-family authority. Unless you arrange for child care services informally with family, friends, or neighbors, be aware that child care programs in most states are regulated by laws and standards designed to protect your child. Always check the credentials of the person or persons running the program and determine if the program is licensed and in good standing with the state. Persons who have an associate or bachelor's degree in child care and are CDA Certified (CDA stands for *Child Development Association,* a child care credentialing organization in Washington, DC) are professionals who have met standards to provide child care and have been recognized as competent by an academic, professional, or governmental agency.

Parenting Assistance. Sometimes parents need more help than can be provided by attending parenting classes. They need someone to be more directly related to their family functioning. Three types of programs that may be available in this regard are *Parent Networking, Parents in Need,* and *Parents Without Partners.* Parent Networking is a concept that can be implemented formally by schools, community agents, or mental health workers who want to bring parents together in supportive networks to help each other with common problems. This type of program has been particularly helpful with adolescents around such issues as curfews, parties, and the use of alcohol and drugs. Parents themselves can mobilize this kind of support by contacting parents of their children's friends for the purpose of developing guidelines that have a commonality across families of their children's peer group.

Parents in Need is a volunteer organization which provides resource persons to serve as parent aides. Matches are made based on the need and developmental level of the family and the experience and resources of the parent aide. The parent aides are volunteers who are interested in participating as a service to the community.

Parents Without Partners is an organization formed to meet the needs of single parents. The organization sponsors educational programs and social activities and generally provides support to single parents in various forms from informal relating to parent support groups.

Support Groups. Support groups are an emerging form of assistance based on the principle of developing a peer support system among persons experiencing similar problems and difficulties. As a result, support groups are available or can be formed with respect to almost any type of difficult circumstance or problem that can afflict a marriage or family. Some of the more common support groups are grief and loss support groups, battered women and battering men support groups, women's and men's support groups, parent support groups, and alcohol and chemical dependency support groups. Support groups that have emerged recently are groups for children of divorced families and groups for adult children who are caring for aging and/or infirm parents. In some sense, *Alcoholics Anonymous (AA)* and its offshoots *Alanon* (for partners of alcoholics), and *Alateen* (for children of alcoholic families) are the most sophisticated and well-known examples of the support group concept. *Gamblers Anonymous* and *Weight Watchers* are other programs that function along similar lines, using peer support dynamics as their primary means of providing help and assistance.

Women's Resource Centers. Services and assistance for women are becoming more and more available in most communities. Assistance may vary from support groups and classes that teach assertiveness to services which assist women getting back into education or the work force. Most higher education institutions have women's resource centers or may have programs that are designed to help older women returning to school (sometimes called *Non-Traditional Student Services).* Community women's programs may have names like *Working Opportunities for Women, Chrysalis, The Women's Project,* or other similar names that attest to both the clientele they serve and the nature of their services.

First Call for Help. Couples and families who recognize a need for help often run into the problem of where to get it. Nothing is more frustrating, discouraging, or tension-producing than to have taken the first difficult step of recognizing a need and then being unable to take the next step of doing something about that need. For that reason many communities have instituted telephone services such as the *United Way's First Call for Help.* This program provides free information on health, welfare, social service, and educational and recreational resources in the area and refers people to appropriate public or private providers. Such a telephone service likely is available in your area and can facilitate that second step by giving you vital information and direction.

Couples and Families in Crisis

Resources identified in this section will be differentiated on the basis of nature of service and service provider, or type of crisis involved. In many cases extensive overlap exists so that if you contact a crisis center or program of any type, you will be able to get assistance regardless of the specific nature of your crisis. In crisis the key is contact, not debate over whether or not you are contacting the right place.

Crisis Phone Lines. Most communities have crisis telephone numbers which are listed in the front of your phone book or publicized through local media and information services. Persons answering the phones are trained in crisis intervention with skills related to suicide prevention and intervention in ongoing crises. They provide human contact and support, have information for crisis services, and can mobilize outside intervention.

Crisis Intervention Centers. Larger metropolitan areas have comprehensive crisis intervention programs with the capability of dealing with the full gamut of human crises. Differentiated expertise is housed under the same program and contact with the center usually will result in immediate referral to the type of crisis services you need. For example, *The Crisis Intervention Center* of Hennepin County (Minneapolis) is attached to the Hennepin County Medical Center. It has 24-hour walk-in service, an emergency room, Crisis Homes, crisis lines for suicide, child abuse and other problems, sexual assault services, home visits, and can mobilize other services associated with potential crisis situations if need be. Contact with such a center will likely provide a suitable source of assistance.

Sexual Abuse. Sexual abuse is a crisis that may emerge from within the family or be inflicted upon the family. In either case, specific services designed to deal with sexual assault or abuse are available in your area. A distinction may be made by providers between sexual assault (rape) and family sexual abuse (incest). In any case, services are always available through local social services agencies and through programs that may have names such as *Victims of Sexual Assault, Rape and Sexual Assault Center, Sexual Assault Services (SAS),* or *Sexual Offense Services (SOS).* Other programs may be specifically identified as *Family Sexual Abuse Programs.*

Crime Victim Centers. Police and citizens groups with the help of governmental and private agencies have been actively developing crime victim centers in many communities. These centers are open 24 hours a day and are committed to immediate and direct service when contacted. They mobilize psychological and practical assistance to victims, provide prevention programs and information, and facilitate police and legal action.

Physical Abuse. Physical abuse in the family (referred to as domestic abuse) may involve wife battering or child abuse or both. Consequently, most communities have "safe houses" which can temporarily shelter victims who have suffered physical abuse or be used as a protective measure. Programs for both men *(Men in Violent Relationships)* and women (support groups for battered women) are available. These programs may be labeled: *Turning-point, A Safe Place, Domestic Abuse Project,* or the *Woman's Advocacy Program.* Counseling programs for men who batter women, for women involved in violent relationships, and for parents who physically abuse their children are usually available through these agencies.

Youth Emergency Services. Many communities have omnibus emergency services housed under the general umbrella of *Youth Emergency Services (YES).* These programs are designed and publicized as services to youth and their families. They have the full gamut of crisis and emergency services and can be contacted for assistance by either the parents or the children or brought into contact with the family through other community agents (police, social workers, school counselors, and so forth). These services can be helpful in working with children who are "throwaways," "runaways," "stayaways," or truant. They assist with parent-child conflicts that tend to emerge during the adolescent phase of family development and provide resources directly to young people who feel their families cannot help them or who are experiencing problems they do not want to expose to their parents.

Alcohol and Drug Abuse. Probably the most visible and available of all resources to couples and families are those associated with alcohol and drug abuse. Schools have alcohol and chemical dependency prevention programs. The work setting has *Employee Assistance Programs (EAP)*. The community sponsors a host of preventive and interventive programs, all encompassing the issue of chemical use and abuse. *Alcohol and Other Drug Abuse (AODA)* has garnered national attention as a major problem of individuals and families. Services span the continuum from education to inpatient treatment for chemical dependency. Alcohol and drug abuse is labeled alternately a disease and a social problem, but in either case, chemical abuse damages marriages and families. Schools, employers, churches, local hospitals, and social service agencies all have information on services available. Certified alcohol and chemical dependency counselors provide counseling, facilitate interventions, and teach courses to facilitate prevention. Most chemical dependency treatment programs still operate from an individual treatment modality (Barnard, 1981), but are increasingly incorporating spouses and families into the treatment process. For example, the well-known *Hazelden Treatment Center* in Center City, Minnesota has a week-long program which spouses and family members can attend while the identified patient is getting treatment. Other programs such as that at Fairview Southdale Hospital in Minneapolis, called *The Family Renewal Center,* incorporate the family directly into the treatment. In any case, services in the area of alcohol and other drugs are generally readily accessible.

CONCLUDING COMMENTS

We realize that the hopes of every couple and family are that none of the previous resources or the problems they represent will ever emerge as part of their marital or family experience. However, we wish to re-emphasize the importance of seeking outside assistance when necessary, and doing so early rather than late. Keep in mind the point that was emphasized at the beginning of this chapter: *"The healthy family (and marriage) admits to and seeks help with problems."*

The facts of the matter are (1) problems are a reality in marriages and families, (2) resolving them is what strengthens marriages and families, and (3) this book would never have been written had not couples and families had the courage and taken the initiative to seek help when needed. They have done their part, now the rest is up to you.

REFERENCES

Barnard, C.P. (1981). *Families, alcoholism and therapy.* Springfield, IL: Charles C. Thomas.

Barnard, C.P., & Corrales, R.G. (1979). *The theory and technique of family therapy.* Springfield, IL: Charles C. Thomas.

Baruth, L.G., & Huber, C.H. (1984). *An introduction to marital theory and therapy.* Monterey, CA: Brooks/Cole Publishing.

Carnes, P. (1981). *Understanding us: A family development experience.* Minneapolis, MN: Interpersonal Communications Programs.

Coogler, O.J. (1983). *Structured mediation of a divorce settlement.* Lexington, MA: Lexington Publishing.

Curran, D. (1983). *Traits of a healthy family.* Minneapolis: Winston Press.

Dinkmeyer, D., & McKay, G.D. (1976). *Systematic training for effective parenting (STEP).* Circle Pines, MN: American Guidance Services.

Framo, J.L. (1982). *Explorations in marital and family therapy: Selected papers of James Framo.* New York: Springer.

Gordon, T. (1970). *Parent effectiveness training*. New York: Plume.

Guerney, B. (Jr.). (1977). *Relationship enhancement: Skills-training programs for therapy, problem prevention, and enrichment*. San Francisco: Jossey-Bass.

Kaplan, H.S. (1974). *The new sex therapy*. New York: Brunner/Mazel.

Lewis, P. (1980, April 11). Family working overtime to survive. *Washington Star*.

Mace, D. (1982). *Close companions: The marriage enrichment handbook*. New York: Continuum.

Mace, D. (1972). *Getting ready for marriage*. Nashville: Abingdon Press.

Mace, D. (1977). Marriage enrichment: The new frontier. *Personnel and Guidance Jounal, 55* 520-22.

Mace, D., & Mace, V. (1977). *How to have a happy marriage*. Nashville: Abington Press.

Masters, W.H., & Johnson, V.E. (1966). *Human sexual response*. Boston: Little, Brown.

Masters, W.H., & Johnson, V.E. (1970). *Human sexual inadequacy*. Boston: Little, Brown.

Miller, J., Nunnally, E.W., & Wackman, D.B. (1976). *Couple workbook: Increasing awareness and communication skills*. Minneapolis: Interpersonal Communications Programs.

Olson, D.H., Druckman, J.M., & Fournier, D.G. (n.d.). *PREPARE*. Minneapolis: Prepare/Enrich, Inc., P.O. Box 190.

Roberts, W., & Wright, H.N. (1978). *Before you say I do: A marriage preparation manual for couples*. Eugene, OR: Harvest House Publishers.

Rueveni, V. (1979). *Networking families in crisis*. New York: Human Sciences.

Sager, C.J., Brown, H.S., Crohn, H., Engel, T., Rodstein, E., & Walker, L. (1983). *Treating the remarried family*. New York: Brunner/Mazel, Publishers.

Speck, R., & Attneave, C. (1973). *Family networks: Rehabilitation and healing*. New York: Pantheon.

Visher, E.B., & Visher, J.S. (1979). *Stepfamilies*. New York: Brunner/Mazel.

Yates, J. (1979, October). The ties that bind can also heal. *Prevention*, 45-53.

INDEX

INDEX

makes the difference 77
Eliot, G. 43
Empathy 47
Engel, T. 252, 253, 262, 275, 283
Environment
    makes different folks 65-94
    work 84-90
Erickson, E. 8, 10, 12, 18
Eros 135
Ethnicity 69-72
    impact 70-1
Evaluating, experiences 103
Evolution, father 218-20
Ewy, D. 223, 237
Exchange theory 131-2
Excitement/attraction 124-5
Exconnections 259-60
Experiences
    choosing 103
    rejecting 103
    stressful 2

F

Faber, A. 223, 237
Factors, affecting marital choice
    140-7
Fairytale approach 127
Family 191-236
    see marriage
    see remarriage
    adolescent 230-1
    against the culture 195
    aging 234
    as a launching pad 232-3
    as a resource 105-6
    as an orchestra 207-8
    availabilty of help 270
    boundaries 200-6
    breaking away 118-20
    checkups 276
    contradictions in 194
    counseling and therapy 268-9, 274-6
    crisis, in 279-81
    crisis intervention 269-70
    culture 67
    defining 193-5

developmental stages 225-34
disengaged, 204-6, *Figure* 205
disintegration formula 115-8
education centers 271
enmeshed, 203-4, *Figure* 203
enrichment 267-8
enrichment programs 273
enrichment resources 272
extended 114-5, 187
finance 106
financial resources 247
first 113
for the culture 195
frontier of 239-62
government 91-3
growth 267-8
growth resources 272
healthy traits 235-6
homeostasis 196-7
individual in system 206-8
life 208-25
life cycle 225-34
morphogenesis 197-8
need 267-70
nuclear 114, 116, 240, 241-2
of origin 121-49
ordinal position 106-13
organizational patterns 202-6
origin of 121-49
parenting 208-25
place in 106-13
planning 271
pre-school 227-8
provides experiences 100-5
reconstruction 242
reconstituted 241-2, 254-5
remarriage 251-61
resources available 270-81
reunions 273
school age 229-30
second 113
single parent 240, 246-51
single parent, types 246
step 240
sub-systems 198-9
super-systems 199-200
support services 268
system 195-200, 206-8

K

Kaplan, H. S. 274, 283
Katz, L. 240, 262
Kiefaber, M. W. 223, 237
Knapp, M. 55, 64
Kohlberg, L. 11, 18
Kubler-Ross, E. 243, 262

L

Laing, R. D. 100, 120
Language
    developing a common 175
    learn each other's 175
Langway, L. 218, 219, 237
Larson, C. 55, 64
Lauer, J. 137, 150
Lauer, R. 137, 150
Leading-supporting, *Figure* 169
Leany, E. C. 218, 237
Lederer, W. 140, 150
Legacy 96-7
    contents 99-100
    definition 97
    like a revolving slate 103
    relationship 97
Lewis, P. 223, 237, 266, 283
Life cycle
    developmental stages 225-34
    family 225-34
Lifestyle 187
Limerance 138-9
Listen, see communication 52
Love 134-40
    altruistic 138
    attachment 139
    companionate 137-8
    essential ingredients 171-3
    infatuaton 139
    limerance 138-9
    passionate 136-7
    romantic 135-6
Loyalty 97-9
    connection 99
    invisible 97-9

Luck of the draw 128
Luft, J. 48, 49, 64

M

Mace, D. 188, 270, 272, 283
Mace, V. 188, 272, 283
Macklin, E. D. 147, 150
Magic approach 127
Manipultion types 60-2
    Figure 61
Marriage
    adjustment difficulty 159-60
    age at 2-3
    areas of conflict 185-7
    blueprint for 100-5
    ceremony 154-7
    checkups 276
    component parts 162-71
    conflict, areas of 185-7
    conformity, as a 141-2
    counseling 272, 273-4
    courtship phase 121-49
    crisis of 158-61
    cross-racial 68
    dating phase 121-49
    dissolution 241-2
    encounter 272
    enrichment 272
    essential ingredients 171-3
    evolution, as a 146-7
    factors affecting choice 140
    female 3
    finishing process, as a 140-1
    functions of sex 181-5
    geographical location 78-82
    growth aspect 166-71
    healthy 187-8
    impulse, as a 146-7
    jailbreak 144-6
    leading-supporting 168-71
    life after 151-88
    male 2-3
    negotiations after 158-9
    on-the-job training 128-9
    preparation for 270-1
    principles facilitating 161-2

Types
    manipulative 60-2
    Figure 61

U

U.S. Bureau of the Census 1, 2, 3, 18,
    147, 150, 211, 238, 246, 247, 263
Understanding 47-8

V

Values
    acting 31
    choosing 31
    prizing 31
Visher, E. B. 240, 254, 255, 263,
    271, 283
Visher, J. S. 240, 254, 255, 263,
    271, 283

W

Wackman, D. 54, 55, 64, 181, 189,
    273, 283
Walker, L. 252, 253, 262, 275, 283
Walsh, F. 158, 189
Warmth 47
Watchel, T. 223, 238
Watzalawick, P. 57, 64
Wedding, significance 155-6

Wedding and beyond 151-88
Weiner, M. B. 182, 189
Win-lose continuum 59-60
Witmer, J. M. 177, 189
Wolpert-Zun, A. 239, 241, 242, 263
Women
    age at marriage 3
    divorce 2
    re-enter work force 3
    sexual development 10-11
Work 27-30, 84-90
    benefits 29-30
    career couples 87-8
    dual career 28
    environment 84-90
    mobility 30
    occupations requiring travel 88-9
    policies 29-30
    relatonship to family 84-90
    seasonal 90
    shift 89-90
Wright, H. N. 271, 283
Wyden, P. 148, 150

Y

Yates, J. 273, 283
York, D. 223, 238
York, P. 223, 238
Youth emergency services 280-1

Z

Zuk, G. 172, 189, 219, 238

ABOUT
THE
AUTHORS

James P. Trotzer, Ph.D.

James P. Trotzer is a licensed psychologist, marriage and family therapist and Executive Director of Renew Counseling Center in Rye, New Hampshire. He is a clinical member and Approved Supervisor of the American Association for Marriage and Family Therapy. Other professional organizations in which he is active include the American Association for Counseling and Development, American Psychological Association and American Family Therapy Association.

Jim received M.A. and Ph.D. degrees in counseling with special emphasis in group counseling from the University of Colorado. He spent a post-doctoral year training in family therapy in Family Psychiatry Department of Eastern Pennsylvania Psychiatric Institute in Philadelphia with additional work at the Philadelphia Child Guidance Clinic.

Professional writing by Jim includes sixteen articles, two monographs, and one book—*The Counselor and the Group: Integrating Theory, Training, and Practice* (Brooks/Cole Publishing). The book has been translated into Chinese and published. He also has contributed a chapter to *The Group Worker's Handbook* (Charles E. Thomas Publishers) and has served on the editorial boards of the *Journal for Specialists in Group Work* and *Journal of Psychology and Theology*.

In addition to a private practice in marriage and family therapy, Jim is actively engaged in consultation, training, and education. A professor of counselor education for 14 years at the University of Wisconsin—River Falls, he has served as a guest lecturer at Temple University, The Johns Hopkins University, and Rosemead School of Psychology, Biola University. He also has been a visiting professor to Japan and Taiwan. A noted workshop leader and public speaker, he divides his professional time between clinical practice, teaching, and writing.

Toni B. Trotzer, M.A.

Toni B. Trotzer is a National Certified Counselor with private practice experience in marriage and family counseling. Her M.A. in Guidance and Counseling is from the University of Colorado plus additional graduate work from University of Wisconsin—River Falls. She is a professional teacher as illustrated by having taught in kindergarten, elementary school, and college. She has taught psychology, human relations, and counseling at the graduate and undergraduate levels.

She has held appointments at University of Wisconsin—River Falls, Northern Essex Community College, and Taiwan Provincial College of Education.

Jim and Toni are parents of three children, all of whom are involved in school and related activities. The family concept is an important aspect of their marriage.